LEADERSHIP AND POWER IN INTERNATIONAL DEVELOPMENT

LEADERSHIP AND POWER IN INTERNATIONAL DEVELOPMENT

Navigating the Intersections of Gender, Culture, Context, and Sustainability

Edited by

RANDAL JOY THOMPSON
Excellence, Equity, and Empowerment, Inc., USA

JULIA STORBERG-WALKER
George Washington University, USA

United Kingdom — North America — Japan — India — Malaysia — China

Emerald Publishing Limited
Howard House, Wagon Lane, Bingley BD16 1WA, UK

First edition 2018

British Library Cataloguing in Publication Data
A catalogue record for this book is available from the British Library.

ISBN: 978-1-78754-116-0 (Print)
ISBN: 978-1-78743-880-4 (Online)
ISBN: 978-1-78743-999-3 (Epub)

ISSN: 2058-8801

ISOQAR certified
Management System,
awarded to Emerald
for adherence to
Environmental
standard
ISO 14001:2004.

Certificate Number 1985
ISO 14001

INVESTOR IN PEOPLE

CONTENTS

Contents

PART 5: LEADERSHIP LESSONS TO REFLECT ON

ABOUT THE AUTHORS

Josh P. Armstrong, PhD, is a Faculty Member and Director of the Comprehensive Leadership Program for undergraduate students at Gonzaga University. Dr Armstrong's research interests include servant leadership, intercultural competencies, and adaptive leadership. Through the past decade of directing a study abroad program in Zambia, Josh has developed his skills at driving in the African bush, dancing, and slowing down to stay for tea.

Maria Beebe, PhD, is an Applied Sociolinguist whose research interests include critical discourse analysis, women's leadership, and information communication technologies for development. She co-edited *AfricadotEdu*, *DISRUPT. Filipina Women: Loud. Proud. Leading without a Doubt* and *DISRUPT 2.0. Filipina Women: Daring to Lead*. Based on 20 years of international development experience, Dr Beebe created Global Networks to foster collaborations for a sustainable world.

Kathleen Curran, Global Leadership Coach, Trainer and Consultant, is the Founder of Intercultural Systems, established in Singapore in 1996, and specializes in developing global leader identity and boundary spanning capacity. Holding MAs in Intercultural Communication and Human and Organizational Development, she is completing her PhD, focusing on global talent development in Asia.

Dick Daniels, D.Min., is the President of the Leadership Development Group. In addition to organizational consulting and executive coaching, he hosts a Linkedin online community of 26,000 global leadership practitioners: The Leadership Development Group. Daniels recently published a nationally awarded book, *Leadership Briefs: Shaping Organizational Culture to Stretch Leadership Capacity*. He currently serves as the Vice President of Consulting Services for Right Management of Florida and the

Caribbean, and is an Adjunct Professor in the EdD program in Organizational Leadership at Stockton University in New Jersey.

Amanda Ellis, Senior Sustainability Scholar, ASU Julie Ann Wrigley Global Institute of Sustainability, is a development economist who was the first woman to lead the New Zealand Aid Program as Deputy Secretary in the Ministry of Foreign Affairs and Trade. Previous roles include New Zealand's Ambassador to the United Nations in Geneva, Lead Specialist (Gender) for the World Bank Group, and Chair of the Global Banking Alliance for Women. Ellis is the author of two best-selling books, *Women's Business, Women's Wealth and Woman 2 Woman*, and five research titles on gender and growth in the World Bank Directions in Development series.

Ashley N. Lackovich-Van Gorp, PhD, is a Scholar-practitioner and a Writer who works globally to create, facilitate, and evaluate girl-centered programming. As the Director of Mercy Corps' Regional Center for the Advancement of Adolescent Girls, Ashley collaborates with her team on creating new modes of girl engagement. She is also the co-founder of Enhance Worldwide, a girl-centered nonprofit operating in Ethiopia, and a blogger for Girls' Globe.

Kathryn B. Mangino is a Development Professional with more than 15 years of experience using practical and academic approaches in gender, capacity building, participatory qualitative data collection and analysis, facilitation and designing, and delivering participatory training. Her experience includes working throughout Asia, Africa, and the Middle East with both bilateral donors and local NGOs. She holds a PhD from Waseda University where she researched the intersection between women's empowerment and male engagement.

David Mashzhu-Makota is a Humanitarian Practitioner with more than 14 years in humanitarian response in East and Southern Africa, Middle East, and South Central Asia. He holds an MA in Leading, Innovation, and Change from York St John University, UK. He is married to Christine and has two children, Chiedza and Mutsawashe. David is very passionate about serving the most deprived and vulnerable communities hence his work has mainly been in fragile contexts.

Patricia McLaughlin is completing her Ph.D. at Eastern University in Organizational Leadership. Her leadership career, which spans the United

States, Middle East, North Africa, Sub-Saharan Africa, and Western Europe, has been centered in the education sector, working in international development, private international schools, and American public schools. Her doctoral dissertation seeks to understand the factors that influence the success, or lack thereof, achieved by expatriate leaders in international development projects they manage through a grounded theory study.

Keba T. Modisane is a Scholar-practitioner in HRM and HRD. Her areas of research interest are in leadership development, gender studies and diversity, ethics and morality, education, and innovation management. She holds a PhD from Renmin University (Beijing, China). Modisane previously worked for 16 years as an HR Manager and currently works as Research Manager at BA ISAGO University in Botswana. She is passionate about issues of nature and religion and believes in positivism.

Iyabo Obasanjo, PhD, teaches Public Health at the College of William and Mary (Williamsburg, VA, USA). She has a PhD in Epidemiology from Cornell University (Ithaca, New York, USA). She worked as a Project Manager in Clinical Research and then as the Commissioner for Health in Ogun State, Nigeria from 2003 to 2007. She won election to the Nigerian Senate from 2007 to 2011, where she was the Chair of the Senate Committee on Health.

Nicole Rouvinez-Bouali is a Neonatologist, passionate about global health, holding a Masters of Management (IMHL). As the Clinical Director of a Global Development Alliance co-funded by USAID-Benin, she developed a sustainable education curriculum to reduce neonatal mortality. She is a founding member of the International, Inter-University Diploma in Perinatology.

Anne M. Spear is a PhD Candidate in the International Education Policy program at University of Maryland. She is an Instructor in the Leadership Studies Minor Program. Anne holds an MEd in Education and Social Change from the University of Miami. Her doctoral dissertation examines teachers' responses to gendered violence in Burkina Faso's school systems through a vertical comparative case study.

Debby Thomas, PhD served as a Missionary and Development Specialist in Rwanda with Evangelical Friends Mission for 18 years focusing on holistic community development. She is presently an Assistant Professor of Management at George Fox University as well as a Leadership and Management Training Facilitator.

Éliane Ubalijoro is the Executive Director of C.L.E.A.R. International Development. She is a Professor of Practice at McGill University, a Member of Rwanda's National Science and Technology Council, a Fellow of the African Academy of Sciences, a Board Member of the International Leadership Association and a Member of the Board of Trustees of WWF International. Éliane is a Member of Rwanda's Presidential Advisory Council. A former biotechnology executive, she has co-led Gates Grand Challenges Exploration grants.

Nila Wardani has over 20 years of expertise in gender and social inclusion, capacity building, participatory qualitative research and analysis, facilitation, designing, and delivering participatory training. Using her expertise in grass-roots facilitation, she established her own women's empowerment NGO. She has additional experience with a variety of international donors, local government, and INGOs. She holds a Master degree in Rural Development with a focus on social capital issues from the University of Sussex, UK.

Gordon A. Zook earned a BS in Food Systems Economics and Management from Michigan State University, an MS in Agriculture Economics from Cornell University, and more recently a PhD in Organizational Leadership from Eastern University. He has worked for Mennonite Central Committee for 18 years in Bangladesh, Haiti, and India along with his wife Carol, primarily in country program leadership. His primary interest focuses on assessing and improving organizational effectiveness, particularly for international NGOs.

PREFACE

*We talk about Sustainable Development Goals (SDGs) which for
me is excellent! As individuals working in international
development, have we taken the time to think and talk about our
Personal Development Goals (PDGs)? Do we demonstrate on a
daily basis how our day-to-day activities contribute to the
achievement of the SDGs? Be the change you want to see in the
global space? Let us build our personal capacities for global action!*

Benjamin Kofi Quansah[1]

The United Nations' call in 2015 to work together to achieve 17 sustainable
development goals by 2030 has reignited the global discussion regarding the
need to continue to improve the lives of a large part of the developing world.
Leaders in international development face an enormous challenge to coordinate their actions, bring resources to bear, and determine the most successful
approach to achieve the vision implied by the SDGs. How leaders should
best lead becomes a critical question.

We decided to pursue this volume because we saw a gap in the leadership
literature related to leaders in international development. Such leaders have
been included in the literature on project management to a certain extent,
but we believe that their leadership extends far beyond the realm of projects.
We also believe that leaders in international development, as significant as
they are in determining the future of the global order, have not been
acknowledged adequately in the academic, practitioner, or public milieus.

Based on our belief that models and theories of leadership should be built
up by practice and that personal reflection is a powerful approach to understanding practice, we put out a call for proposals that asked contributors to
write their leadership stories. Furthermore, we asked authors to highlight
particular leadership moments and examine those moments in terms of four
factors which we determined were key in this profession: gender, context,
culture, and sustainability. We were interested to determine whether their

gender influenced their leadership, especially since leaders in this profession encounter a wide divergence of attitudes toward gender in the countries in which they work. We wondered whether the social, economic, political, or personal context in which they lead impacted their leadership. Culture, of course, is a huge factor in international development leadership and we wanted contributors to reflect on how they adapt their leadership to different cultures and how they cross borders and develop agility to move from one culture to another. Lastly, since a key focus for international development currently is on sustainable development, we wanted leaders to inform us how this focus has impacted their leadership.

Of the many proposals submitted by international development leaders in response to our call for chapters, we selected 18 leaders based on their extensive and sustained work in the international development field. The 14 women and four men originate from Africa, Asia, Europe, and North America, and they represent a diverse array of cultures, leadership histories, and perspectives. Their leadership roles differ and include a former senior-level government official from a developing country; a humanitarian aid worker; a policy maker in influential donor organizations and the United Nations; leaders in faith-based organizations; project implementers in bilateral aid organizations, non-government organizations, and corporations; university professors; a physician; an interculturalist; and an HR executive in a development organization. The diversity of the authors has provided a kaleidoscope of perspectives that together offer a comprehensive view of leadership in international development. Some surprises emerged such as the need for leaders in international development to challenge culture, not only adapt to it. These leaders had to decide to work with existing power structures or try to change them. Expatriate women as a sort-of "third gender" in some countries and the paradoxes that are a constant reality for leaders in this profession, were among another surprise.

From the rich stories of the complexities, uncertainties, pressures, and victories of the authors, we closely reviewed each chapter in a comparative manner to identify commonalities, differences, themes, and patterns. The process we used bridges the practitioner/scholar divide by offering a tentative framework for leading in international development based on actual practitioner stories from the field. Typical qualitative research data analysis methods were used, including the use of qualitative data analysis software and modified grounded theory methods. The result is the presentation, in

Chapter 1, of a tentative model or theory of leading in international development contexts.

Our intention and hope is that this volume will initiate a new dialogue between practitioners and scholars in this important area of leadership and that both emerging and veteran leaders in this profession will gain valuable insights from the chapters.

Randal Joy Thompson
Julia Storberg-Walker
Editors

NOTE

1. Benjamin Kofi Quansah, CGMS, is a Ghanaian leader in international development. In 2017, he was awarded the prestigious 2017 Newton award from the US National Grants Management Association for his outstanding contribution and performance in the field of grants management. This quote was retrieved from: https://www.goodreads.com/quotes/tag/international-development.

ACKNOWLEDGMENTS OF
THE EDITORS

The journey of putting together this volume has been made possible and immeasurably more enriched by the support and commitment of a number of individuals to whom we are deeply indebted. The honest self-reflection and commitment to the betterment of the world of the chapter authors have made this book both possible and promising. We as editors have benefitted from a life-enhancing learning process catalyzed by the leadership stories of these contributors.

The editors also owe a huge debt of eternal gratitude to Debra DeRuyver, Communications Director of the International Leadership Association (ILA). Debra was with us every step of the way, offering sound advice and guidance based on her many years of experience. We also would like to thank the staff of ILA for their faith in us and support for our work. We hope we met the expectations of Cynthia Cherry, CEO, who announced our book at the 2017 ILA Conference in Brussels. We are ever thankful to Shelly Wilsey, COO, for her wordsmithing and Bridget Chisholm, Director of Conferences. They and the rest of the ILA staff provided the foundation for making this book possible and providing us with the opportunity to make an impact.

We would also like to acknowledge all the readers of this volume who we invite to join us on this journey of exploration of leadership in international development. We look forward to engaging in a dialogue with all of you and in advancing our understanding of the factors influencing leadership in this profession as well as the values, principles, and competences that will help us all work together for a better world.

ABOUT THE EDITORS

Randal Joy Thompson is an International Development Professional and Founder and Principal of the consulting company Excellence, Equity, and Empowerment. As a US Foreign Service Officer for 28 years, she advised senior government officials on policy changes and helped to change systems to improve health, child welfare, education, social science research, and program evaluation in all regions of the world. As a Certified Performance Technologist, she has also worked to improve organizational and human performance. She has chapters in *Breaking the Zero-Sum Game: Transforming Societies Through Inclusive Leadership*; *Grassroots Leadership and the Arts for Social Change*; *Theorizing Women & Leadership: New Insights & Contributions from Multiple Perspectives*; and *Women and Leadership Around the World* and many academic journals and books.

Julia Storberg-Walker is an Associate Professor in the Executive Leadership Program of the Graduate School of Education and Human Development at George Washington University, and an Affiliate Faculty and Advisory Board Member at George Washington's Global Women's Institute. Julia served as Editor-in-Chief of *Human Resource Development Review* from 2014 to 2017. She is an Associate at the Taos Institute. Her publications include *Theorizing Women and Leadership: New Insights and Contributions from Multiple Perspectives; Authentic Leadership in HRD: Context and Identity Matter! Critical Explorations on Leading Authentically*, and many chapters, articles, and global presentations on theoretical development for applied disciplines. She received the International Leadership Association's Women and Leadership Affinity Group's Outstanding Scholar Award.

DEDICATIONS

To all my Colleagues and Friends in International Development who have
dedicated their lives to creating a better world and to those I worked with
who were murdered doing so, including James Foley and
Lisa Marie Akbari.

And to my sons Devin and Patrick who grew up around the world, are true
survivors — Devin of an attempted coup in Cameroon and Patrick of an
attempted murder in Ukraine — and are leaders in their own right, working
toward justice and equality.

Randal Joy

I dedicate this book to all of the leaders who get up every day in the name
of peace and equality. "The best way to find yourself is to lose yourself in
the service of others." — Gandhi

Julia

OVERVIEW PART 1

ON LEADING IN INTERNATIONAL DEVELOPMENT

Randal Joy Thompson

Leaders in international development work on the cutting edge of the global order, striving to create a world where everyone can live a life of dignity with access to resources and services to meet their fundamental needs. Such leaders rarely have the chance to tell their stories. How they lead most effectively in various contexts and cultures has not often been told, nor have the qualities and approaches they employ to achieve success been systematically studied. The purpose of this volume, then, is to fill this gap by sharing these stories and proposing a tentative theory of leading in this context. In addition, the volume offers an innovative practitioner/scholar collaboration model for generating new knowledge directly from the stories and anecdotes of leaders.

We (the co-editors) decided to combine our practitioner and scholar skills and together developed a vision for this unique volume. Chapter 1, Toward a Theory of Leading in International Development, describes the specific steps undertaken to combine research and practice; our goal was to create a vehicle for stories from this leadership area and then analyze the stories to identify commonalities, differences, and critical leadership issues. From the analysis, our goal was to offer a tentative new theory of leading in this context that can be used to inform future research and leader development initiatives. As Chapter 1, Toward a Theory of Leading in International Development, makes clear, the leader stories provided a rich depth of leader experiences to draw from, and a new theory of leading in this context is offered.

Leadership and Power in International Development: Navigating the Intersections of Gender, Culture, Context, and Sustainability provides 18 leaders from Africa, Asia, Europe, and North America working in various aspects of international development the opportunity to describe their challenges, successes, and failures in leading change in different countries, different sectors, and at various levels, including national, local, and individual. This overview illustrates the complexities related to leading in this context. We believe that this under-researched area is a critical area for leadership scholars and practitioners, and as such we seek to shed light on key elements of this profession. Specifically, this overview provides a brief examination of leading in international development and then provides a brief discussion of some of the specific issues and experiences faced by the authors in this volume.

The first section, entitled "On International Development Leaders," posits a preliminary definition of what leaders in international development do. The second section, entitled "The Architecture within which International Development Leaders Lead" describes the organizational context of their leadership. "Approaches to International Development," the third section, summarizes different approaches to achieving development that leaders have implemented over the years. The fourth section, "How do the Leaders in This Volume Practice Leadership?" highlights leaders' conception of leadership as well as their reflections on the four factors we initially identified as possibly influencing leadership in this profession, namely gender, culture, context, and sustainability. Power emerged as a dominant factor in leadership in international development in virtually all the stories of the authors. In the Overview Part 2, Anne M. Spear presents an overview of the broader context of the issue of power in this domain and a commitment by the authors to a leadership practice that sincerely focuses on equalizing power relations and creating global harmony.

The introductions to each of the five parts of the volume also highlight some of the key findings regarding leadership in international development. Part 1, Challenges in International Development, of the volume includes stories that introduce the reader to some of the most common challenges faced by leaders in international development. Part 2, Leadership for Women's Empowerment and Equity, describes the leadership moments of leaders who have devoted their career to promoting women's empowerment and equity. Part 3, Spirit-filled Grassroots Leadership, describes leadership by faith-based leaders who work at the grassroots level. Part 4, Leading Major Donor Projects, contains stories by leaders who work for major donors or their projects. Finally, Part 5, Leadership Lessons to Reflect On, provides leadership lessons for the reader to reflect on.

ON INTERNATIONAL DEVELOPMENT LEADERS

Who Are Leaders in International Development?

One of the hopes of this volume is to initiate a conversation about how to conceive of a leader in international development. At this point, we begin with the assertion that *a leader in international development is a change maker dedicated to transforming complex systems and their components in developing countries (and by implication in the global world) such that all individuals in the world can live in equitable societies, free from want, able to achieve their aspirations, and in harmony with the environment.*

What Is Unique about These Leaders?

What leaders do in international development is unique in many respects. When expatriates, they cross sovereign borders, bringing know-how, resources, and technologies, as well as principles, values, assumptions, ways-of-doing things, and worldviews to bear on the change they wish to make in the developing countries in which they work. What they bring with them may clash with what leaders in developing countries carry or what the society can manage and adjust to. They often represent a power and privilege imbalance, the result of which can appear overbearing and authoritarian and arrogant. They may be offering an unwelcome change or a change only supported by certain groups in the developing countries. They can disrupt power relations and cultural norms that either will be resisted or may cause instability. When leaders of development come from within their own countries, they may represent certain powerful groups that may oppose providing benefits to groups that could disrupt the power hegemony. Or, they may come from disenfranchised groups that may threaten the powers-that-be.

These various characteristics of what leaders in international development do and who they are, the impact of their leadership, and their effectiveness are explored by various authors in their chapters.

THE ARCHITECTURE WITHIN WHICH INTERNATIONAL DEVELOPMENT LEADERS LEAD

Leaders in international development lead within a complex global architecture of international and national organizations established shortly after World War II, which has evolved over the years through various phases driven by changing theories of how to catalyze international development and alter geo-political relationships as well as by vehement critiques of the sometimes negative impact of the practice of development on the lives of its beneficiaries. Although human, financial, and material resources and know-how have traversed global boundaries throughout history by migrations, cross-border trade, conquests, war, technical assistance, humanitarian aid, and religious zeal, the contemporary era of "international development" and "foreign aid" is generally considered to have begun with the words of US President Harry S. Truman delivered in his Inaugural Address on January 20, 1949:

> *More than half the people of the world are living in conditions approaching misery...Their poverty is a handicap and a threat both to them and to more prosperous areas. We must embark on a bold new program for making the benefits of our scientific advances and industrial progress available for the improvement and growth of underdeveloped areas... Greater production is the key to prosperity and peace. (Truman, 1949)*

International development or global development historically has been closely linked to the concept of economic growth, although its definition has been broadened over the years to include human development and, more recently, sustainable development. Such development is directed by the policies, programs, knowledge, and resources within developing countries augmented by transfers of financial, technological, informational, and human resources from more developed ones. Leaders in international development are responsible for these transfers.

At the time of Truman's speech, the foundational architecture of international organizations that would play key roles in international development and foreign aid had already been built with the creation in 1944 of the International Monetary Fund (IMF) and the International Bank for Reconstruction and Development (now part of the World Bank Group), and in 1945 the United Nations. Further, the Marshall Plan for the Reconstruction of Europe was initiated and the Organisation for European Economic Cooperation (OEEC) was created in 1948 to administer the Plan. The Marshall Plan served as a significant step forward in the advent of international development by focusing on the provision of technical and humanitarian assistance while at the same time creating a political and economic bloc opposed to the Soviet Union that would play an important role in international development henceforth. The conceptual foundation of development during this period and during the 1950s was the modernization theory posited by Walt Rostow and other American economists (Rostow, 1960, 1990).

Foreign Aid as an Essential Tool of International Development

The 1960s era of the independence of former colonies marked the advent of Western countries creating foreign aid organizations. Canada, France, and the United States led the way and other countries followed suit in subsequent years. In the United States of America, an advocate of foreign aid, President John F. Kennedy pushed for the enactment of the Foreign Assistance Act in 1961 that established the United States Agency for International Development (USAID). The establishment of USAID by Kennedy ushered in a new stage of development in the US. Kennedy's 1961 Alliance for Progress focused on increasing gross national product (GNP), establishing democratic governments, ending adult illiteracy, land reform, and social planning guaranteed by US$20 billion.

Whereas predecessor US agencies such as the Technical Cooperation Agency, the Institute of Inter-American Affairs, and the US Department of Agriculture doled out highly technical programs, USAID required a new kind of development professional. No longer "well drillers" who worked at the community level, the new professionals were economists, loan officers, planners, senior technical advisors, private sector business executives, and professionals who could undertake policy discussions with ministers and heads of nations (Askin, 2012, p. 29). Development became the focus of "studies, theories, and program approaches and helped usher in what many later characterized as the 'Golden Age of Development'" (Askin, 2012, p. 30).

Given the advent of bilateral aid donors, the Development Assistance Group (DAG) of the Organisation for Economic Cooperation and Development (OECD) was established on January 13, 1960, in order to track aid flows of its members to developing countries. The OEEC was reorganized in 1961 to become the OECD, whose 35 members from mostly high-income countries include some non-Western states. The Development Assistance Committee (DAC) was the renamed version of the DAG and focused on promoting development policies to improve economic and social well-being as well as to track resource flows, analyze data to predict future trends, and set international standards.

The United Nations agencies have also played a key role in international development. The United Nations Development Programme (UNDP), the United Nations Population Fund (UNFPA), the United Nations Children's Fund (UNICEF), the United Nations Educational, Scientific and Cultural Organization (UNESCO), the Food and Agriculture Organization (FAO), the World Health Organization (WHO), and others have developed key international policies and negotiated with governments to make changes for the betterment of their people.

The architecture has evolved over the years as previously so-called developing countries have become middle-income countries and emerging powers and have become donors in their own right. Further, developing countries have increasingly formed a "Southern bloc" to negotiate for more effective aid and a stronger role in managing it, through the Aid Effectiveness movement and resultant Paris Declaration, Accra Accord, Busan Partnership Agreement, and the Partnership for Effective Development Cooperation.

Multiple Identities of Donors

Within the international architecture of international development, donors are generally categorized into multilateral, bilateral, non-governmental, corporate, and individuals. Multilateral donors, whose funds come from many countries, include the UNDP, the World Bank, and international development banks, among many others. Bilateral donors represent individual countries. Currently, the DAC members are the largest donors. However, China is a growing donor as is India, Brazil, Mexico, and several of the Arab states.

International Non-government Organizations (INGOs) include Oxfam, Save the Children, World Vision, Catholic Relief Services, CARE, Mercy Corps, and hundreds of others, funded by a combination of donations and government funds. Missionary groups are also generally included in this category. Private foundations and philanthropic donors include, among many others, the foundations of ex-US presidents such as the Carter Center, the Clinton Foundation, and the Obama Foundation, and private philanthropic foundations such as the Soros, Rockefeller, and the Bill and Melinda Gates Foundations. Many national non-government organizations (NGOs) also serve as donors.

In addition to the above donors, there are a myriad of private sector organizations that deliver aid provided by multilateral and bilateral donors and who work on the front lines of delivering aid directly to developing countries through a number of different funding mechanisms that will be discussed later. Corporations also have social responsibility strategies that are considered as aid. Further, private corporations provide the majority of resource transfers in recent years from developed to developing countries to stimulate international development, but those transfers are not considered as official aid.

Leaders work in all these various types of organizations and at all levels of this system, including political decision makers, policy makers, program designers, and project implementers in the field. The authors in this volume include leaders who work or have worked for developing country governments, for developing country development organizations, for major multilateral and bilateral donors, and for international and national nongovernmental organizations. They have led at the political level, the policy level, the organizational level, the community level, and the individual level.

APPROACHES TO INTERNATIONAL DEVELOPMENT

Depending upon what part of the development architecture they work in, leaders in international development either influence changes in or respond to changes in the currently popular approaches to development assistance. They also develop projects and other mechanisms to implement the currently popular approach. Approaches to such assistance have evolved since the Marshall Plan. The decades of development, hence, have been variously characterized. The technical expertise of leaders throughout these various periods has sometimes changed as has the concept of what types of interventions truly lead to the betterment of humanity and society. The magic key to development has yet to be found in this practice. A brief but not exhaustive summary of the overarching approaches is provided below in order to frame the intellectual context within which leaders in this profession have worked.

Although conceived to serve particular political agendas, until the 1990s, development assistance has been treated as a purely technical endeavor (Carothers & De Gramont, 2013; Eyben, 2014). Development professionals, including an array of strategic planners, economists, agronomists, public administration experts, and public health and education experts, purposefully eschewed the political and considered international development as catalyzed by technical innovation and know-how. In the 1950s and 1960s, the emphasis was on stimulating economic growth in the Third World, hoping that "fostering economic development in poor countries would inoculate them from leftist [i.e., Communist] subversion" (Carothers & De Gramont, 2013, p. 256). Thinkers in the developing countries and newly independent colonies began to identify "dependency theory," which contended that resource flows from the developing world to the developed world exceeded those in the opposite direction due to prejudicial terms of trade and that development assistance exacerbated this inequality, resulting in the unfair exploitation of developing country resources by donor-countries (Carothers & De Gramont, 2013; Eyben, 2014).

In the early 1970s, criticism swelled against the strictly macro-economic and industrialization approach of early international development, contending that the quality of the populace's life was not being improved. The basic needs approach emerged with sectors such as health and education, and micro-technology being highlighted as critical to development. Development professionals also began to promote programs directed at women, who heretofore had been the invisible beneficiaries of development assistance.

The 1980s marked the inception of the market centered, neoliberal economic era. Development assistance focused on restructuring the economic systems of developing nations to foster private sector development and minimize the state's expenses for the provision of the social safety net. This was the era of the IMF's structural adjustment loans, which offered money for meeting strict economic restructuring. A countermovement took place at the same time that promoted "bottom up approaches" including appropriate technology and Rapid and/or Participatory Rural Appraisal, an empowerment approach currently employed by two of the authors in this volume. Complex, integrated community development projects became popular. Increasingly, emphasis was also placed on integrating women into mainstream development programs, including as private sector entrepreneurs.

During the 1990s, post-communist period, capitalism was assumed to be the dominant global paradigm. Poverty became the focus of development rhetoric and programs. Efforts were made to establish public–private partnerships and to incorporate private capital into the development assistance mix. Politics finally became an open strategy. As Carothers and De Gramont (2013, pp. 257–258) explained: "Faced with the frequent experience of market policies floundering in developing countries because of weak state capacity to implement reforms, endemic corruption, and inadequate legal protections for market activity, the mainstream aid community embraced the need to strengthen state capacity." Further, building up civil society to both monitor states as well as to provide services that states could no longer afford became a major focus.

By 2000, the United Nations published the eight millennium development goals (MDGs), which were promoted as the overarching goals to be achieved by 2015 that all development organizations and professionals should be working toward. These included: eradicate extreme poverty and hunger; achieve universal primary education; promote gender equality and empower women;) reduce child mortality; improve maternal health; combat HIV/ AIDS, malaria, and other diseases; ensure environmental sustainability; and global partnership for development (United Nations, n.d).

Following the September 11, 2001, attacks on the World Trade Center, international development became part of the US National Security Plan and development assistance was viewed to a large extent as an important weapon to stave off radicalism and terrorism. An important aspect of this view was the need to democratize countries so that citizens could wield more influence over the decisions that impacted their lives and hence be less motivated to turn to violence.

By 2015, sustainable development had become the operating paradigm. The 17 sustainable development goals (SDGs) in the areas of health, quality education, water and sanitation, gender equality, poverty alleviation, and energy have been posited as the ideal unifying vision of a future that we all should be working toward.

According to economist Jeffrey Sachs (2015), sustainable development is both an intellectual and a normative pursuit. Intellectually, sustainable development (Sachs, 2015) "tries to make sense of the interactions of three complex systems: the world economy, the global society, and the Earth's physical environment ... Normatively, [sustainable development] recommends a set of goals to which the world should aspire ... calls for a world in which economic progress is widespread; extreme poverty is eliminated; social trust is encouraged through policies that strengthen the community; the environment is protected from human-induced degradation" (p. 3). To achieve sustainable development, Sachs (2015) adds other objectives of good governance and the provision of social services, infrastructure, promotion of science and technology, and regulations to protect the environment.

How Development Assistance Is Delivered

Leaders in international development deliver assistance in several forms, including cash transfers to developing country governments with conditionalities, through loans, grants, cooperative agreements, programs, and projects. Projects have been the most common form of promoting development and have been the focus of much of the critique of development. Projects are a temporary, time-bound, resource-bound system with specific objectives, which provide funding, training, and technical assistance to change complex systems in developing nations (Thompson, 2015).

Leaders in this volume have been responsible for implementing projects in health, education, agriculture, business, energy, social welfare, technology, humanitarian aid, and other sectors as well as working toward individual and community transformation.

Leading in a Milieu of Intense Criticism

Leaders in international development lead in a milieu that has been the object of extraordinary criticism from many different corners, justified by many different theories and reasons. Leaders have been blamed for poor development designs and results (Cassen, 1986; Easterly, 2006, 2013;

Eyben, 2012, 2014; Foreman, 2012; Moyo & Ferguson, 2010; Riddel, 2007), for forcing inappropriate and unsustainable Western solutions on developing nations (Easterly, 2006, 2013; Thompson, 2015, 2016), for patronizing and neo-imperialist attitudes toward the developing country stakeholders (Biccum, 2005; Easterly, 2006, 2013; Riddel, 2007), for living lavish lifestyles while purportedly helping the poor (Coggins, 2012; Eyben, 2014), and for an array of other reasons.

As expatriate experts, leaders in development often come to developing countries with the stance of the "authority-right-we, as against the alien world of illegitimate-wrong-others" (Perry, 1998, p. 59). Several of the authors in this volume have noted this stance and attributed to it some development failures. Eyben (2014) notes that the majority of leaders in international development who are sincerely interested in making a positive difference in the lives of others have reflected on the possibility that they may have promoted an inequitable system instead of changing it. Faced with the dilemma of having a perception of herself different from how others in developing countries perceive her, a common paradox, Eyben (2014) proposed reflexive thinking as a way of examining one's own assumptions and issues and possible shadow sides. One of the hopes of this volume is that we will be able to offer leaders in international development a self-reflexive approach to leading that positively impacts the transformation of the global system and sincerely improves the lives of all peoples.

HOW DO THE LEADERS IN THIS VOLUME PRACTICE LEADERSHIP?

The leaders in this volume, as described in Chapter 1, Toward a Theory of Leading in International Development, write with heart and generosity about their leadership failures, successes, and the influence of four critical factors surrounding leading in this context, namely gender, culture, context, and sustainability. This following section of the overview offers a summary review of these experiences in order to set the stage for the diversity of stories you are about to read. As illustrated below, our leaders hold a diverse array of views about leading, change, relationship building, power, and the four critical factors surrounding their work.

How Is Leadership Conceived Of?

The authors in this volume have posited a number of different conceptions of leadership in international development that we hope will serve to initiate a dialogue regarding what leadership may be most successful in this profession. Table 1 includes the various conceptions expressed by the authors in this volume.

The overall focus of the above leadership conceptions is on taking the "other" into consideration for all decisions and actions and leading to facilitate the growth and development of the other, often through a process of discovery and co-creation. Leadership is a cooperative and communal activity built on connection, or what Kathleen Curran calls "Global Resonance" in Chapter 18, Developing Global Resonance for Global Leadership. The notion of individual leadership does not make sense. Leadership is always in relationship, and hence, it is critical to transform the "I-you" duality intentionally into a "we" in order for positive and successful change to take place. As we as leaders influence others, they influence us. As we make decisions, the well-being of others is unavoidably part of the equation. We do nothing without input from others and we fool ourselves if we think we do. Further, authors illustrate clearly that leadership is a value-laden activity. The principles and values that the leader holds dear are inevitably manifested in his or her leadership decisions and actions.

How Leaders in International Development Initiate Change?

As change makers, international development leaders introduce change at many different levels and in a number of different ways, including at the policy level of donor organizations and developing country governments; in entire social and industrial systems; in developing country organizations; in communities; and within individuals.

Chapter authors present different approaches to catalyzing change at each of these levels, generally beginning with an emotion-laden mental transformation of certain key individuals that is variously described by the authors as an opening of never imagined opportunities, a new sense of personal power, a mindset change, an opportunity for a new way of doing things that will reap a better life, or an unleashing of personal creativity. As authors describe in their chapters, such a transformation is catalyzed by

Table 1. Conceptions of Leadership Expressed by Authors.

Leadership	Author and Chapter
Leading requires one to be much more focused on others than self, and for me, this is a magnet in drawing people to my side and has given me the opportunity to understand them better, their fears, their joys as well as their aspirations	David Mashzhu-Makota, Chapter 2
I use multidimensional leadership approaches, largely situational but also democratic	
Leadership of international development requires the level of deftness to be able to lead from behind and help steer the communities along the roadmap for the achievement of the SDGs	
Leadership in international development, in my view, basically has to do with hammering on the ideals relevant to the organizational vision and mission as well as aligning with critical legitimate stakeholder interests	
Leadership in this sector also requires flexibility and quick thinking because there is a lot of fluidity in situations, and things change, we need to move very fast forward but without losing sight to our goals	
Entering a room and subtlety reading the room is part of leadership and opening yourself up to changing your assumptions quickly as things change. Admitting errors immediately is also important for legitimacy	Iyabo Obasanjo, Chapter 3
Knowing yourself and what you stand for and what you believe in is a critical aspect of leadership	
Leadership is designing safe spaces for others to take risks, to fail toward success, to blunder away from shame toward creativity and innovation	Éliane Ubalijoro, Chapter 4
Leadership is making the vulnerable a powerful bridge for others' authenticity to emerge stronger, bolder, and more caring	
Being able to bring people along (a more feminine leadership trait) while also focusing on task execution, this capacity to hold polarities creates safety for those who are often scapegoated to bring their best ideas and abilities forward while ensuring that voices that are often dominating or charismatic are held under check	

Table 1. *(Continued)*

Leadership	Author and Chapter
Leadership strategies and tactics differ with context and desired goals that are expected. I believe that the context of leading staff to learn a new process is different from chairing a disciplinary hearing and is equally different from conducting a training program and even from functioning as an arbitrator	Keba T. Modisane, Chapter 5
I argue for a leadership model in which the development community acts as a culturally savvy mediator between the international and local communities rather than a dictator, in order to support and activate local organic leadership. By local organic leadership, I mean leadership that is authentic and originates from incentives developed by community members to make change and not motivated from top—down instructions from outside sources	Anne M. Spear, Chapter 7
We believe in leadership through encouragement, support, networking, and valuing others. We believe that true, sustainable leadership comes from acts of humility and trust; humility in the recognition that we "development professionals" do not have all the answers; and trust in a belief that all women have the capacity to lead if given the appropriate context, tools, skills, and network	Nila Wardani and Kathryn B. Mangino, Chapter 8
Now women can identify the real functions of leadership — influencing others, protecting those who need protection, making hard decisions, and directing others to a better future	
Being a leader is an identity, a persona that one must embody	Ashley N. Lackovich-Van Gorp, Chapter 9
My leadership is an evolving and reiterative practice in which I observe, learn, and interpret the situation and then mold my style, strategy, and tactics accordingly	
I believe that accompaniment and leadership are intrinsically tied together for those who want to serve and work in developing nations	Josh P. Armstrong, Chapter 11
Jesus told his disciples that their leadership needed to be different than what was found in the world	Gordon A. Zook, Chapter 12

Table 1. (*Continued*)

Leadership	Author and Chapter
The second philosophy is that of servant leadership which views the leader's role as developing other people through serving them. The leader functions from a desire to be a servant, which then leads to leadership as a way of serving others and the larger group or society. The servant leader desires to see others develop their ability to be leaders and draws true satisfaction from seeing this happen	
Intuitive leadership is leading with one's heart while allowing one's mind and gut to process all the information gathered from others through intuition and critical thinking and making decisions always from the perspective of the "we."	Randal Joy Thompson, Chapter 16
Over time I learned that leadership combines positive influence and effective action	Dick Daniels, Chapter 17
Leadership in international development is a journey of humility	
But the transformative moment of leadership is giving without an expectation of getting back	
Clearly, global and international development leadership is not an individual, independent activity. Such leadership is, notably, an interdependent and facilitative one, whether in business, education, or international aid	Kathleen Curran, Chapter 18

trusting relationships accompanied by data to show the benefits of the change; an empowering process where participants achieve mental break-throughs, new knowledge and skills, or similar happenings. Daniels contends in Chapter 17, Leadership Musings, that, in organizational change, cultural change is the initiating factor that proceeds visioning and strategic planning.

Following the initial openness to change, the transformational process is continued through creating buy-in from other key stakeholders, providing the knowledge, skills, resources, and support needed to support the change.

In Chapter 6, From Marginal to Mainstream: Leadership in Integrating Gender into Private Sector Development, Amanda Ellis recounts her approach to policy change regarding the need to finance private sector ventures of women as consisting of three levels that varied significantly based on the social cognitive model of change. She calls her approach at the most senior organizational levels "a transformational deep dive approach to expose unconscious bias." This approach, she recounts, was essential to help all the executive team become role models and visible advocates of the need for change. They also needed to be convinced of the business case for the change.

For mid-level staff, Ellis concludes that the business case was the most successful approach to obtaining buy-in. Front-line staff bought in through video training that taught them how to comply with the policy in terms of service delivery. Without direct positional power, Ellis recounts that she had to develop a collaborative strategic approach to engage those with power at the top of the organization to own the agenda and then use their directive power to create change through the hierarchy. Measuring results helped drive a positive cycle of change.

Relationship Building

An essential component of change is the building of close relationships with other leaders and stakeholders involved in or impacted by the change. Every author in this volume emphasized the importance of relationship building prior to even initiating any change efforts at any level in developing country systems. The primary focus on relationship building has not been the focus of international development practice, which instead has focused on "getting the job done." The importance of trustworthy relationships is a universal cultural and human value, and hence, it is baffling how little attention has been spent on this in the international development literature. Chapter 1, Toward a Theory of Leading in International Development, provides more evidence of the importance of relationships and connection in leadership in this profession.

IMPACT OF FOUR FACTORS ON LEADERSHIP

As I stated at the beginning of this overview, we requested that authors reflect on the influence of four factors on their leadership, namely gender, context, culture, and sustainability. Highlights of their reflections are presented in the sections below.

Gender

Most of the authors in this volume interpreted the gender factor to refer to how their own gender affected their leadership access and effectiveness rather than to whether their gender impacted the way they lead. Only Éliane Ubalijoro openly embraces feminine leadership in Chapter 4, Transforming Community through Feminine Leadership, and summarizes its key attributes for her. Interestingly, several of the women leaders practice leadership that exemplifies these attributes, without identifying them as feminine. Several of the male leaders in this volume recognize their privilege and also the reality that women bear a disproportionate cost of poverty, conflict, and underdevelopment. Women leaders describe the gender discrimination they have experienced, but also note that their gender gives them access to people and places men cannot go. As such, women leaders can join women's groups where men cannot go and develop an understanding of their needs.

Expatriate women leaders can also enjoy a special status and be excluded from complying with cultural prerogatives required by local women to a certain extent but not completely. As Anne Spear recounts in Chapter 7, What about the Grassroots Leaders? A Model for Culturally Appropriate Leadership through Empowering Local Women, they can be considered as a sort-of "Third Gender" with a culture of their own that provides limited access to where local women dare not go.

Culture-adapters and Culture-challengers

Leaders in international development, as the authors in this volume emphasize, must understand and adapt to the cultures within which they lead. Leaders need to be perceptive of cultural values and practices and agile to move from one to another. As Éliane Ubalijoro writes in Chapter 4, Transforming Community through Feminine Leadership in the African Context, "The idea that culture eats strategy for breakfast keeps me focused on understanding the contexts in which I am working. Understanding culture is primary to any task where leading with trust is intended. How change processes are designed, addressed, and implemented need a strong foundation of listening, observing, and seeing patterns that create cultures." Or, as Iyabo Obasanjo explains in Chapter 3, Leadership in International Development, "I am a product of African traditional Yoruba culture and Western culture and so in Africa I lead differently than I lead in the West. I have to be able to change from one cultural perspective to the other without missing a beat."

However, these leaders also point out that they are required to be "culture challengers" when certain practices negatively impact life. As David Mashzhu-Makota says in Chapter 2, Chronicles of a Humanitarian Worker, challenging a cultural practice may include

> *Finding innovative ways of creating new meanings where some*
> *cultural practices have become obsolete and are also a violation of*
> *some fundamental rights...One has to explore the best ways of*
> *engaging the communities without antagonizing them by getting*
> *down to their level to understand why they should insist on such*
> *practices and then providing them the narrative of the potential*
> *harm of such practices...Because they saw me as one of their own,*
> *I have been able to lay bare some of the unhealthy and also*
> *dangerous cultural practices such as female genital mutilation*
> *(FGM). The role played by men in such societies is very crucial and*
> *hence they need to be engaged as part of the solution to some*
> *problems afflicting the women and communities in general.*

In Chapter 3, Leadership in International Development, Iyabo Obasanjo argues that "if a cultural practice kills, it can be changed (or it must be changed). Most cultural rituals have a reason in days of old and now are just rituals with no purpose so they can be changed." However, to reinforce the elimination of a cultural practice, Obasanjo points out, alternatives must be available. For example, Ashley Lackovich-Van Gorp, author of Chapter 9, Leading with Girls, has spent much of her career working to change the cultural practice of child marriages and does so conscious of the cultural factors that justify such practices. As an African, Obasanjo cautions that options need to be available to change the motivation for such marriages. As she says, "saying that someone shouldn't give out their 15-year-old in marriage when there is no secondary school in an area and girls are considered unmarriageable after about age 20 without solving the school and other social issues is what I can interpret to the development worker."

Context

The context of international development, including the social and economic status of a country or its stability, may influence leadership, and hence, we asked authors to reflect on this factor. Noteworthy to highlight is the influence of conflict situations on leadership and the requirement that leaders not escalate conflicts. Further, as David Mashzhu-Makota points out in Chapter 2, Chronicles of a Humanitarian Worker, "security and access play a significant role in development, and as such, insecurity limits access to society, making it impossible for new knowledge and practices to reach these communities. Inaccessible locations are usually associated with underdevelopment."

Further, in such locations, far from formal systems, all issues are managed through traditional community structures requiring leaders to, as Mashzhu-Makota adds, "find ways of breaking through the social system and begin to develop awareness about basic human rights, children's rights, women's rights, and all other matters to help communities develop a much more egalitarian social order."

Sustainability

Authors interpreted sustainability differently, and it became clear from the authors that the United Nations has not clarified how the SDGs are to be interpreted or obtained consensus among leaders regarding how they are to be achieved. The SDGs have impacted the leaders in various ways including being more conscious about the impact of their work on the state of the world and the environment. As Éliane Ubalijoro comments in Chapter 4, Transforming Community through Feminine Leadership in the African Context, "What the SDGs reinforce for me is that respect for environment/ emotional space/built space/design are critical to humanity's thriving in ways that do not hurt the planet. The SDGs have made things that were seen as 'soft stuff' take on more importance today and give my leadership greater credibility. I am not seen as a soft feminine leader but as a leader who believes in the interconnectedness of all."

Marie Beebe emphasizes that "sustainable development presumes balancing economic, social, and environmental considerations." Iyabo Obasanjo and Ashley Lackovich-Van Gorp stress the essential role of women in the achievement of the SDGs and highlight especially SDG 5. Lackovich-Van Gorp reflects on the disproportionate impact of climate change on women and girls. Obasanjo and Nicole Rouvinez-Bouli emphasize that the most important SDGs focus on health. Dick Daniels argues that "the 17 SDGs and 169 targets within those goals demonstrate the need for collaborative partnership. This leadership competency requires the interpersonal savvy and cultural sensitivity to work across typical borders and boundaries to serve a greater purpose together."

Power

Power was not a factor that we requested authors to address but it emerged, not surprisingly, as a significant factor that influences leadership at all levels and in all sectors of international development. Power is an essential factor in the theory that Julia Storberg-Walker presents in Chapter 1, Toward a Theory of Leading in International Development. Expatriates representing Western nations or even INGOs enter developing countries and cross-country borders representing various power positions. And they, too, encounter individuals in developing countries also representing specific power positions.

Several authors discuss the need for leaders to more self-consciously reflect on their own power and privilege and to assess the power structures and make a determination whether to work within the given power structures or to become "power challengers" in order to achieve a more equitable society. International development leaders may face political grandstanding by local leaders whose power base is threatened and their organizations may even be asked to leave the country. Anne Spear contends in Chapter 7, What about the Grassroots Leaders? A Model for Culturally Appropriate Leadership through Empowering Local Women, that some of the failures she has noted result because "development leaders fail to become skilled at 'playing' with and around power, and development organizations themselves are unwilling to concede power and influence, refusing to challenge harmful power dynamics, particularly regarding gender inequalities."

She offers an analysis of wider power relations that influence leaders in Part 2, Power in International Development Leadership, of this overview.

NOTE

1. Gustavo Esteva is a Mexican activist who founded the University of the Earth in Oaxaca, Mexico, a network of learning, study, reflection, and action. He is a well-known advocate of post-development.

OVERVIEW PART 2

POWER IN INTERNATIONAL
DEVELOPMENT LEADERSHIP

Anne M. Spear

WHAT IS POWER IN INTERNATIONAL
DEVELOPMENT LEADERSHIP?

In a recent speech at the 2018 Comparative and International Education Society Conference in Mexico City, Gustavo Esteva[1] addressed a room full of international development leaders (Esteva, 2018). His message followed the conference theme of dialogue between the North and South, in which he suggested that dialogue must not be "just to hear, but to be transformed." How successful the international development community is at being transformed through listening and exchange is often debated and is a source of tension. Many scholars, including Esteva, contend today's development organizations and leaders charge ahead as new age colonialists with neoliberal capitalist agendas, doing harm despite vocalized good intentions. Highlighting the connection between development, politics, and economy, Collins and Rhoads (2010) explore neocolonial and neoliberal issues, "the former conveying new forms of global hegemony advanced by powerful nations and their institutions, and the latter representing an economic ideology by which weaker nations may be brought into greater alignment with global trade initiatives" (p. 182). In research examining the relationship between universities in developing nations and the World Bank, the authors conclude that development leaders in the World Bank were aware of such accusations, but maintained current policies do not contribute to a neocolonial agenda. Further, there was evidence of individual commitments to disrupting political and economic inequalities. Despite such expressed individual commitments, systemic ideologies can, and do, often benefit the privileged.

There is no shortage of theories exploring the impact of development, which is often made up of well-intended, good-hearted individuals. Critical scholars continue to draw on Gramsci and Freire to frame arguments in dependency, post-development, post-structural, and postmodern theories that construct notions of continued hegemonic oppression and dominance perpetuated through development institutions' ideologies. These theories and critiques cannot be ignored, at least in part, due concerning evidence of the increased global inequalities.

There are many complex power relationships within the field of international development. The chapters in this book attempt to explore some of these contradictory relationships, while acknowledging intersections of identity and marginalization. Authors examine leadership in development through on-the-ground lived experiences and through the way that shifts in development approaches allow for more successfully confronting power dynamics. This book contributes not just another assertion that context matters, but takes the critiques a step further, toward the demonstration of the application of successful projects, which challenge the standardization of development.

EXPLORING THE CONTRADICTIONS: CONTEXTUALIZATION VERSUS STANDARDIZATION

There is a practical logic behind the practice of standardization. Standardization allows for standards and comparisons in measurements and outcomes, as well as the ability to replicate and scale up projects. While there are benefits to standardization, there are also dangers, often at the expense of the disadvantaged. In *The World Bank and Education: Critiques and Alternatives* (Klees, Samoff, & Stromquist, 2012), education scholars rail against the World Bank's approach to standardize education development. Specifically, the institution's claim as a "knowledge bank" is challenged. The idea of a knowledge bank as a collection of "knowledge" for a variety of actors to draw on is perhaps well intended. However, it raises the question of whose knowledge is being validated, collected, interpreted, and disseminated. Knowledge also can represent an unequal power relationship.

A concrete example of the tension around the idea of "banking" universal knowledge is found in exploring the contextual view of gender roles in precolonial Africa. African women scholars assert that women were defined not by feminine aspects but by roles they played in their communities. Women, such as in the Igbo tribe of Nigeria, were involved in public life, including being active in political systems. Colonial influences brought prescribed ideas about femininity and the notion that women were not fit to participate in public life (Edbung, 2016; Ifamose, 2016). Others imply that colonial influences only reinforced existing gender norms of femininity in West Africa rather than creating such norms (Harsch, 2017). Today, Okafor and Murove (2016) declared, "One wonders how an African society can progress and establish the liberation of the enslaved others if it adopts the Western feminist agenda which perpetuates antagonism; the fight for self-assertion will never end" (p. 43). They go on to discuss that existing African values such as *Ubuntu* are more appropriate to apply to confront gender inequalities as opposed to outside development discourse. Further, Connell (2016) acknowledges, along with African feminists such as Patricia McFadden (2007, 2010), the disruption and influence of postcolonial development on gender norms and dynamics, such as the introduction of a western dominate prototype of masculinity in postcolonial Africa. Lugones (2007, 2008) goes further to term "gender coloniality" for the postcolonial construct of gender. She not only rejects the definition of gender but also emphasizes that the concept does not apply to the southern continents.

The above example, regarding an important concept in international development, demonstrates the complexities of context. How, if at all, can a "knowledge bank," aimed at syncing and standardizing "knowledge" to promote accessibility, be contextualized appropriately? This example of the different analyses of history of and influences on gender roles, and the certain views that have been privileged, aims to highlight the importance of development leaders' ability to address power relations and dynamics within their work. This book offers examples of how individual leaders can challenge the dominant discourse and systems and redirect power relationships within international development.

REDISTRIBUTION OF POWER: RECOMMENDATIONS THROUGH LIVED EXPERIENCES

As a post-development theorist, Esteva urges us to go "beyond development" toward "hospitality." He defines this as, "accepting, respectfully, that the other exists." In an age where he contends that there is a new social class — one made of the "disposable people" — it is imperative that leaders seek to be "hospitable" to the truth and knowledge of marginalized groups that current politics and economic ideologies discount. Concepts such as empowerment and grassroots participation can be employed to challenge the notion that anyone is disposable. We, as a collective and as individual leaders, have the ability to reject ideologies that bring such a class to existence by being aware of power dynamics and then demonstrating an active commitment to disrupting them.

Readers of this book will find a variety of suggestions to employ when engaging in development projects. Themes around respect of culture, context, meaningful relationships, empathic listening, and humility are presented throughout this book as means to demonstrate appropriate, responsible leadership in international development. Applied theories such as grassroots leadership, accompaniment, and the seven qualities of feminine leadership frame different approaches to implementation of projects through the development of relationships. It is within the acknowledgment of individual limits, particularly surrounding identity and privilege, that power can be redistributed and equalized.

The majority of the contributors of this book would emphatically agree with Esteva; we must not just listen but aim to transform. Within these pages, we receive lessons learned on how to reset harmful power dynamics and encourage readers to open up to new and old innovative ways of working with others. Whether as gatekeepers or allies, each person is a leader in defining how the world should look. To transform power relations that have led to inequalities is a massive task, but this book examines successful, applied approaches to slowly transforming unequal dynamics through connection and mutually respectful relationships that seek harmony and the achievement of common goals.

REFERENCES

Askin, P. (2012). The great turnaround in Latin America. In J. Ballantyne & M. Dugan (Eds.), *Fifty years in USAID: Stories from the front lines* (pp. 29–30). Arlington, VA: Arlington Hall Press.

Biccum, A. R. (2005). Development and the "new" imperialism: A reinvention of colonial discourse in DFID promotional literature. *Third World Quarterly*, 26(6), 1005–1020.

Carothers, T., & De Gramont, D. (2013). *Development aid confronts politics: The almost revolution*. Washington, DC: Carnegie Endowment for International Peace.

Cassen, R. (1986). *Does aid work?* Oxford: Clarendon Press.

Coggins, R. (2012). The development set. In J. Ballantyne & M. Dugan (Eds.), *Fifty years in USAID: Stories from the front lines* (p. 21). Arlington, VA: Arlington Hall Press.

Collins, C. S., & Rhoads, R. A. (2010). The World Bank, support for universities, and asymmetrical power relations in international development. *Higher Education*, 59(2), 181–205. doi:10.1007/s10734-009-9242-9

Connell, R. (2016). Masculinities in global perspective: Hegemony, contestation, and changing structures of power. *Theory and Society*, 45(4), 303–318. doi:10.1007/s11186-016-9275-x

Easterly, W. (2006). *The White man's burden: Why the west's efforts to aid the rest have done so much ill and so little good*. New York, NY: Penguin.

Easterly, W. (2013). *The tyranny of experts: Economists, dictators, and the forgotten rights of the poor*. New York, NY: Basic Books.

Edbung, I. E. (2016). Women' s political empowerment in Nigeria: A reading of Akachi Ezeigbo's the last of the strong ones. In T. Falola & W. S. Nasong'o (Eds.), *Gendering African social spaces: Women, power, and cultural expressions* (pp. 79–92). Durham, NC: Carolina Academic Press.

Esteva, G. (2018, March). *Beyond education*. Speech given at the meeting of the Comparative and International Education Society conference, Mexico City, Mexico.

Eyben, R. (2012). Struggles in Paris: The DAC and the purposes of development aid. *European Journal of Development Research*, 25(1), 78–91.

Eyben, R. (2014). *International aid and the making of a better world: Reflexive practice*. London: Routledge.

Foreman, J. (2012). *Aiding and abetting: Foreign aid failures and the .07% deception*. London: Civitas.

Harsch, E. (2017). *Burkina Faso: A history of power, protest, and revolution*. London: Zed Books.

Ifamose, F. O. (2016). Gendering the political space in Nigeria: The contradictions between theory and reality. In T. Falola & W. S. Nasong'o (Eds.), *Gendering African social spaces: Women, power, and cultural expressions* (pp. 17–35). Durham, NC: Carolina Academic Press.

Klees, S. J., Samoff, J., & Stromquist, N. P. (Eds.). (2012). *The World Bank and education: Critiques and alternatives*. Boston, MA: Sense Publishers.

Lugones, M. (2007). Heterosexualism and the colonial/modern gender system. *Hypatia*, 22(1), 186–209. doi:10.1353/hyp.2006.0067

Lugones, M. (2008). The coloniality of gender. *Worlds & Knowledges Otherwise*, 2(2), 1–17. doi:10.1207/S15327949PAC0603_5

McFadden, P. (2007). African feminist perspectives of post-coloniality. *Black Scholar*, 37(1), 36–42. doi:10.1080/00064246.2007.11413380

McFadden, P. (2010). Challenging empowerment. *Development*, 53(2), 161–164. doi:10.1057/dev.2010.15

Moyo, D., & Ferguson, N. (2010). *Dead aid: Why aid is not working and how there is a better way for Africa*. New York, NY: Farrar, Straus, and Giroux.

Okafor, N. I., & Murove, F. M. (2016). The Nwanne paradigm as liberative panacea to the patriarchal Nigerian Igbo society. In T. Falola & W. S. Nasong'o (Eds.), *Gendering African social spaces: Women, power, and cultural expressions* (pp. 37–55). Durham, NC: Carolina Academic Press.

Perry, W. G. (1998). *Forms of intellectual and ethical development in the college years: A scheme*. San Francisco, CA: Jossey-Bass.

Riddel, R. (2007). *Does foreign aid really work?* Oxford: Oxford University.

Rostow, W. W. (1960). *Stages of economic growth: A non-communist manifesto*. New York, NY: Cambridge Press.

Rostow, W. W. (1990). *Theorists of economic growth from Hume to the present: With a perspective on the next century*. New York, NY: Oxford University Press.

Sachs, J. D. (2015). *The age of sustainable development*. New York, NY: Columbia University Press.

Thompson, R. (2015). Dying to lead: Women leaders in Afghanistan. In S. Madsen, F. Ngunjiri, K. Longman, & C. Cherrey (Eds.), *Women and leadership around the world*. Charlotte, NC: Information Age Publishers.

Thompson, R. (2016). Theorizing women's ways of knowing and leading for international development projects: The adaptive transformational system leadership model. In J. Storberg-Walker & P. Haber-Curran (Eds.), *Theorizing women and leadership: New insights and contributions from multiple perspectives*. Charlotte, NC: Information Age Publishers.

Truman, H. S. (1949). Second presidential inaugural address. Retrieved from https://trumanlibrary.org/whistlestop/50yr_archive/inagural20jan1949.htm

United Nations. (n.d.). Millennium goals 2000−2015. Retrieved from http://www.un.org/millenniumgoals/

1

TOWARD A THEORY OF LEADING IN INTERNATIONAL DEVELOPMENT

Julia Storberg-Walker

The chapters in this edited volume were written with courage and heart. Courage because it is not often that we are given the opportunity to peer into leader challenges and failures and learn about the power of reflection and resilience. Heart because the stories expose the various sources of strength and commitment to lead in international development contexts. Through courage and heart, I believe the authors are generously giving of themselves and sharing their experiences to help the rest of us continue to learn and develop. We have the opportunity to learn how to be more compassionate, reflective, and effective leaders through reading their stories. Whether the context is HIV-Aids, economic empowerment for women, education, or agriculture, the stories offer an intimate glimpse of the micro-moments of leading as well as the power of critical self-reflection and continual learning.

Based on these stories, the purpose of this chapter is to offer an evidence-based preliminary theory for leading in international development contexts. While the leadership industry has offered countless theories, principles, guidelines, and leadership development programs, the industry has also been critiqued as Western-focused, gender-biased, and replete with normative values. As described by Karsten and Hendriks (2017), leadership is often viewed as "... heroic, wilful, decisive, rather masculine" (p. 166) and research on leading has identified the disconnect between the solutions offered by the leadership industry with the everyday leadership experience. For example, Karsten and Hendriks' (2017) study of Dutch mayors found "… we join a growing body of literature now emerging from Anglo contexts that challenges the heroic notion of leadership and that highlights the collective, nondecisive aspect of leadership …" (p. 168). Following this trend, this chapter is one attempt to ground new knowledge about leading from the actual experience of people in the field, doing the work of leading.

Consequently, we (the editors) designed this volume to bridge *leading* and *researching* and to provide an innovative alternative to the scholar/practitioner divide. As will be described later, qualitative research methods were used to generate new understandings culled from the leadership stories of the chapter authors. Much like interview data typically used in qualitative research, the chapters were the "data" from which the new ideas about leading in international development contexts emerged. Newer genre leadership research was consulted in order to identify differences and commonalities between the self-authored stories of leaders (e.g., the chapters) with the new scholarly ideas about leading and leadership. Ultimately, this chapter offers the beginnings of a theory of leading in international development and identifies specific implications for leader development, leader practice, and next-generation leader research.

This chapter is presented in four sections. First, the methods used to generate the emerging theory of leading in international development contexts are described. Second, the findings from the data analysis are presented. The analysis identified three critical elements challenging international development leaders: *power, connections*, and *paradox*. In addition, the analysis illuminates the complex relationships between *gender, culture*, and *leading*. The emerging theory is defined and illustrated, along with key principles and ideas culled from the data. Third and finally, the chapter concludes with implications for next-generation leading, leader development, and research.

METHODS

In scholarly research, clearly defined and highly cited scholarly references are used to support research methods decisions. One of the goals of presenting methods is to allow readers the opportunity to see into the processes used, to gain transparency, and therefore to gain trust in the researcher's process and ultimate findings. As we (the co-editors) worked on blending scholarly with practitioner interests, we developed a modified or blended research methods approach designed to offer tentative but research-informed findings able to be used for future research and practice needs. A critic could perhaps argue that this approach is far from the rigorous and pure archetype of social science research – and we would agree. But that is not our focus or our goal. We believe that new knowledge and new ways of knowing can be generated from multiple and diverse practices, that new knowledge is always tentative and context-dependent, and that new knowledge cannot be separated from the power structures surrounding the research (the researcher and her context) and the researched (the leaders, in this case, and their diverse contexts).

The seventeen chapters in this volume represent the data used to generate a new theory of leading in international development contexts. Seventeen chapters written by different authors may have generated a different perspective; just like the analysis conducted by a different researcher would have impacted the findings. From my experience over the years as a qualitative researcher, I know that to some people this is considered a "biased" or "fruitless" exercise because it can't be generalized. If new knowledge can't be generalized, why do it? I suggest that generalized knowledge is extremely limited – and possibly counterproductive – when the focus is on a deeply human experience like leading. To me, leading is an in-the-moment practice that cannot be divorced from the context within which the leading is happening. Scores on a leadership questionnaire are limited when a leader faces paradox, incommensurate choices, power differentials, and human frailties (including the frailty of the leader!). Consequently, one of the best things we can do is to understand leaderful experiences through stories and then try to discern the key elements that shaped the story. What we believed we needed to do as editors, then, was to develop strategies to gather a good set of stories about leading in international development contexts.

Data Collection Methods

To get the "best" stories for this volume, we (the co-editors) deliberated at length about the call for chapter authors and what types of stories we believed would trigger the biggest opportunity for learning. Starting with the lead editor's extensive career in international development, we created a list of cutting-edge topics we wanted to be included in the chapters. Then, leveraging the co-editor's extensive research on theorizing, we consolidated the list and created a series of questions or prompts we wanted each author to address. We wanted to cast a wide net to get a diverse array of stories from different positions, contexts, and countries. We were explicit with the authors that the questions and prompts needed to be used to catalyze their thinking and writing.

Ultimately, 43 chapter proposals were submitted. After reviewing the proposals, 17 were selected that represented the wide range we were hoping for. The chapter authors submitted numerous drafts that were reviewed by the lead editor and revised based on the lead editor's comments as subject matter expert, and ultimately the final drafts were sent to me (co-editor) for analysis and theorizing. As the theorist, other than generating the questions and prompts, I did not have a role in reviewing or commenting on in-progress chapters. This separation was important because it strengthened the legitimacy of the chapters by ensuring any biases or assumptions I may have about leading would not influence the actual creation of the chapters.

Data Analysis Methods

I used two methods of data analysis to understand the leadership stories in each of the 17 chapters. First, aligned with the questions/prompts that guided each chapter author, the chapters were read for stories related to the key topics of gender, culture, leadership journey, and sustainability. (Note: as described earlier, these topics were selected based on the lead editor's extensive international development expertise combined with the co-editor's leadership theorizing expertise.) The process of pulling out selected pieces of the story (chapter) is called *coding* in qualitative research.

Second, the chapters were read and re-read to identify important elements not predefined in advance. I wanted to identify, within each story, any overarching leadership themes, principles, or beliefs not captured explicitly by the guiding questions/prompts. This process is a modified *open coding* or *in vivo coding* process used by qualitative researchers.

From these two analytical processes, I then reviewed and re-reviewed each code, began to clump like codes together, see patterns between codes, and began to piece together a tentative meta-story that could represent the individual stories. Remember, the goal is not for "truth." Instead, the goal here is to offer one way to understand and build on the collective and unique experiences represented in this volume. This process illuminates one potential interpretation, based on modified research techniques, that permits a deeper understanding of the in-the-moment experience of leading.

FINDINGS: THE EMERGING THEORY OF LEADING IN INTERNATIONAL DEVELOPMENT CONTEXTS

Based on the review and analysis of the 17 chapters, 3 critical elements of leading emerged as most relevant (albeit in different ways) to our international development leaders. The elements are *power, connecting*, and *paradox*. After describing these three elements, a discussion of how these relate and interact will be presented as an emerging theory of leading in international development contexts.

Fig. 1. A Tentative Theory for Leading in International Development Contexts.

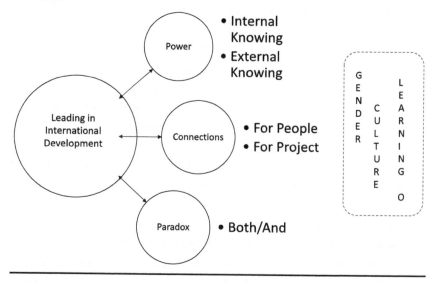

The illustration above attempts to show that all three elements are active when leading in international development contexts. Notice that the large circle uses the word *leading* and not *leadership*. This is intentional and is an important distinction that highlights the *doing* of leading rather than the *thinking about* leadership. Thinking about leadership is important – ideas from servant leadership, for example, are ideas that many of the leaders in these chapters think about in an aspirational manner, or to make sense of their decisions. However, in the moment – during the practice of leading, abstract ideas like servant leadership are not so helpful when one is faced with paradox. Leading signifies being a leader, and leading is a verb – action oriented and future directed. The double arrow between the elements and the large *leading* circle suggest a fluidity and interactive effect; at times, *power* is more salient and at times, the *ability to hold paradox* is most important.

Power, *connecting*, and *paradox* are fluid elements that ebb and flow, sometimes in the background and sometimes in the foreground, but they are always present in some way. Power contains two subelements – the level of internal and external knowing about the power dynamics swirling around you. Internal knowing (again, the – ing is intentional – knowing is a verb that implies movement and action, unlike "knowledge of" which signals cognition based on past experience) includes your philosophical view of power and its use/deployment in international development, your level of understanding of your own privilege and the power that is bestowed on you by norms and expectations, and your level of assuredness and centeredness in terms of your source of power (e.g., your personal mission or vision for your work). The external knowing points to the importance of knowing about the seen and unseen power structures around you as you work in international development. Always fluid in the background, leaders have some ideas about power structures and by including this "always moving knowing about power" in the emerging theory grants this important knowing the legitimacy it has in practice.

The element of connecting includes two sub-elements – connecting for people and connecting for the project. Both types of connecting are important for international development success – connecting for people signals the importance of building human to human relationships, honoring recipient and donor alike, and treating all with human dignity. Connecting for the project adds the layer of strategic intent to the human to human relationship – connecting for the project means that you develop human relationships with individuals with the skills, passion, and/or expertise to help you further your project goals.

Paradox is a word not used by any of the authors in this volume, but in each and every story, there seems to be some bit of paradox either in full view or partially hidden. Paradoxes are within us because we need to lead (e.g., be strong) and be humble at the same time; we need to, in some sense, maintain control, while at the same time empower others. Paradoxes are also within organizations – the need for stability at the same time the need for change; the need to complete the project on time and on budget while at the same time be responsive to the recipient country. According to the Center for Creative Leadership, paradoxes are "… described as dilemmas, conundrums, polarity, competing values or contradiction" that "… show up in all facets of organizational life including leadership (control vs. empowerment), teamwork (tasks vs. relationships), strategy (competition vs. collaboration), structure (centralized vs. decentralized), and within ourselves (work vs. home)."[1] Paradoxes challenge leaders to question their default either/or decision-making and struggle with living with the reality of international development.

The final element of the emerging theory is the dashed-line rectangle on the right side of the image. The rectangle illuminates three always-present background influences that are at play in some degree or another; the three are *gender*, *culture*, and *learning orientation* (learning o in the figure). Gender influences include the gender of the leader, the gender of the project recipients, and the gender(s) of the project team. Culture influences are great and included here are postconflict, postnatural disaster, and postsuffering influences. Culture, as illuminated in the chapters in this volume, is embedded in and touches on all aspects of international development. Learning orientation highlights the influence of passion to learn and willingness to be open to learning through experience. According to John F. Kennedy, the "… link between leadership and learning is not only essential at the community level. It is even more indispensable in world affairs."[2] The stories in this volume offer rich and intimate looks at learning through failure, learning by examining internal blocks, or learning just by paying attention. Learning is always happening to some degree while leading in international development contexts.

Ultimately, the emerging theory assumes an always moving, always dynamic flow of information, energy, focus, decision-making, anchoring, recalibrating, and relating while leading in international development. The stories in this volume suggest that power, connections, and paradox are the three critical elements of leading; and that always swirling in the background are issues related to gender, culture, and learning. It is important to note that Spear (Chapter 7) suggests that the traditional approach to international development has not been successful, in part, due to not understanding the importance of these elements:

> ... *three ways I have observed that the traditional approach to*
> *international development has failed, within the context of power*
> *and privilege: 1) the failure to build relationships creates missed*
> *opportunities; 2) development leaders fail to become skilled at*
> *"playing" with and around power, and 3) development*
> *organizations themselves are unwilling to concede power and*
> *influence, refusing to challenge harmful power dynamics,*
> *particularly regarding gender inequalities.*

Hopefully, the emerging theory offered here will contribute toward greater success for all stakeholders.

Critical Element #1: Power

The international development leaders in this volume represent a wide range of perspectives on power in terms of how it is manifested in their work as leaders. Perhaps it is because some of the leaders are interested in power, they naturally wrote more about it; others may be less interested in power and more focused on the mission or vision of their work. Some authors offer reflective critiques of their own misunderstandings of power and lessons learned, while others implicitly describe using power to set a development agenda without commenting on the mechanisms or belief systems supporting their power. Despite this diversity, in each chapter stories illuminated power differentials between entities (e.g., donors and recipients) or between people (between staff on projects or between leaders and recipients). Power, as illuminated by the stories in these chapters, matters to leading, implementing, evaluating, and sustaining projects.

One author, voicing a critique of leadership writ large, wrote:

> ... *leaders in many domains unwittingly encounter the same pitfall*
> *and create hegemonic relationships and processes for achieving*
> *goals that have been interpreted by an entity external to the context*
> *in which implementation would occur and do not take all party's*
> *priorities into account. (Curran, Chapter 18, this volume)*

This critique points to power over decision-making, agenda setting, and goal planning and highlights a reoccurring theme: international development professionals can use their power to decide what the problem is and how to fix it. This power lives and breathes throughout human society, and it is especially impactful in leadership contexts with multiple entities across multiple cultures – like the international development context. Curran goes on to explain:

> *Intercultural philosophy originating in Western cultures has also often been critiqued as historically distorted due to unjustified and unquestioned claims of superiority, rationality, and universality. Philosophically and in practice, therefore, the tendency to employ the expert "helping model" in international development, global business, education, or other contexts may be explained but not excused. Many examples of leadership in practice show a tendency to default to the outdated, yet well intentioned, albeit unjust and unsustainable positions of rushing to solutions developed, owned, and delivered by experts.*

Scholars who are interested in identifying and exposing hidden assumptions have wrestled with the issue of power and may have interesting ideas to offer leaders of international development projects. For example, Ziai (2017) advocates for "postdevelopment" thinking in order to "… critique different kinds of power relations … and contribute to a non-Eurocentric and more power-sensitive theory of positive social change" (p. 2550). Ziai's critique invites us to consider how we "normalize" power relations between people and challenges us to rethink or question our assumptions. In addition, Ziai brings up an important focus on the need for deeper understanding and enactment of non-Eurocentric views of change. This focus invites us to recognize and begin to label development practices, institutions, and infrastructure as built from Euro-centric perspectives and logics that may not "fit" with the perspectives and logics of non-Eurocentric cultures and contexts.

Another critique that can add value to international development thinking is found in Cooke (2003). Here, the argument is made that empowerment (a term so valued in the west as a signal of progressive intent) began as a tool used by colonial administrators to maintain control.

> *Achieving empowerment through participation was at its very beginning, therefore, subject to the colonialist's asserted sovereign*

power, and the limited autonomy it granted was a means of
maintaining that power (p. 47).

I have to admit that reading Cooke's argument made me a bit
uncomfortable – as a scholar and activist I fostered a sense of pride in my
"empowerment" initiatives. At the same time, I am slowly gaining a deeper
perspective of my privileged position in terms of "empowering" others,
and I believe continued critical reflection on my role as change agent will
continue to deepen my understanding of my power (granted to me by
social norms and taken by me as a change agent) as a northern, White,
educated woman. I believe all leaders will be well served by continually
challenging themselves and asking tough questions about how they understand power – how it is distributed, why it is distributed, who gets it, and
who does not.

McLaughlin (Chapter 15) shares my view and nicely captures the importance of a continual focus on learning and growth as a leader:

> *Among the most valuable leadership lessons I have learned is the*
> *importance of self-awareness and self-reflection. Awareness of how*
> *I am perceived by others helps me relate effectively and knowing*
> *what gives purpose to my work helps me find joy in it. Reflection*
> *helps me find answers buried within me.*

Likewise, Lackovich-Van Gorp (Chapter 9) shared an intimate look at
her ongoing journey to understand her own power and privilege:

> *Once a colleague from the Global North actually said, "the*
> *problem is the Ethiopians cannot think for themselves." I was so*
> *shocked and appalled by this comment that I could not gather my*
> *thoughts fast enough to respond. I should have recognized this*
> *man's racism long before this comment, but I was naïve and*
> *embedded in my own privilege, not realizing his level of bias*
> *because his bias did not directly impact me ... I remember that I am*
> *allotted certain privileges as a White, well-educated and financially*
> *well-compensated individual from the Global North and need be*
> *acutely aware of imbalances of power. I pay attention to micro-*
> *aggressions and I seek feedback from national staff and project*
> *participants to ensure that my privileged position is not obscuring*
> *my perceptions ...*

Power shows up differently in the stories presented in this volume. For example, contrary to Cooke's (2003) critique, in Chapter 8, empowerment is viewed as critical to

> ... the grassroots woman; the unrecognized every day leader who is brave enough to question traditional gender norms, and works for gender equality in small ways in her household and community (p. 151).

This view of empowerment seems to contradict the view that empowerment is a tool of colonizers and instead empowerment here is viewed as a tool of resistance. Wardani and Mangino, in Chapter 8, write that

> ... it was considered shocking to think that rural women had the capacity to take on serious issues such as infrastructure, resource management, or agriculture. The development world assumed that in order to complete a community diagnosis there needed to be an NGO or donor-led intervention ...

To Wardani and Mangino, empowerment seems to be a strategy to subvert or resist what they viewed as a power imbalance between donors and communities. What is different in this view seems to be the intent behind deploying an empowerment strategy; the authors view

> ... our role in development (is) as motivators working to bring out the leader in the everyday rural woman. We believe in leadership through encouragement, support, networking and valuing others. We believe that true, sustainable leadership comes from acts of humility and trust; humility in the recognition that we "development professionals" do not have all the answers, and trust in a belief that all women have the capacity to lead if given the appropriate context, tools, skills and network.

Spear (Chapter 7) relies on an empowerment model to help us understand more about the different types of empowerment leaders of international development projects need to be aware of:

> A clear understanding of the process of empowerment will help development leaders to determine what type of support is needed

for each female leader or group. I am employing Stromquist's
(2015) categories of empowerment: psychological, knowledge,
economic, and political. These four categories address different
areas of need for women to gain access to a variety of resources.
Psychological empowerment gives women the self-confidence to
take action and enter public spaces, traditionally only reserved for
men. Knowledge empowerment includes access to knowledge
either from formal and nonformal education. Economic
empowerment includes access to material goods, financial
resources, and economic rights. Examples of economic
empowerment include legal protection to own land and get bank
loans, as well as to access economic markets and enter the labor
force. Political empowerment comes from women's ability to use
their voices in their community, often in local politics or
community organizations.

The quote above illuminates the close relationship between power and gender, as cultural expectations (who gets to decide, who has a voice in public
forums) and leadership behavior (heroic, agentic, and independent) are
male-normed. Lackovich-Van Gorp (Chapter 9) described how she navigates
gendered power differentials while working as a leader between cultures:

Although much research indicates that women lead differently
than men, I do not believe that I do. I think that leadership is
more individualized than it is gendered, but cultures perceive and
label women's leadership differently due to norms, stereotypes
and expectations. Moving from context to context I witness
perceptions of me and my leadership change according to the
culture and situation. This constant shift in perception has taught
me that my struggle is not me, but the context and so I mold my
response to these challenging perceptions to the specific situation.
For example, sometimes I need to listen more and talk less, or
vice versa. Sometimes I develop personal relationships with
colleagues, other times I recognize a need to keep relationships
professional in order to be respected. There are times I need to be
assertive, times I need to be passive. Over time I have learned to
be perceptive and gain insights into how I am viewed to select

specifically how I can best affirm my voice and make a powerful, lasting impact on the lives of girls.

Another example of the relationship between power and gender appears in the actual work of doing international development, as described in Chapter 7:

I have personally witnessed how NGO workers contribute to the support of harmful power dynamics at a local level, often unknowingly. Many people desire to work with development organizations because there is usually an exchange of money, resources, and power. Thus, many corrupt leaders become opportunists and make themselves quickly visible to development organizations in order to be part of projects. These leaders do not have the right motives and are often not trusted by their communities. The foreign workers do not know this, at least in the beginning, and they inadvertently contribute to the power and influence of a negative leader as well as set up local implementation of projects to suffer (p. 140).

Taken as a whole, the issue of power lies between the lines of every page of this volume – either explicitly or implicitly – in all of the stories, anecdotes, and remembrances. International development leaders who continually challenge themselves, expose their assumptions, and remain open to learning and critical self-reflection about power will likely have a deeper tool box for doing this important work.

Critical Element #2: Connections

In each and every chapter, leaders describe the various networks, relationships, connections, and allies needed to be successful. Whether the need is diverse expertise, stakeholder information, or access to resources or legitimacy – the power of connections in international development cannot be overstated. Ellis, in Chapter 6, illuminates the importance of making connections as a change agent: "I knew I needed to quickly make the business case, engage the CEO as both ally and advocate, and create a network of powerful influencers across the company who would support the new Women in Business program." Rouvinez-Bouali (Chapter 13) describes *collective intelligence* as a product of connections:

> *Through our educative approach, I have fostered the creation of a "neonatal-perinatal network," where healthcare workers from one unit share their success with others and enquire about what they can do better. Networking has been key in facilitating the dissemination of helpful interventions in Benin … I do believe that significant change will come from this improved collaboration in the coming years.*

Rouvinez-Bouali also describes the importance of finding shared values as the basis for connecting with others:

> *Partnerships need to be based on values, instead of technical support alone. There is no financial incentive for partnership based on values, so that actions based on values are more likely rewarded as they engage local partners in a true partnership. Finding common values is key to improving the capacity to develop projects with low-resource country partners, who sometimes denigrate international help, based on the perception that international help mostly serves foreign interests, instead of those of the low-resource partners themselves.*

Beebe (Chapter 14) describes the connections needed for accomplishing international development work "Collaboration required the exchange of information, joint implementation of activities, sharing of resources, and capacity building of local organizations." And in a beautiful narrative, Spear (Chapter 7) describes the important learning that is the product of building relationships one by one:

> *One day, with not much "work" to do, I sat and shelled peanuts with some women. One of the women turned to me and expressed how pleased she and the others were that I was sitting with them and practicing Moore, the local language. I started to do this more often and began to see development from their view of the world: White SUVs that drove by to talk to the most privileged male politician in the village; money and projects, which never touched their lives; new buildings remaining empty; women who stood in the hot sun to watch celebrations honoring foreign guests that were seated in the shade of a tent; and women walking home as the wealthy guests and local male leaders went to a private reception*

with chicken and soda. This is what development looked like to these women. I soon realized that spending my time with them was what they valued most of all in order to build relationships.

Likewise, Armstrong (Chapter 11) shared this touching and heart-felt moment of making a connection, and learning (again!) the importance of relationships:

> *With a bucket full of water and an agenda to complete, I walked swiftly by a village elder sitting in the shade of an enormous tree. This man called out to me, and I remember feeling bothered by his intrusion to my work. After pulling up a chair for me, he proceeded to ask about our project. After satisfying his curiosities, I found myself pausing and finally entering into this moment of true dialogue. We shared stories of families and communities. I heard about his work, his history working for Zambia's independence, and the dynamics of leadership in Mize. I surprisingly found myself sharing about my own feelings of inadequacy in leading this community project, particularly after a lifetime of abundant water supply. After some time together, I invited him to join our classes and continue the relationship.*

Through the stories in these chapters, we are provided with many different ways to understand the power of connections in international development leadership. Connections can be made for information, to coordinate, to build trust, to gain power, and to gain legitimacy. Networks are formed to improve practice, to build coalitions, and to gain support. Leaders who understand the limitations of their own knowledge and ideas turn to others, form communities, and understand that the power of the collective is much greater than the power of the individual. Leaders, like many in these chapters, learn to become more discerning about when, why, and who to partner with. As Obasanjo described in Chapter 3:

> *When I was younger, I felt I needed to know everything in my different fields of interest. Now I intentionally ask myself how I can partner effectively for success and fulfillment. How do I choose the right partners so success does not come at the detriment of fulfillment? In the past, my focus on great technical skills blinded me to the adaptive leadership capacity of people I partnered with.*

> *This blind spot in turn brought more rigidity to work that required*
> *space for emergence to occur to tackle hard problems and*
> *unnecessarily lead to failures I had to own up.*

Blending connection with self-knowledge/self-reflection, another author offers a rather startling lesson learned about connecting to others:

> *My biggest failure as a leader of international development*
> *projects has been confusing people who were eager to benefit*
> *from my networks but were not necessarily interested in working*
> *with me and did not hold the same intentions for the work we*
> *were doing together. People often want to "help" but not all help*
> *is good or needed. Becoming more intentional in how I partner*
> *has improved the quality of my collaborative leadership ...*
> *Bringing people who are unaware of their neediness and see*
> *themselves as giving creates a savior syndrome that can bring*
> *toxicity to group work in international development. A person*
> *that takes on a messiah archetype is actually driven by*
> *unprocessed hidden wounds. This creates a blind spot that makes*
> *authentic reciprocity impossible. Need for control takes*
> *precedence to helping others become independent as well as get*
> *their fair due. However when a wound is conscious and not*
> *hidden from self, this can bring vulnerability and authenticity to*
> *collaborations that allows self-actualization while also helping*
> *empowerment of others.*

These chapters illuminate the power of connections over and over and over, and it seems to be truth at the grassroots level all the way up to the highest reaches of International Non-Governmental Organizations (INGOs). Forming partnerships, connections, and allies is a critical issue for leading international development projects.

Critical Element #3: Paradox

As described in the introduction to this section, the word paradox was not used by any of the chapter authors; however, reading between the lines *para-dox* was present in almost every story and leadership experience. Consider the expression *less is more*. We may have used this idea at some point in time as a leader – taking a back seat at times may generate more success in a project; or when coaching someone saying less may be more helpful to the client's growth and development than telling the client the answer. In international development, the paradoxes are numerous and ever-present, and include donor versus recipient needs/expectations, strong leader versus servant leader, individualistic versus communal culture, cultural norms of donor country versus cultural norms of recipient country, and empowering versus directing leadership style. The outcome of project you are leading may not be desired by the recipient community; for example, Lackovich-Van Gorp (Chapter 9) describes her challenge of working to help girls in a patriarchal culture:

> For example, in most places in the Middle East, preference for sons and the culture of masculinity make it very challenging to speak about the needs of girls without acknowledging the needs of boys. "What about our sons!?!" one male community member asked during a discussion on the unique needs of refugee girls who are prone to child marriage. Noting in my head that the mere act of asking about sons in a workshop on girls indicated the gender imbalance, I quickly addressed the challenges facing boys. Acknowledging that this culture is more open to equality than equity, I have integrated messaging about adolescent boys into my presentations on girls as a way to make the audience more receptive of girl-centered messaging. I am seen as being a very "balanced leader" who "treats boys and girls the same." Thus, I am able to have deep, meaningful, and intentional conversations about girls with some of the most gender-blind audiences.

Lackovich-Van Gorp's description of the paradox between her work (girl focused) and the culture she worked in (patriarchal) is clear and her ability to navigate the paradox proactively contributes to her success. Rather than polarizing girl versus boy, Lackovich-Van Gorp's strategic decision was to be able to tailor her communication methods and style to different audiences while maintaining her anchor in her passion for helping girls. In other words, Lackovich-Van Gorp's understood that if she did not attempt to depolarize the paradox, her project would be at risk. She used typical communication tactics and skills that were guided by her understanding of paradox and her commitment to diminishing the negative consequences of the paradox. This type of response — using typical communication or people management tactics — is one way to minimize potential harm when facing paradox.

Obasanjo, in Chapter 3, highlights the paradoxes inherent between donor/recipient as well as the perception versus reality of her expertise and knowledge. As a highly educated, senior level government official she writes:

> *I have worked on both ends of the international development, as a recipient of international development projects working in the Nigerian government and as part of donor projects. I believe my unique contribution to this book is from the perspective of the recipient since I believe most donor organizations do not see recipient institutions, structures and individuals as equals, and this holds back success in international development projects in many ways. As a Senator in Nigeria from 2007 to 2011, I was the chair of the Senate Committee on Health and this afforded me a front row seat in the interactions with development organizations. Almost all international agencies that came to advocate to me came with a prepared speech based on the fact that I had no knowledge or data or information on health outcomes in general and in my country in particular. Many times they came with a local Nigerian officer and neither would have researched my background education or anything. The assumption was that to be working in a developing country, a host country national must be a moron and be ill informed. I was better educated than many of the international folks that came to lecture me.*

Scholarship on paradox has been burgeoning over the last three to four years, and it has emerged in response to increasingly complex and incommensurate trade-offs in global issues like climate change, technology/security, and globalization. Johnson (2014) made the argument we needed to know more about this important aspect of leading:

> *Whether we call it Paradox, Dilemma, Polarity, Tensions, Dual Strategies, Positive Opposites, The Genius of the "And," Managing on the Edge, Yin and Yang, Interdependent Pairs, or some other name, there is an underlying phenomenon that works in predictable ways. The more we understand about the elements of*

this phenomenon and the dynamics by which it functions, the more effective we can be at leveraging its energy. This leveraging can support us in pursuing our most expansive dreams and addressing our most chronic issues—as individuals, families, organizations, nations, and humanity. (p. 206)

Human resource and management scholars agree and suggest that "navigating paradox has become the next wave in the evolution of leadership effectiveness" (Ulrich, Kryscynski, Ulrich, & Brockbank, 2017, p. 53). Navigating paradox is a combination of sensemaking, change, and innovation (Jay, 2013; Nelson, 2018) that requires specific leader skills, including "cognitive complexity, confidence, conflict management, and communication" (Nelson, 2018, p. 70). Paradoxes can show up between people, cultures (e.g., global/local), project goals, and time horizons (short term fix versus long term harm). Learning to anticipate paradoxes and plan mindfully will provide international development leaders a much deeper tool box for success.

CONCLUSIONS AND IMPLICATIONS

I have argued in this chapter that leading is a practice in the moment and that an analysis of the leadership stories in this volume suggests there are three critical elements to leading: *power, connecting*, and *paradox*. I have offered a tentative theory of leading in international development contexts (See figure 1, page 33) combining these three elements and I have suggested that always in the background are the swirling forces of *gender, culture*, and *learning*.

Understanding leadership as a practice in the moment is not new. Raelin (2017) offers a move away from a role- and influence-based understanding of leadership toward a collective understanding of leading:

To find leadership, then, we must look to the practice within which it is occurring. The practice view in a nutshell depicts immanent collective action emerging ... in the moment and over time among those engaged in the practice. By its nature, it challenges our traditional views of leadership because it does not rely on the attributes of individuals nor need it focus on the dyadic relationship between leaders and followers, which historically has been the starting point for any discussion of leadership (p. 216).

Raelin calls this L-A-P, or Leadership-As-Practice, and emerging scholarly literature suggests that LAP could offer both leadership scholars and leader developers with new and innovative ways to think about leading. In my view, LAP is not a typical leadership theory, *per se*, but rather a way to understand the emergence of collective leading. It differs from the theory offered in this chapter because it focuses more on the *how* (how does leadership emerge?) and less on the *what* (what do leaders need?). LAP advocates for equality, empowerment, and has democratic roots.

Specific to the international development context, LAP seems aligned with the type of values toward relationships and connecting found in the stories in this volume. For example:

> ... it (leadership in the LAP view) cannot be based on a philosophy of dependence in which followers without discretion follow leaders even if the latter are empowering. Empowerment in this instance still requires an empowerer, whereas in a philosophy of co-development, people discover and unfold from within themselves. The practice of leadership is not dependent on any one person to mobilize action on behalf of everybody else. The effort is intrinsically collective. The parties to the practice engage in semiotic, often dialogical, exchange, and in some cases for those genuinely committed to one another, they display an interest in listening to one another, in reflecting upon new perspectives, and in entertaining the prospect of changing direction based on what they learn (Raelin, 2013). Not requiring prespecified outcomes, practice can actually precede agency while focusing on a process that can be inclusive of participants' own communal, shared, and exploratory discourses. (Raelin, 2017, p. 217)

However, it is clear that the LAP "intrinsically collective" view of leading is not outside of hierarchical forces that exist in international development projects and that specific steps, actions, and principles would need to support LAP efforts. It would be important to discern what is not said or done as much as what is, to be cognizant of which voices are included and which are not, and to be aware of the forces (cultural, political, and economic) that enhance or diminish participation in leadership. That said, adopting a LAP view of leadership may well offer leaders in international development with tools for empowerment and emancipation:

By focusing our attention on the group in practice, however, L-A-P is witness to the formation of community within which members through social critique, contestation, and reflective emancipatory dialogue may have a better chance to resist oppression and other forms of inequitable social arrangements (Crevani et al., 2010; Raelin, 2014). Indeed, L-A-P potentially represents an alternative critical discourse to the mainstream personality approach to leadership, which tends to incarnate the individual leader as a beacon of prosperity and moral rectitude. (Raelin, 2017)

Implications for Leader Development

Both the emerging theory of leading in international development contexts and the LAP participative/process approach to leading can offer leader developers with new ideas for curriculum, activities, and strategies for developing effective and resilient leaders. Immersive activities in real-world situations could provide the diversity of experiences needed for leading, and participative or action learning technologies could be deployed. Individual and collective reflection on lessons learned could expose hidden assumptions (e.g., about power, gender, or culture). A focus on reflection combined with an open-hearted learning orientation can help leaders uncover hidden blind spots and assumptions. Adopting the LAP view would suggest that learning about collaborations and relationship development would be critical.

Facilitated discussions on power – both seen and unseen – would seem to be a priority based on the emerging theory. All of us, because we are human, are on a learning curve in terms of understanding the world and our place in it. Thinking about our power – the power that we take and the power granted to us by social/cultural norms – can well serve leaders in international development.

Implications for Research

From the emerging theory, combined with the LAP perspective, I see three areas for future research focusing on the how, the why, and the why me of leading in international development contexts. Research on how leadership is done, from the LAP perspective, would require deep case studies of the processes of leading groups and teams. Research on the why leadership is done could likely produce more diverse leadership stories, and thus, they could add to, extend, or change the emerging theory of leading in international development contexts. Finally, research on the "why me" of leading could focus on leader identity development across cultures and projects, taking into account power, connecting, and paradox. These research initiatives could help to fill the gap in the field of international development with more research- and evidence-based understandings about leading in this dynamic, complex, and fluid environment.

NOTES

1. https://www.ccl.org/articles/leading-effectively-articles/manage-paradox-for-better-performance/

2. https://www.jfklibrary.org/Research/Research-Aids/JFK-Speeches/Dallas-TX-Trade-Mart-Undelivered_19631122.aspx

REFERENCES

Cooke, B. (2003). A new continuity with colonial administration: Participation in development management. *Third World Quarterly, 24*(1), 47−61.

Jay, J. (2013). Navigating paradox as a mechanism of change and innovation in hybrid organizations. *Academy of Management Journal, 56*(1), 137−159.

Johnson, B. (2014). Reflections: A perspective on paradox and its application to modern management. *The Journal of Applied Behavioral Science, 50*(2), 206−212.

Karsten, N., & Hendriks, F. (2017). Don't call me a leader, but I am one: The Dutch mayor and the tradition of bridging-and-bonding leadership in

consensus democracies. *Leadership*, *13*(2), 154–172. doi:10.1177/
1742715016651711

Nelson, J. A. (2018). *Here be dragons: How global business executives
navigate change and paradox* (Doctoral dissertation). Retrieved from
Dissertation Abstracts International. (10747735)

Raelin, J. A. (2017, Fall). Leadership-as-practice: Theory and application –
An editor's reflection. *Leadership*, *13*(2), 215–221.

Ulrich, D., Kryscynski, D., Ulrich, M., & Brockbank, W. (2017). Leaders as
paradox navigators. *Leader to Leader*, *85*, 53–59.

Ziai, A. (2017). Post-development 25 years after *The Development
Dictionary*. *Third World Quarterly*, *38*(12), 2547–2558.

PART 1: CHALLENGES IN INTERNATIONAL DEVELOPMENT

The four authors in Part 1 introduce us to many of the typical challenges leaders in international development contend with as the result of gender, context, culture, and sustainability. These authors set the stage for the remaining chapters by highlighting themes that we will see repeated a number of times throughout this volume.

In Chapter 2, the first chapter in this section, David Mashzhu-Makota, leading on the "humanitarian front line" begins our journey by characterizing international development leadership as "both depressing and exciting." He highlights the contradiction of being in contact "with people overwhelmed with suffering and whose dreams are shuttered" and the "opportunity to partner with them to rise from the depths of despair and lead a new normal life with hope for the future." Mashzhu-Makota bemoans the uneven impact of poverty, injustice, and conflict on women. As a leader working primarily in countries at war, a growing context for leaders in this profession, he discusses the importance of being neutral and not adding to the conflict as well as the difficulty leading when an area is too dangerous to travel to. He reminds us that leading "requires one to be much more focused on the others than self"; entails "empowering both staff and communities with knowledge, skills, and competencies"; and requires integrity, conflict-resolution skills, and making tough and fair decisions. While he recognizes that leaders need to understand, honor, and adapt to culture, he notes that leaders must also become "culture challengers" in certain situations, an important theme that continues throughout the book. In his case, his organization opposes child marriages. Power wielded by local politicians and others who pretend to support development is also an important challenge faced by leaders as well as the possibility that a government may ban a non-governmental organization that they feel has too much political influence. Mashzhu-Makota reminds us leaders that we need to be diligent in ensuring that our interventions do not have negative unintended effects, as in the cash transfer program he describes.

Iyabo Obasanjo, in Chapter 3, says that her "unique contribution to this book is from the perspective of the recipient since I believe most donor organizations do not see recipient institutions, structures, and individuals as equals, and this holds back success in international development projects in many ways." As a former member of the Nigerian Parliament, a PhD epidemiologist, and a senior official in the Nigerian Ministry of Health, Obasanjo has been involved both in leading international development projects as well as in being on the recipient end. She recounts experiences being made to feel like a moron and her disappointment in not being able to pursue successful projects she designed in conjunction with the World Bank. Her leadership is contextual and responsive to the people she is leading, and is always based on "being fair," "building trust," and being knowledgeable. Obasanjo highlights the importance of understanding people's values and their cultures as well as one's own. As she says "working in different cultural milieus with varying value systems means you have to know your value system or you will be drifting in the wind with each environment in which you find yourself." Like Mashazhu, she believes that leaders need to challenge cultures that are life-destroying. Finally, she makes a strong case for a central focus on women and health in international development as the foundation of all progress in developing countries.

In Chapter 4, author Éliane Ubalijoro begins with a heartfelt remembrance of her mother who gave Ubalijoro her first example of sustainability-focused leadership. A professional with "multiple identities that all have been soothed by my mother's smile" derived from living in Rwanda, Europe, and Canada, Ubalijoro has concluded that "leadership is designing safe spaces for others to take risks, to fail toward success, to blunder away from shame toward creativity and innovation. Leadership is making the vulnerable a powerful bridge for others' authenticity to emerge stronger, bolder, more caring." As she contends, "when a leader is in alignment in mind, body, and spirit, decision-making is about serving something greater." Ubalijoro introduces leaders to the importance of being aware of one's shadow side and how it impacts one's competency. Like Obasanjo, she has been disappointed by some people she has worked with who treated locals with impatience and disdain and who apparently have a "savior mentality." She was forced to recognize that "people who want to help sometimes need more help than they are aware of and this lack of awareness creates unnecessary tensions in work environments. Bringing people who are unaware of their neediness and see themselves as giving creates a savior syndrome that brings toxicity to group work in international development."

In Chapter 5, the final chapter in Part 1, Keba T. Modisane introduces herself as a product of the Botswana government's emphasis on women's education and empowerment. First an HR Director in a Botswana government organization to foster local innovation and development and then as Manager of the School of Graduate Studies and Research at BA ISAGO University, Modisane focuses on intra-organizational leadership. She speaks of the importance of upholding cultural values in organizations and of the devastating effects when organizational climatic conditions become stormy. She assigns organizational leadership the responsibility of controlling these climatic conditions, a theme repeated in Chapter 16 of this volume, and asserts that "ethical and authentic leadership practices that shun unethical behaviors and practices" forms the foundation of a successful organization. Modisane implemented an internal development project to bring awareness to staff of HIV/AIDs, which has ravished Botswana. Overcoming the resistance of staff who criticized her for "entering their bedrooms," Modisane hired health professionals to design and implement the program to legitimize it. Results were positive and employees reached out for counseling, testing, and family support. As Modisane concludes, "I believe that helping others, displaying love of neighbor (including love of fellow employees), and caring for them in a small way (during their darkest hour) is a God-given gift we can all display no matter what our position is in the organization hierarchy and in the society."

2

CHRONICLES OF A HUMANITARIAN WORKER

David Mashzhu-Makota

International development leadership can be both depressing and exciting. On one hand, it brings you in direct contact with people overwhelmed with suffering and whose dreams are shuttered. On the other hand, the excitement lies in the opportunity to partner with them to help them rise from the depths of despair and lead a new normal life with hope for the future. Having worked in some of the most difficult and fragile contexts such as Darfur, South Sudan, Yemen, and Afghanistan, there is a pattern in which conflict tends to ravage the communities. Women and children, especially, bear the brunt of this savagery. Even though I never experienced the brutality of conflict as a child, a fair amount of my encounters resonate with some of the children I have come across now as a leader. These encounters make me reminisce about my childhood and it is amazing to realize how far I have come.

As early as in high school, I guess the potential to be a leader was in me. I grew up on the knees of my maternal grandmother and went on to start primary school a little earlier than the average age of 10, because most of my peers were already in school and my mom felt troubled by the fact that I was very lonely in the village during the school term. Even though I was seven, I was lanky and that made me a little tallish. The head teacher asked me to stretch my right hand over my head to reach my left ear.[1] He smiled at me and muttered something to the fact that I was admitted. I went into class and joined the rest of the kids immediately.

In high school, I still had the little boyish face and was the youngest in my class. In those days, prefects were big tough guys. I'm not sure whether this was the main criterion but I guess much had to do with that. Though I didn't become a prefect, I was a "Table Head." This sounds funny but in those days in a boarding school being a table head was a most prized role, because during all meals, table heads were first in the dining room, collecting the food for their allocated tables from the main kitchen and dishing it out in the plates for the other students. Gosh, you had to be close to the table head to get favors for "top layer[2]." This was the *crème de la crème*.

During my time in college and my early years of employment first as a teacher, whenever there were situations that required someone to stand up, I found myself rising up to the occasion. As a result, I grew more and more confident, and people around began to accept my leadership, believing, and trusting in my potential to influence positive change.

GENDER DISPARITIES IN INTERNATIONAL DEVELOPMENT LEADERSHIP

In my current professional field as a humanitarian worker, I have come across so much human suffering and discrimination of all sorts, which I can simply describe as pathetic, both in work places and directly in communities that I have served in. What has surprised me most is not necessarily the existence of these vices; rather, it is the, sometimes, uncompromising resistance to change by some of the supposedly key stakeholders. Also equally shocking is the level of complaisance by some of the victims.

Take for instance, while gender inequality pervades community life and naturally extends into formal work life, in theory, workplaces have policies and procedures which promote workplace equality. Unfortunately, the platform for the implementation of these policies is cast upon a number of constraints all rooted in the cultural milieu. For example, on the one hand, men generally battle with the idea of accepting women leadership in work places, in particular their national/local counterparts. And on the other, local women seem to be oblivious of their imperceptible subservience to their male counterparts and that chips off their self-confidence at an individual level to stand before men and challenge their views. Therefore, the context tends to limit the extent to which one can promote gender equity because the society appears to perpetuate the gender disparities in numerous ways such as placing less emphasis on educating females. This action creates the shortage of educated and experienced female cadres who can compete alongside their male counterparts in formal employment. The other cultural drawbacks are entrenched in how the role of women is perceived. Little girls are looked at as potential wives and not as future doctors, engineers, and so on. As leaders, we analyze the causes of these disparities and advocate for context-appropriate cultural practices and policies that do not endorse these inequalities in order to bring about equality and sustainable community development.

CONTEXTUAL ISSUES IN GOVERNANCE AND LEADERSHIP

In international leadership roles, we often grapple with the dynamics of contextual issues, particularly conflicts that arise as a result of different interests such as sustained levels of inequality, ethnicity, gender disparities, and many others. As leaders, we have to think through the impact of our actions, decisions, and programs to avoid perpetuating or escalating the conflict. Some of our actions may involve balancing staff appointments in key positions for example and also looking at projects to be implemented in communities and how these are leveraged to promote community collaboration and peace. Security and access play a significant role in development, and as such, insecurity limits access to society, making it impossible for new knowledge and practices to reach these communities. Inaccessible locations are usually associated with underdevelopment.

In ensuring sustainability, as leaders, we frequently place a premium on program design as a critical component to sustainable development. This involves designing projects that promote livelihoods, skills development, education, employment creation, poverty alleviation, and peaceful co-existence. We are also mindful of the cultural context and community aspirations around promoting positive cultural ethics such as child safeguarding and of course special interest groups incorporating issues of disability, minorities, and above all advocating for equal rights for all. I have an openness that allows people of all walks of life to feel comfortable to meet with me personally and discuss their concerns especially those deemed to be confidential where people may be hesitant to follow through the laid-down organizational reporting protocols. People have had trust in me and are generally fairly assured to confide in me.

Every so often as leaders we find ourselves leading people who are encumbered with a lot of baggage, sometimes all sorts of brokenness, such as pain, anguish, grief, poverty, and hopelessness. I am a little bit more empathetic knowing the background behind some of these people. I use multidimensional leadership approaches, largely situational but also democratic. Often I have realized that now and then, circumstances demand specific styles to dispense certain decisions – both those with positive implications and those with negative implications for individuals – which also require taking into consideration the character of individuals that I am dealing with.

I am mostly inclined to getting the processes right before the results, because then, when it comes to results, whatever the outcome, one can be sure that at least there was integrity throughout, and this diminishes the potential of unexpected skeletons in the closet. Sometimes, people get good results but they may use unethical means and no one may notice these because the outcomes may look wonderful and fantastic. However, integrity for us is not just a word we use to feel righteous but it's a part of our core values, and it defines our transactional relationships with all stakeholders. Several times, there have been attempts either through some of our service providers or staff for underhanded deals – usually in procurement processes – which, when discovered, have led to the termination of the service providers and our staff who were involved.

I have been instrumental in advocating for empowering both the staff and communities with knowledge, skills, and competencies. I value skills development because it has been most difficult in certain situations to get suitably qualified staff to handle some basic roles and responsibilities, this has led to sustainable community development in a number of projects that my organizations launched. In some communities for instance, some single women were being persecuted as they were viewed as potential suitors to the married men. This was an extension of the unfortunate and obvious situation of gender discrimination which is an intergenerational disparity. The fight now pitted women versus women, and the losers were still women. We ran programs that provided knowledge and information through educational campaigns on women's empowerment and gender-based violence. We also demonstrated through our staffing that women can occupy significant leadership responsibilities and lead from the front in some of our projects. In certain constituents, sociocultural barriers tended to limit the extent to which women were recognized as leaders; we, however, found ways of engaging all stakeholders in appreciating the value of what individuals could bring to the table without necessarily focusing on whether or not they were this or that gender.

Looking back at some of the failures experienced in leadership, a cash transfer program in one underprivileged community I served in a few years ago stands out. This project appeared to have been very well conceived to provide options for beneficiaries in terms of the household necessities to support their families. This programming had a lot of advantages over the traditional food and nonfood item distributions. It was more cost-effective, faster, and allowed beneficiaries to procure items that they specifically needed, besides it empowered beneficiaries to determine their own standards. The previous traditional baskets had witnessed an assortment of donated items making their way on the local markets as beneficiaries sold these to get money in order to buy the things they needed most.

The targeted beneficiaries lived in conditions of extreme deprivation and child poverty was severe. A significant number of school age children had either dropped out of school or had never been to school in their lives. This cash programming had been piloted elsewhere with very successful results, and therefore, we were all cautiously optimistic about its potential for success in this community. The program inception was marked with a sense of dignity and self-assurance and some of our beneficiaries' hopes had risen high, in the euphoria of celebration and excitement.

As our monitoring teams began to go around the community and provide feedback on the progress of the program, certain unanticipated details began to surface, much to our amazement. We learned that the majority of beneficiaries were investing the cash in buying khat[3] − a flowering evergreen shrub that contains two alkaloids, cathinone, and cathine, which act as stimulants. The users of khat chew the leaves and in our program it was shocking to realize that instead of tackling the major issues of household nutrition, children's education, as well as other social basic needs, our program was now perpetuating undesirable practices. To make matters worse, even children below 10 years old were participating in chewing khat as the product became more available in their homes.

It was very clear that we did not do a proper context analysis in our assessments and program design as these omitted the critical issues of the community culture. We had to face up to our donors and answer serious questions. This was particularly challenging and painful, as a leader. I felt culpable because certain critical facts had eluded our minds in determining the suitability of our design.

In view of the challenges that confront leaders today, the next generations of leaders have a difficult proposition because a lot of things are evolving, such as donor fatigue, and global economic challenges which have taken over the purses of many would-be charitable individuals and corporations. In the past, funding was not that too difficult to secure as compared to nowadays, where there is a great deal of competition among International Non-Government Organizations (INGOs), and this is coupled with the emerging of locally based NGOs also slowly taking up the space.

The next generation of leaders will have to live with the fact that resource mobilization will always be difficult for the unforeseeable future. Organizations will have to seek creative ways of programming that set out very clear proposals with high quality content that is not only relevant to address the current needs of beneficiaries, but also include sustainable solutions and innovations that speak to very contemporary issues, such as climate change. What can be funded by multilateral institutions will be influenced by the competing priorities. Conflicts and wars continue to create serious humanitarian needs. Unfortunately, most of the funds are spent on the war itself instead supporting the vulnerable communities impacted by the war (Schippa, 2016). Humanitarian leaders of the future will need to ensure that they continuously review ways of working. For example, sometimes in conflict zones, we have to work with local partners who are able to access dangerous areas of fighting because they have networks within the war zone. On the other hand, while INGOs maintain humanitarian principles such as *nonrefoulement*,[4] it is becoming much more difficult to support programming of refuges in foreign lands.

Depending on the societal values, gender can influence how people perceive one's leadership. I have essentially been brought up by women from the days of my grandmother, my mom, and my sisters. Even at work, most of my leaders have been females. This has helped me to be sensitive to others and be compassionate as well as rationale. I was fortunate to have been under the tutelage of female leaders, especially during my early years because I was able to absorb values of respect and integrity. It is worth noting that women have tended to have solid values because society's expectations for their discreet behavior seems to be very high.

Sometimes, people have stereotypes and this tends to create some gaps in terms of expectations. For example, being male, people in male-dominated communities are more accepting not because they necessarily agree with me, but because the patriarchal orientation dictates that men should lead. I have, on occasion, been able to meet with community leaders to discuss critical matters and share knowledge and information. One of the most notable was the launch of the gender-based violence program in one remote community. Initially, this was perceived as an attempt by women to use the platform of INGOs to settle scores with men, but when the elders heard my explanation, they appeared to have taken my words to heart because they were coming from a man. The fact that gender-based violence is not necessarily only per-petuated by men on women, but that it is violence against any gender, helped them understand how certain backward cultural beliefs may have dis-torted the real values of social relationships, like marriage, for example. I remember one man, standing up before a small crowd saying that "some-times, it is necessary to control our women so that they do not become too wild, and if need be they can be disciplined just like the children." There was a murmur in the small crowd but one could notice that he wasn't the only one who subscribed to this view. Explaining the role of both men and women as a man to other man makes a real big difference in some of these conservative communities. It is more like confronting oneself in the process and similar reflections appear to resound with every one of the men.

Being a man definitely does not give one the privileges to relate very closely at the level of women's' challenges. In spite of special care and con-sideration, I have noticed that I am restricted in a variety of ways. To begin with, there are no moments of confiding in me because of the cultural sexual sensitivities and the apparent differences. I obviously cannot appreciate how certain experiences feel to a woman and can only speak to these in ways that I can relate to. Nonetheless, men play an important role in helping resolve some of the challenges burdening women such as the unhealthy and danger-ous cultural practices like female genital mutilation (FGM).

The humanitarian sector has influenced my leadership in a variety of ways. Looking at governance issues for instance, where the principle of col-lective authority has been established, participation of all concerned parties is required before final conclusions are made. As an organization, we have set up frameworks to address issues of transparency, integrity, and accountability. As we deliver our programs to the community, we involve them to determine the nature of programs suited to their contexts and accordingly take cognizance of sustainability measures. The lessons learned from the cash programming that ended up perpetuating the addiction of *khat* has become like case law. In the current programs, we support community members much like consultants do, helping to shape the destiny of communities and also providing the support in terms of a variety of resources that are necessary to achieve the agreed targets. I have to assume a variety of styles to enable the organization to connect with the people at their different levels of articulation in accordance with the needs for program delivery.

Take for instance at a macro-level, what the Paris Declaration[5] has brought about, in my view, is not necessarily that which was not known, but rather that which was not being consciously and deliberately addressed. I have coined the acronym "MAARHO" to refer to the five principles of the Paris Declaration (Mutual Accountability, Alignment, Results, Harmony, and Ownership). MAARHO as I would like to refer to it consolidates the concepts of quality of aid delivery and positive impact in humanitarian programming. In some ways, this declaration has put in place a mechanism for a broader cultural shift involving critical core values that underpin the backdrop of funding by donors.

In terms of how MAARHO influences my leadership, the effect has been to awaken the need for collaborative approaches to leadership. For instance, joint efforts such as consortiums are now making a great deal of sense because they also help to harmonize our focus on community development and humanitarian support, extending the boundaries of humanitarian and development footprints. There has been a noticeable shift also in donor mapping with some contexts becoming less attractive and hence the frequency of funding shortfalls; this means that organizations will need to do more with less and this requires creative leadership. For example, in our country program, we sought to revive the reading culture that had been lost due to internal conflicts that destroyed the infrastructure for provision of quality education. Working with schools, local communities, local writers and line ministries we organized and printed more than 4.5 million copies setting up 6,000 reading corners across the country that enabled us to reach out to more than 1 million children.

CULTURE INFLUENCES AND DECISION-MAKING PROCESSES

It is important to appreciate the role of culture in shaping our societies. Culture has influenced my leadership in innumerable ways. In the first place, sometimes my reactions are instinctive. I don't have to sit down and think through every detail of my responses for ad hoc situations. I have a personality that people have gotten accustomed to which is both part of my nature and to some extent is couched in the key organizational values, with the latter being calibrated to my role and not necessarily what I may think as a private individual. For example, in a context where homosexuality is taboo, I will choose not to engage in this debate to avoid unnecessary controversies, which may undermine my organization's mission.

Leadership in international development in my view, basically has to do with drilling down on the ideals relevant to the organizational vision and mission as well as aligning with critical legitimate stakeholder interests. For example, in one community where I worked, we recruited local staff for most of the lower level jobs and my organization had zero tolerance for any marriage to girls under the age of 18 years and all our staff were expected to comply with these regulations. However, in their communities, marriage is not necessarily initiated by men alone, but rather by women as well. Girls are encouraged by their parents to present themselves to suitors. A 13- or 14-year old girl will brave the early morning dew and sit by the doorway at the dwelling of the suitor. When the man comes out of the hut and sees the young girl by the door way, he has to call on the elders in the home stead, and if he indicates to the elders that he does not want to get married to the girl or that he is not ready yet to marry, the elders will have to take the girl back to her parents. They will not go back empty handed. Instead, they will have to bring with them two to three cows as payment for the humiliation suffered by the girl due to the rejection by the man. The cows are seen as the restoration of dignity. If the girl is returned without payment, her parents will not accept her back.

In addressing the challenges around this issue of cultural complicity for marrying off young girls, my organizational values were pivotal in determining the minimum acceptable standards and also aligned to international children's rights, together with all our staff; we never tolerated any violation for whatever conceivable reason. In terms of reaching out to the communities, we used various methods to provide information, sometimes launching education campaigns and awareness programs with different age groups, use of visual materials, and mobile cinemas portraying the effects of early marriages on children. We established adult literacy classes, and in these classes, we also taught basic human rights.

SUSTAINABLE DEVELOPMENT, CONCEPTS, AND EXPERIENCES

Sustainable development is the key to unlocking community value and is central to the development agenda for any programming initiatives that can bring about positive changes in the human development index (HDI).[6] For me, this concept speaks to my personal and professional responsibility to model good practices that put people at the center of problem-solving, through the practice of ethical behavior, good governance, transparency, integrity, and accountability. In addition to these, there must be a real drive to create new ways of simplifying processes with value addition while retaining good cultural practices. For example, in some communities, people experience seasons of plenty and of lack. Fruits in certain places grow in abundance and they ripen all at the same time, giving so much plenty and with little room to store. Sometimes, these fruits are affected by fungal diseases and rot during the periods of ripening with little left for suitable human consumption. Traditionally, people have dried these fruits, but sometimes, the methods used diminish the quality of the fruit, and this affects their marketability. There is usually a lot of wastage that could be reversed with better methods and approaches such as simple technologies that can retain quality of produce and also create economic value for the communities.

Sadly, it seems there has not been much exciting news about the processes of the United Nations Sustainable Development Goals (SDG) implementation. The negative news perhaps stems from a variety of fronts like the challenges arising out of the limitations and deregulations imposed by some governments (states) on the humanitarian and development sector, but of course the most recent sexual scandals by some INGO employees have not helped either. The former, seems to arise when the state perceives that it has lost control of its constituents and thus been weakened politically. In a bid to reassert its power, certain less progressive legislations are enacted forming barriers impeding humanitarian support making access cumbersome and frustrating. These include, for example, requirements for rigorous registration processes for humanitarian agencies, inflexible memorandum of agreements, and unrealistic demands for financial scrutiny. For example, where an INGO will be distributing winter kits to communities, government protocols demand that any gathering of community members for whatever reason should be approved by the state. When approval has been obtained, dates are set for the function, and as part of the protocols, a senior government official should be invited and invitations are sent a month in advance with subsequent follow-ups. Sometimes a day or two before the distribution, you are informed to postpone the distribution because the minister will not be available and you are supposed to postpone the distribution for a further three weeks. Imagine the impact to the beneficiaries who will have to brave the biting winter without sufficient blankets for the next three weeks while awaiting the minister's official ceremonial presence for the blankets hand-over. This also affects the period of implementation agreed with the donors, sometimes resulting in unnecessary requests for no-cost extensions, which is an indication of failure to implement within specified project timelines.

OTHER CRITICAL ISSUES IN INTERNATIONAL DEVELOPMENT LEADERSHIP

Leadership in international development requires a lot of maturity and patience because sometimes moving an inch can be a painstaking experience that costs so much of the resources but with relatively less impact. It is the will power to make a difference that can spur leadership in humanitarian development as opposed to the desire for a high salary package. The majority of organizations in INGOs pay very modest remuneration due to limited budgets. Sometimes when news media reports that such and such an organization has received US$10 million funding, for example, members of the communities begin to imagine that all the monies will be shared among the INGO leadership. There is a lot of financial accountability in humanitarian organizations and with key risk management systems in place. International development leadership demands a very high level of integrity because that is also a key part of the credibility aspect in attracting donor funding. Leadership in this sector also requires flexibility and quick thinking due to a lot of fluidity in situations, and when things change, we engage in fast forward without losing sight of our goals. Be prepared to encounter both joys and heartaches and be ready to move on because your daily occasions can range from attending a funeral, to visiting bedridden persons and celebrating a function, and most probably hosting a high-level delegation for funding support.

I acknowledge several criticisms about humanitarian aid and rightfully so. A sizeable chunk of the critics' arguments has been relevant in general terms over the years, such as limited accountability, high staff turnover, competition for humanitarian market share, and the dilemma of neutrality (Branczik, 2004). In accepting these arguments, it must be understood that with the passage of time, the majority of humanitarian agencies have created much more robust management systems, especially in such as areas as financial integrity and accountability, which has become the currency for organizational sustainability.

The dilemma of neutrality is very much a reality that humanitarian leadership grapples with on a daily basis especially in conflict contexts. This issue creates a great deal of anxiety in everyone and we all have to be guarded in the way we speak or comment on any issues in public. This is the standard all over, and in fragile contexts, the impact of any utterances can be easily magnified or deliberately taken out of context to settle scores by our detractors.

Sometimes, leaders are required to practice remote management due to insecurity preventing us to access operational areas. This makes accountability extremely difficult because a lot of resources can go missing, making our work very challenging. Such losses impact very negatively on beneficiaries who are mostly vulnerable especially during these moments. As an organization, we have put in place business continuity plans to take care of volatilities and also train key staff on remote management to allow some form of practical sustainability in our operations.

International development leadership has everything that a leader requires to grow and consolidate his/her role in society. One of its distinct elements is that sometimes, there is a lot of uncertainty, and hence, one has to develop a reservoir for flexibility and adaptability. Fainthearted leaders would struggle to survive in these assignments, as the issues one juggles require mental strength and bravery. It is nonetheless an exciting and personally fulfilling career because one can immediately realize a positive impact on the human lives that one touches during the course of the assignments. There is nothing more satisfying than seeing a smile on the face of someone who has been overwhelmed with grief or burdened with hunger and sorrow.

The legacy I have left with both the staff and the communities that I have worked with is one of empowering them with knowledge, skills, and competencies. I value skills development because it has been most difficult in certain situations to get suitably qualified staff to handle some basic roles and responsibilities; furthermore by developing critical skills, this has led to sustainable community development in a number of projects that my organizations launched. Among some of the key successes that I am proud of is one of gender equity, much more so with regard to existing intergenerational community disparities. We ran programs which provided knowledge and information through educational campaigns on women empowerment and gender-based violence. We did not just campaign for the communities, but also employed women in leadership responsibilities, taking charge of some of our projects. In certain constituents, sociocultural barriers tended to limit the extent to which women could be recognized as leaders, but often we found ways of engaging all stakeholders in appreciating the value of what individuals brought to the table without necessarily focusing on whether or not they were this or that gender.

NOTES

1. Typically in precolonial Zimbabwe, very few children would get birth certificates at birth, and they would go on to enroll in school without a birth certificate. Head teachers, therefore, had a hard time in determining the actual age of the children. Hence, this system of stretching one's hand to touch the other side of the ear was kind of a yardstick to indicate that a child was old enough to be enrolled.

2. When beef stew or vegetables are prepared in big pots before being dished out, the oil or fat settles at the top and in dishing students would scoop the top part referred to as top layer. The bottom part would be watery

3. *Khat* is a flowering plant native to the Horn of Africa and the Arabian Peninsula. It is used as a stimulant, and it is a controlled substance in many countries. The World Health Organization classified it as a drug of abuse.

4. *Nonrefoulement* is an international principle of law that prohibits countries from returning refugee-seekers to their countries if they would be in imminent danger.

5. The Paris Declaration was signed in 2005 at the Second High Level Forum on Aid Effectiveness in order to establish better principles of cooperation between donors and developing countries and to improve the impact of international aid.

6. The human development index (HDI) is a composite statistic that measure life expectancy, education, and per capita income in countries in order to rank them into levels of development,

REFERENCES

Branczik, A. A. (2004). Humanitarian aid and development assistance. In G. Burgess & H. Burgess (Eds.), *Beyond intractability*. Boulder: Conflict Information Consortium University of Colorado. Retrieved from http://www.beyondintractability.org/essay/humanitarian-aid

Schippa, C. C. (2016). *Director, institute for economic and peace.* June 2016 Global Peace Index Report. Retrieved from https://www.weforum.org/.../2016/.../the-world-continues-to-spend-enormous-amount

3

LEADERSHIP IN INTERNATIONAL DEVELOPMENT

Iyabo Obasanjo

I was born in Southwest Nigeria, to the Yoruba ethnic group. The Yorubas traditionally revered birth order above gender. For example, in the language there is no gender denotation of siblings as in brother/sister but siblings are spoken of as either older or younger (*Egbon, Aburo*). Names are also rarely gendered although mine is, since it means "mother has come back" and only a female can be a reincarnated mother. I am the oldest child in a family of six children. As the first born in a Yoruba family there is a lot of responsibility placed on you, the refrain is that "as the first child goes, goes the rest." You are expected to lead and act responsibly as an example to your younger siblings and sometimes even to cousins and extended relatives. So, I always felt like a leader and that I needed to guide and help others and set an example. I was never formally told this but it was the expectation of everyone around me.

From a young age, I knew part of my responsibility was to succeed so that my siblings following would have someone to look up to. Professionally, managing people was what made me realize concretely that I was a leader since that meant I had to help people in their own career development and help them do their jobs better. It required me to care about them and learn about their lives outside work to understand what were their hindrances and help find solutions. This happened early in my career when I helped manage a veterinary clinic and the veterinary technicians and staff

71

reported to me and also when I was a project manager in the pharmaceutical industry in a matrix structured organization. I had direct reports, but I also had people reporting to me for a project deliverable, though I had no management responsibility over them. I had to have a good relationship with them to ensure that they would deliver on my project on time without having the responsibility of disciplining them if they missed their deadlines. This taught me that you could build good working relationships based on mutual trust and respect. I went on to manage a state Ministry of Health in Nigeria and serve in the Nigerian Senate and each role meant I had to make decisions that affected the lives of others.

I develop legitimacy as a leader by being fair and building trust. I currently teach and sometimes when a class meets for the first time I see the skepticism in the students' faces, a middle-aged Black woman teaching them. After a few weeks, I begin to see respect in their faces and that is because I know the material very well. After taking my exams and they that see I grade fairly but strictly, they again have a level of respect and see me as legitimate. So, I build legitimacy by showing my proficiency so that even if you don't like me for any reason, you have to accept that I am knowledgeable and know what I am doing. I try to be fair but not be a pushover. So I will listen and care but that does not mean I will leave room for you to get away with not doing what is expected of you.

How I decide what style, strategy, and tactics to use as a leader depends on the people I am leading. I have managed doctors and managing them is different from managing my office staff of five in the Nigerian Senate or leading as a university teacher. In all situations, people want to know you care about them. Helping doctors with continuing education opportunities is as important as helping undergraduates or graduate students with the next steps in their education or career choices but the level of independence of the person and the knowledge they have about the world and opportunities available are different.

Advising a student requires asking about parental issues involved, for example, a student may want to go on to graduate school but will the parents have the resources to pay some of the cost? How do I help the student find information on scholarships? For a medical doctor, I am going to assume more independence of action and ability to find information on their own. Also, sometimes leadership styles change with feedback. So I can assume some independence but if the person comes with added questions then you provide more. I also believe being able to notice situations in a way that requires the use of emotional intelligence is important. Entering a room and subtlety reading the room is part of leadership and opening yourself up to changing your assumptions quickly as things change. Admitting errors immediately is also important for legitimacy. I think when one makes a mistake and tries to hide it, it limits one's legitimacy.

In terms of my greatest success as a leader, I am most proud of people I have mentored or taught who went on to have great careers or do further studying due to my influence. My greatest failure as a leader in international development has been assuming that culturally, everyone wants the same things. I do still believe all human beings want the same things, that is, their children to do better than them, good health and safety and security for themselves, family, and property, but how these are perceived is clouded by the cultural milieu. As a person who grew up in Africa and moved to the US for graduate education and then went back to Africa to lead, I found that assuming people followed my way of seeing things was wrong. I was no longer truly African in my thinking and this was from my Nigerian education and from living in the US. Education fundamentally changes your value system. I didn't really understand people's value system and they didn't understand mine either.

I am a product of African traditional (Yoruba) culture and Western culture and so in Africa, I lead differently than I lead in the West. I have to be able to change from one cultural perspective to the other without missing a beat. I believe immigrants, in general, have this ability to function expertly in various cultural milieu. It also allows me to be able to deal with diversity in the work environment in the US. It also allows me to teach differently since I have various perspectives to choose from and I don't have a narrow worldview. In Africa, I can have meetings with development experts with a Western perspective and move to a local political meeting with another way of looking at things. I feel that translating each group to each other is also part of my leadership. For example, saying that someone shouldn't give out their 15-year-old in marriage when there is no secondary school in an area and girls are considered unmarriageable after about age 20 without solving the school and other social issues is what I can interpret to the development worker.

I learn to lead in different cultures by understanding that people all over the world are the same but the incentives in their environment dictate how they go about reaching their goals. For example, every parent wants a successful child but what constitutes success depends on how society incentivizes. If there are no women in leadership roles and only marrying a rich man is how a woman is considered successful then that will be the goal for parents but if there is an opportunity for an educated girl to reach leadership in her own right then parents will pursue education for their daughters. Instead of looking at the outcomes, I look at the incentives that make the decisions rational within the cultural milieu. So I lead by that knowledge and I know that the culture I observe has an incentive system that is rational in the system it operates in.

Culture is never static and even when people say, "this is our culture," you can historically trace the "culture" to some event. Humanity has been adopting culture from other groups since the beginning of mankind. As individuals and society groups, we adopt seamlessly and forget that what we now do we got from some other group or some individual. Humans are great at mimicry of what we like, so as individuals, we copy behaviors of people we like and as societies, we copy from other cultures we interact with. No culture is pure. It is an amalgamation of so many other cultures, including some that can no longer be traced. Even indigenous practices have origins and meanings long lost. So when people tell me something is their culture, I say if it is killing you then it is changeable. For example, during the Ebola outbreak in West Africa, people were told to stop burials since it was a source of passing the virus to others and to start cremating. And people did. So burials and the rituals around them was the culture. If a cultural practice kills, it can be changed (or it must be changed). Most cultural rituals have a reason in days of old and now are just rituals with no purpose, so they can be changed.

If anything I lead at cannot go on without me then it is unsustainable. All development efforts must be able to go on without development workers involved. The most important goals of the United Nation's (UN) Sustainability Development Goals (SDGs) to me are those that are about women and children. SDG Number 5 deals specifically with gender and to me is the foundation for all the others. An educated woman produces educated children with less chances of the children living through poverty or hunger with the know-how to get resources for good sanitation, clean energy, good jobs, and sustainable lifestyles. So sustainable development led me to focus on women as the source of creating a sustainable future for mankind. Knowing yourself and what you stand for and what you believe is a critical aspect of leadership. Working in a different cultural milieu with varying value systems means you have to know your value system or you will be drifting in the wind with each environment in which you find yourself.

REFLECTIONS ON INTERNATIONAL DEVELOPMENT

I have worked on both ends of the international development, as a recipient of international development projects working in the Nigerian government and as part of donor projects. I believe my unique contribution to this book is from the perspective of the recipient since I believe most donor organizations do not see recipient institutions, structures, and individuals as equals, and this holds back success in international development projects in many ways. As a Senator in Nigeria from 2007 to 2011, I was the chair of the Senate Committee on Health and this afforded me a front row seat in the interactions with development organizations. Almost all international agencies that came to advocate to me came with a prepared speech based on the fact that I had no knowledge or data or information on health outcomes in general and in my country in particular. Many times they came with a local Nigerian officer and neither would have researched my background education or anything. The assumption was that to be working in a developing country, a host country national must be a moron and be ill-informed. I was better educated than many of the international folks that came to lecture me.

One day when I was extremely busy, I stopped the lecture and turned to the Nigerian representative and asked, "Do you know what my education is?" As an epidemiologist, I love data and they were relating maternal mortality data, which I knew very well. I asked the foreign representative whether she would go to visit a member of parliament in her own country without doing some research on the individual, and we all fell silent, a little embarrassed. I then said:

> Please let me know how you want me to help.

> We are on the same side and lecturing me won't help your cause. Let me know how you think we can work together and I will be honest with you about the barriers and constraints if any, I face.

There were two exceptions to foreign donors talking down to me. The first was when Ted Turner, famously of CNN, came with a delegation of the UN Association and wanted to know how they could have effective interventions on measles vaccination to go with the ongoing polio vaccination. From the discussions, I realized they had some information on my background and did not assume I knew nothing about the topic and the interaction was more of a discussion than a lecture. The second organization was Engender Health led by Ana Langer who was from South America and not from a developed country. I think this fact may have led to her not feeling superior to me in our interactions.

My worst experience was with an antismoking organization made up of Nigerian youths who were paid by a US antismoking network. When they came to speak to me, I told them that given the levels of infectious diseases and maternal and child mortality and the low levels of smoking in the country, I felt smoking was not something I wanted to target. Our people still suffer mostly from poverty-related diseases and yes, smoking occurs but not at levels in the West and you have to be stabilized financially enough to eat to be a smoker. There is no local antismoking network in Nigeria. Rather, they are sponsored financially from the US. The organization started a media campaign against me because of my stance. The thing is, if elected officials in Third World countries cannot respond to their own local problems but only the problems as perceived and financed by the West, then we cannot solve our own problems but only solve problems the West deems important.

I lived in the Research Triangle Park region of North Carolina in the 1990s when it was transitioning from a tobacco-based economy to a research- and technology-based economy. The political leaders of North Carolina refused to impose strict antitobacco laws until they were able to transition their economy from depending on tobacco. Unfortunately, leaders in developing countries are not allowed the same privilege but must be dragged into doing whatever donors perceive as important and not what is important economically and otherwise for their own people. It is a double standard that many people think they are helping but are actually creating more problems. Self-determination is important for individuals to succeed and for societies to succeed as a collective. Imposing from the outside reduces self-will and determination and reduces the ability of societies to improve their own lot.

Before I was elected to the Senate, I was Commissioner for Health in one of the 36 states in Nigeria, Ogun State. In that role, I also interacted with a lot of international development and donor organizations, which sponsored specific programs, such as Merck and Onchocerciasis. We had an ongoing Health System Development Project (HSDP) grant from the World Bank. We drew down the money by writing up proposals for specific things we wanted to use the money for. We did things like the renovation of all 32 hospitals owned by the state and starting a roadside ambulance service by buying and renovating ambulances.

However, two projects were especially dear to my heart but the World Bank refused to sponsor both projects. The first started based on an observation I made. During the day, I spent a lot of my time going to meetings or attending to people who came to my office for all kinds of supplications. Some had a sick child they wanted to take to our clinic and had no money. Some were politicians wanting linkages or access. Many just wanted to meet and chat. I ended up doing paper work, that is, actual work in the office from after 5 pm to around 8 to 9 pm and when I got home, I watched TV as I ate dinner.

Without cable, I only had access to the two local TV stations. One was owned by the state government and the other by the federal government, and since I worked for the state government, it felt appropriate to watch the state station. Invariably every evening at prime time they had a TV show by someone calling himself a doctor who was essentially a traditional medicine man in a suit who was selling all kinds of herbal remedies as in-home shopping networks. The day I got infuriated was when he said a remedy was for the liver to function better and pointed at the kidney in the human body organ diagram he had up. I called the Director of the state TV station and asked why he would let a quack hawk medication on TV to unsuspecting citizens especially since the program was in Yoruba, the local language, so he was basically targeting the uneducated. The director replied that the Governor had given him a charge to make the TV station profitable and that the man paid good money to be shown at prime time. I asked if I got the money to put up a science-based factual show in Yoruba, would he remove the man from prime time and put my show on instead? He said, "yes," as long as he got the same amount.

The next day at the office, I talked to my HSDP team and some of the other senior physicians and we devised a one-season Yoruba medical program, which we wrote as a proposal to the World Bank, requesting to use the HSDP money to fund the program. We hired a semi-famous local Yoruba movie director and he hired actresses and actors. We also had a female dancing group who decked out in the local fabric for the program each week and they opened up the show (the quack also had dancing girls). We got a local comedian to weekly introduce the program by interviewing a medical expert on a health issue then there was a break led by the dancing trio and advertisement and then there was a 30-minute drama on a health issue (e.g., a woman not going for ante-natal and having a bad childbirth outcome, or the use of a tainted blade causing tetanus, etc.). The actors and actresses were the same ones in famous Yoruba Nollywood,[1] and the shows were weekly and very popular. It was what most of the local people talked to me about. The movies are generally high drama with awful story lines like soap operas on US TV but it is what the average African watches. Consequently, they would be a good avenue to provide positive health and other information to Africans even in local languages instead of most of the movies that depict witchcraft and other vices that keep people from having better control of their lives. However, the World Bank refused to continue to fund our project. Nollywood could be a development tool but it is over looked because it is not what the elite Africans who international development workers interact with watch. The truth is that those elite Africans have more in common with Western elite than with the local populations in their own countries.

The second intervention that I cherished but was rejected focused on capacity building, which was a major part of the HSDP. The money was mainly used to send senior physicians to the US and Europe for seminars and workshops. When I was first appointed Commissioner, I made it a goal to visit all the 32 hospitals the state ran and toward the end, I would be able to recognize the most senior nurse before she was introduced. It was usually the fattest and most worn out looking uniformed female in the hospital. Many of these nurses had entered the state service as young women and now headed up the hospitals, but were rarely appreciated or recognized. Many were dismissive of my suggestions because as far as they were concerned, I was another in a line of Commissioners who had come and gone and did nothing essentially to improve the hospital system. The ideas for training nurses came to me when I observed the patient intake at one of the hospitals. After taking the patients weight, I asked the nurse if she would calculate the body mass index $(BMI)^2$ and she didn't know what a BMI was.

Back in my office, I spoke to a former nurse who now ran a gym at the stadium in town. We worked together to devise nutrition and weight-management training program for nurses. There was an old nurse's hostel that was abandoned when the nursing school moved to a larger facility at the outskirts of town and it was now derelict. We used HSDP money to renovate it and it could train 50 people at a time. Nurses in the state employment based on seniority and distribution across the state so as not to leave any facility understaffed were selected to participate in the one-week program. They arrived on a Sunday afternoon and were weighed, given their BMI and a gym bag containing two sets of shorts, t-shirt, and running shoes based on shoe sizes they had provided. Each morning they had a 2-mile jog and I joined them many mornings. They then had morning classes on health and nutrition to benefit them but also to use on the patients they saw. They had cooking classes on healthy meals and they also had their own health status measured, for example, blood pressure, cholesterol, etc., and were counseled or provided information to use to consult a physician. I had a few nurses tell me that they had been in the employment of the state for 30 years and no one had ever done anything for them but expected them to selflessly work to better the health of others. Many had no additional training since their initial employment and it was one of the most gratifying experiences I had. Many were diagnosed with illnesses they didn't know they had. We had four nurses whose blood pressure was so high on the first-day screening that they were sent to the hospital immediately.

The development literature is filled with how nurses don't treat people well in developing countries but there isn't a lot on the status and conditions under which nurses work. While doctors have status and many drive to work in rural hospitals but nurses tend to live locally and are really the ones that hold the hospitals together and have direct involvement with patients. To improve healthcare delivery in developing countries, more emphasis needs to be placed on nursing and nurses. Doctors working in rural Africa do so because they want to or have issues or reasons to stay. Doctors are actually international beings and most can immigrate to a developed country or work in a city if they so choose but nurses don't have the same access or privilege. Focusing on nursing and nurses will be the best way to improve health delivery in poor countries. Doctors leave all the time taking their training with them but nurses generally tend to stay in rural areas and within countries more and uplifting and motivating them, should be a priority.

A feature of international development work is interference by government officials. One of the most joyous projects I was ever involved with was the eradication of Guinea Worm (GW) from Nigeria. As Commissioner for Health for one of the states in Nigeria, we worked with the Carter Center point person in Nigeria, General Yakubu Gowon. In 2003, Ogun State was one of two states in Nigeria with active GW transmission. This was due to the extreme rocky nature of areas in two local governments. In all other areas in the state, GW was eradicated by digging boreholes to provide potable water from the ground and having people stop using streams and other fresh water sources that were infected with GW larvae that lay in wait to infect humans who waded into such waters. This breaks the life cycle of the organization and provides clean water. In these two areas, several attempts to put in place boreholes had been unsuccessful because the equipment used to dig the ground had broken from the rocks underneath the soil. Attempts over large areas and even a geologic study to look for areas without rocks underneath had been unsuccessful, so the state public health team went regularly to these areas and taught the people how to filter their water from the river using a white cloth provided through the Carter Center. They would cover the top of the large pots they used to keep water with the cloth before they poured in water they just collected from the infested location.

Another alternative provided in one location was to move the whole village to a spot closer to the road that had clay soil and help rebuild their mud huts with thatched roofs by using burnt clay bricks with tin roofs and indoor toilets. Most of the affected villages had only a few people since there is a tendency for people to move out of rural areas, and about two villages opted for this option. However, even where it was not feasible or the villages rejected the option, we continued to visit the villagers to monitor cases and teach the procedure to filter the infested water. We got notice that General Yakubu Gowon, now retired, was going to pay a visit to the state and visit the two areas to review the work, which was sponsored by the Carter Center. At the Ministry, we prepared for the visit by getting our team ready and having him interact and talk to the villagers and to see the infested water and discuss how to develop a more durable solution. Gowon's people also sent a letter to the Governor's office informing him of the visit. The Governor then called me as the Commissioner and informed me that since he would be out of the country during the visit, his wife would accompany us. This would have been all well and good but the Governor then turned it into a political jamboree, with politicians gathered at each location, women's groups singing his praises at each location. Consequently, an in-depth review of the situation was impossible to carry out. Also, ridiculously, the Governor's wife wore 6-inch heels to the villages and went with us on to the rivers, which were a hike from the villages through muddy paths and sometimes dense forests which meant we cut short going to see the rivers the villagers got their drinking water from. This interference meant we couldn't give the in-depth on the ground assessment to General Gowon which was what he was there for not for a political jamboree.

I firmly believe that women are central to African development and I have therefore focused my work in the last few years on issues of women's leadership and empowerment in Africa. My experience is that in all female spaces the conversations and the passion to see development is different from in mixed gender groups. Women think of what kind of world their children are growing up in, and what kind of world they want their children to inherit. This makes them key to sustainable development. The Swedish Foreign Minister says Sweden will practice Feminist Foreign Policy and I think all international development should be Feminist International Development. All development projects should have a female as the local representative or project leader, and international development organizations should insist on this, or at least a female as the second lead. This will make countries look for and promote women for leadership in such positions. All international development projects should also focus on improving the lives of women. When women's lives are better, then the whole society is better, with healthier and better-educated children and sanitation and environmental issues are seen as important. The best way to assure sustainability in international development projects is to make them female-focused since only societies that figure out how to adequately use the capacity and resourcefulness of women will have sustainable development. One area in which including women is fundamental is health. Data continue to show that in developing countries women's leadership results in better health outcomes. This means that for better health indices, countries only need to put women in leadership positions. Since women are part of the citizenry, this is a much cheaper intervention than most of the ones going on today relying on expensive expatriates and solutions which are in many cases not sustainable or too expensive to broaden to scale.

NOTES

1. Nollywood is extremely popular with our local people. It is what they watch. The average African does not know or care about Hollywood and do not see their lives reflected in those movies. If you see Africans gathered around a TV in Africa most likely they are watching a Nollywood drama. And this is not only in Nigeria. I visited Kenya a couple of years ago and took a taxi from the airport to my hotel, when the taxi driver realized I was Nigerian, he started mentioning all the "famous" Nollywood actors and actresses and if I knew them. I said I didn't and I could tell that his view of how important I was in Nigerian society waned because to him, knowing the actors and actresses meant you were important. I have had South Africans ask me on a visit if I had any Nollywood movies with me. In English speaking Africa, Nollywood movies reign.

2. BMI quantifies the amount of tissue mass (muscle, fat, and bone) an individual has and then determines whether that person is underweight, normal weight, overweight, or obese based on that value.

4

TRANSFORMING COMMUNITY THROUGH FEMININE LEADERSHIP

Éliane Ubalijoro

INTRODUCTION: LESSONS FROM MY MOTHER

My leadership work in international development started when my mother passed away. I was 32 years old at the time, a mother of a 9-month-old, and had been living in Canada for almost half my life. I had come from my homeland of Rwanda at the age of 17 to go to University in Canada and planned to head home as soon as my undergraduate degree was in my pocket. My mother seeded my areas of interest years before, as I saw her decide what to plant, how best to compost, take care of the livestock, and host the most amazing harvest celebrations I have ever taken a part of. Our family had a large farm compared to small holder farmers in the hillsides of Rutongo, where my family home is based and now the final resting place of both my parents. My mother often hired from surrounding areas to accomplish all the tasks needed to keep the farm running, so when I was growing up I always had the impression, the whole hillside was invited to harvest celebrations.

My mother gave me my first example of sustainability-focused leadership. My father was comfortable in books, historical knowledge, dialogue, ancient Greek, and Latin as well as what occupied most of his life, diplomacy. From him, I developed a love of ancient history and studied Latin diligently through middle and high school. The task of running the farm was my mother's business. After years living in foreign capitals around the world, the smile she had standing by her growing fields in Rwanda is something I will always cherish. From her, I learned that nothing was waste but everything could be part of a larger ecosystem that we kept going to nourish the soil, the crops we grew, and the livestock we kept. Coming from a country that has gone through deep trauma and witnessing the resilience that was shown by women in its rebuilding after the genocide in Rwanda, taught me the importance of individual and community rebirth after destruction.

How my mother took back to the land and kept the farm going after being displaced into a refugee camp is the most powerful symbol of flowing with life in the face of suffering that I will ever have. She came back to a home that had been ransacked of anything precious and yet found comfort in the power of the land to restore life. When she died, my husband and I had begun planning when our 9-month-old daughter should get all the needed vaccinations to allow her to fly to Rwanda and meet her grandparents. At that point, my father had been mostly confined to a wheelchair following the effects of a stroke years before. This is how I remember my mother:

My mother didn't just cook
She served you love on a platter
Her love was infectious
Her laugh was infectious
Her smile all-encompassing
From the moment I was born
I knew I was special
I was her only girl
The one she always said
She would leave everything
From the time I was small
She would show me all her jewels
And tell me one day
They would be mine
That was a long time ago
Before the war, before the terror
Before the genocide
In the span of a few months

Starting April 1994
All our dreams died
Jewels were stolen
Dear friends died cruel deaths
And all that was left was
A few precious photographs
They were left behind
In the banana groves
When everything else was taken
Or purposefully destroyed
You see my mom was scheduled
To be killed then
But fate decided otherwise
We were blessed with eleven more years
Of her presence on this earth
During these eleven years
She created opportunities for hundreds
In the form of a good word
Leading to a job
Employment on our home farm in Rutongo
Favors here and there based on trust
She used her business acumen
Not only to create jobs
But to strengthen a community
That did not dare believe in hope
During those eleven years
She was a witness to two of her sons' weddings
Three baptisms of her grandchildren
As well as from a distance
Be part of two of her other children's weddings
Including mine
My mother died March 19th of this 2005
God gave us eleven extra years
Of her earthly presence
When she took in her last breath
My daughter was nine months
I still hear my mother

Whispering to me into the night
Be a happy child of mine
Strive for the best
Persevere, and when all hope is gone,
Persevere some more
Because I will always be
A bright light
In any darkness
That life will bring onto you

FOLLOWING IN HER FOOTSTEPS

It is with a mixture of deep sadness and joy that 12 years after my mother's death, I prepare to take on a role as an international board of trustees for the World Wildlife Fund starting in 2018. Next month, I will attend my first WWF International board as an observer to prepare me for my responsibilities starting next year. I am excited to contribute to reflecting on the work ahead to help scale "partnering for a future in harmony with nature." I am sure my mother would be smiling.

The goals of WWF Global are to "ensure that the world's most important fisheries and ocean ecosystems are productive and resilient and improve livelihoods and biodiversity; the most iconic and endangered species are secured and recovering in the wild; the integrity of our most important forests, including their benefits to human well-being, is enhanced and maintained; freshwater ecosystems and flow regimes provide water for people and nature; a global shift toward a low carbon and climate resilient future is achieved; and that sustainable food systems conserve nature and maintain food security." In 2013, I was the chair of the International Leadership Association's 15th global conference, and in that capacity, I was given the opportunity to choose the conference's theme of "Leadership for Local and Global Resilience." I chose this theme because my life has been a constant bridging of the local and global. In me are bridges to and from my homeland of Rwanda. As a child in a family of diplomats, I loved spending summers covered in the red ocher dust of Africa. I spent winters in Washington, D.C. and Paris, France. I went through years of study from private school to getting my PhD. The arc of schooling took me from nursery school in Kampala,

Uganda to graduate school in Montreal, Canada. I hold in me multiple identities that have all been soothed by my mother's smile. Leadership is designing safe spaces for others to take risks, to fail toward success, to blunder away from shame toward creativity and innovation. Leadership is making the vulnerable a powerful bridge for others' authenticity to emerge stronger, bolder, and more caring. My mother's legacy was all about building safe spaces for people to work, feast, dance, sing, reflect, learn, and flourish in life together. Being able to bring people along (a more feminine leadership trait) while also focusing on task execution, this capacity to hold polarities creates safety for those that are often scapegoated to bring their best ideas and abilities forward while ensuring that voices that are often dominating or charismatic are held under check.

WHAT THE DNA HELIX TAUGHT ME ABOUT MY OWN LEADERSHIP

Being trained as a molecular geneticist and having worked in the biotechnology sector, I have grown to appreciate how innovation cultures emerge from creative ideas. Working in innovation made me realize how critical leadership is to designing and enabling ecosystems that translate creative ideas into sustainable services and products that serve humanity and the earth. My work in climate change has built my capacity to see complexity and systems as opportunities. Feminine leadership has been critical to my path. According to Leigh Buchanan, there are seven feminine qualities that are crucial to great leadership. Leadership centered on these seven qualities is how I live my feminine leadership. I chose to lead with:

> *Empathy: Being sensitive to the thoughts and feelings of others.*
>
> *Vulnerability: Owning up to one's limitations and asking for help.*
>
> *Humility: Seeking to serve others and to share credit.*
>
> *Inclusiveness: Soliciting and listening to many voices.*
>
> *Generosity: Being liberal with time, contacts, advice, and support.*
>
> *Balance: Giving life, as well as work, its due.*

Patience: Taking a long-term view. (Buchanan, 2013)

Building community with other female leaders with reverence for the feminine has been a pillar to my work and gaining a seat at the table. My failures have centered on my unconsciousness related to the feminine shadow. In her 2011 book *Female Leadership: Management, Jungian Psychology, Spirituality and the Global Journey through Purgatory*, Karin Jironet shares with us how she used the seven sins and virtues of Dante's Divine Comedy to coach women executives she has worked with in Holland. Here are the seven sins (that I will refer to as shadows) and their related virtues (that I will refer to as light):

(1) Pride and humility

(2) Envy and generosity

(3) Anger and gentleness

(4) Sloth and zeal

(5) Greed and charity

(6) Gluttony and temperance

(7) Lust and chastity

The more I learn to see and bring light to these shadows in myself and others, the more powerful my feminine leadership has become, the easier it has been to build community with shared values as well as pass on hard-won wisdom to next generations from places I came to with extreme naivety.

The process of owning my legitimacy as a leader has been supported by phenomenal women of diverse origins that have passed on to me the lessons they have learned from their own successes and failures in their respective fields of international development work. Their leadership styles, strategies, and tactics have helped me own my path with greater authenticity and grow my capacity to be of greater service. From the gender-based research I have done funded by the Bill and Melinda Gates Foundation and other organizations, to the role I have as a member of Rwanda's Presidential Advisory Council, the urgency of bringing feminine leadership to international development continues to drive my work as I continuously thrive to become a change maker able to overcome resistance through compassion. The work I do spans food security, advocating for biodiversity conservation, global health, and climate resilience to building knowledge economies in Africa. None of this could be possible or continue to grow in breadth and depth if my cultivation of feminine leadership and a community of global women leaders did not support this journey for me. The values we share related to the socioeconomic empowerment of African women and girls have been central to the dialogues that have enriched my journey and the work I have been able to contribute to with others. My hope is to share the lessons I have learned along the way in this book chapter.

OWNING MY STRATEGIC MINDSET

My style, strategy, and tactics as a leader come effortlessly when I am able to act with compassion without dipping into sentimentality. I have struggled with a tendency to be a people pleaser for most of my life. Leading skillfully requires accepting that not all people will be pleased with what I do. Yet it is my responsibility to execute a decision or task with respect and compassion for all involved. I have favored the cultivation of a compassionately flexible growth mindset. I have had no how-to handbook to face turbulence, but I have done my best to stay present and open to learn moment by moment. I remember occasions when I had to fire individuals, and in each case, it was because the fit was not right with the task and responsibilities of the role. I went into these meetings with a clear sense that parting ways with this person professionally were about freeing them and the company to move toward a more appropriate path. I kept in mind the question of whether we had the "right people on the bus to get where we need to go." This perspective made the related discussions much easier for me. We all want to be on the right bus with the best group of people to journey toward what we want to achieve collectively. I may have been very lucky but for each case, I faced of having to let someone go, I never felt discomfort and pain despite my people pleasing tendencies. I realized that even something unfortunate, such as firing someone, could be done with compassion and respect, and I have found that the feelings were always returned.

When a leader is in alignment in mind, body, and spirit, decision-making is about serving something greater. The humility to ask for help from my teams always fired them up and always astonished me. The more vulnerable I was in service to our collective work, the more my teams gave me in return.

In contrast, when I let feelings get in the way such that being able to honestly tell someone I was dissatisfied with their work became difficult, I failed myself, the person I was having difficulty with and ultimately the projects I led. I once inherited a team member who was performing below standards and as long as I smiled and did not confront the team member, being nice to this person brought absolutely no change. However, when I found the courage to honestly and respectfully bring forth my expectations, what was needed from this person versus what they were delivering, an honest discussion ensued on this person's family issues that were becoming overwhelming. We then had coaching sessions where I helped my team member find ways to both meet our goals and give his family the needed presence they required. Knowing that I was supporting his success on both fronts allowed a new relationship to emerge and flourish.

OWNING MY SUCCESSES AND FAILURES AS A LEADER

My biggest failure as a leader of international development projects has been confusing people who were eager to benefit from my networks but were not necessarily interested in working with me and did not hold the same intentions for the work we were doing together. People often want to "help" but not all help is good or needed. Becoming more intentional in how I partner has improved the quality of my collaborative leadership. I have had situations where I realized some of my well-meaning Western colleagues working in Africa, inadvertently came in with a savior mentality. Initially, this was a shock to me to see this in action with a mixture of amazing benevolence toward poor small holder farmers and a total disdain of the mid-to-low level government civil servant, our only critical link to local farmers. There was a constant impatience with local government colleagues and anger at them that previous recommendations were not implemented. At the same time, these same local colleagues and I had been left out of a critical publication that would have given greater local ownership to the work and its implementation. My hope that things would change, resulted in disappointment until I severed the relationship. What I learned from this experience is that people who want to help sometimes need more help than they are aware of and this lack of awareness creates unnecessary tensions in work environments. Bringing people who are unaware of their neediness and see themselves as giving creates a savior syndrome that can bring toxicity to group work in international development. A person that takes on a messiah archetype is actually driven by unprocessed hidden wounds. This creates a blind spot that makes authentic reciprocity impossible. Need for control takes precedence over help others become independent as well as get their fair due. However, when a wound is conscious and not hidden from self, this can bring vulnerability and authenticity to collaborations that allow self-actualization while also helping empowerment of others.

As a leader, I am humbled and content to see others thrive because I gave them support on their own journeys. I am proud of the power of collaborative projects to accomplish so much more than I could do on my own. I am rewarded by how much I have learned to become a more compassionate leader after my daughter's birth. I learned to see that I needed compassion. Becoming a mother, grieving over the loss of my mother and having to pivot away from a high passed trajectory in the biotechnology sector were a lot of things for me to juggle at the same time. I wanted to explore ways I could thrive professionally in Canada while being of service to my homeland and mothering my daughter. I had studied agriculture as an undergraduate student in the hope of working in the area of food security in Rwanda. The last three decades of history in Rwanda challenged me to find a new path that led to a career in the biotechnology sector in Canada. I had to rethink my career again to create a path for me to take care of my father after my mother's death. This took me back to international development but with the added experience of years working through the biotechnology innovation ecosystem. Over the last 11 years, I have established an international career that combines all I have learned from leadership through innovation as well as through facing the suffering of my country and my own powerlessness faced with the horror that took place there. My journey to grow my love for Rwanda, for the planet, and for humanity has opened me to hold more suffering with the paralyzing effects of depression I struggled with during my graduate studies after the Genocide. Dedication to my work, my collaborations, and to each team member even when I had to let them go, have given me a level of clarity that allowed me to thrive in the biotech sector. Working in international development has required me to stretch my capacity to love and hold suffering beyond anything I could have imagined. I have also learned to dream bigger and widen my horizons because I have opened myself to collaborating with others to accomplish many things beyond my personal expertise.

MY DREAMS FOR THE NEXT GENERATION

What I wish I knew all along is that believing in the power of love is not naïve or innocent but is an act of rebellion in a world that sees material symbols of power and the easy path of significance through force and violence as legitimate. I also wish I understood that reciprocity is the foundation for creating a peaceful and inclusive whole. In my work in international development, I have seen the shadow of giving disempower people when reciprocity is not foundational. Where there is no reciprocity, a power dynamic sets any intent to solve a problem into a path of legitimizing the savior by perpetuating victimization.

I wish I had known that studying and dissecting poverty doesn't create a pathway to prosperity but serves to nurture experts on poverty.

I wish I had known the power of studying positive deviance earlier and the urgent need to find ways to scale these anomalies.

Over the last year, I have had the opportunity to mentor and support young female and male African scientists through the Next Einstein Forum and the African Institute for Mathematical Sciences. I have also had the opportunity to take part in dialogues related to the intersections of gender bias and innovation in this same context. What I want this new generation of African leaders to know is that if they are willing to dream big while they continue to work as hard as they do, being willing to ask for support can often help leapfrog obstacles that are difficult to overcome alone. When I was younger, I felt I needed to know everything in my different fields of interest. Now I intentionally ask myself how I can partner effectively for success and fulfillment. How do I choose the right partners so success does not come at the detriment of fulfillment? In the past, my focus on great technical skills blinded me to the adaptive leadership capacity of people I partnered with. This blind spot, in turn, brought more rigidity to work that required space for emergence to occur to tackle hard problems and unnecessarily lead to failures I had to own up.

REFLECTING ON GENDER IN MY LEADERSHIP

My gender has deeply influenced my leadership style. When I was studying for my PhD, I sometimes was told I would never find a husband because I was becoming "overeducated." It was perplexing to me that while I studied genes and DNA important in the communication between plants and symbiotic fungi, why someone felt my only purpose in life was finding a husband. Decades, later, as a mother to a 13-year-old daughter and wife, I realize how important it is to shape girls' minds to not limit themselves. Studying biases related to gender and professional roles, I have incorporated these insights into my leadership teaching in executive programs. Having been confronted with what some may see as legitimate versus "non-legitimate" pathways I can take, I reflect deeply on how I vision my authentic purpose versus a desire to please or prove others wrong. Because many of the roles I have taken on didn't have role models that look like me that I had easy access to, looking inward has been critical to creating a path that is my own. I am an African female professor, advisor, and consultant, and I look much younger than my actual age. Whether I was lecturing in molecular genetics, leading a research and development team in a biotech company, advising a President, working with executives on their leadership development, I had to learn to own my physical space through the puzzlement of my audience. I had to also learn to trust that the "package" I came in was also a legitimate source of learning.

My gender only limits me if I allow it. When I feel more comfortable blending the best of my feminine and masculine leadership styles, I can bring both compassion and authority to tasks and group work. International development projects often involve transforming reactive vicious cycles into creative virtuous cycles.

WHY UNDERSTANDING CONTEXT HAS BEEN CRITICAL TO MY LEADERSHIP

My first arts-based action research workshop in Rwanda had space for local participants to draw challenges they face. I remember seeing these images of gender-based violence, of memories of the genocide from repeated images and I had to remind myself that beyond my role as a researcher I was working people who had lived trauma up close I had felt from afar. I felt deeply moved by their capacity to hold pain and hope so strongly and with so much grace. The project was ultimately to improve food security but what this reminded me is that we were working with real people, mind, body, and soul and couldn't only focus on what technology-based solutions. The socio-political-economic context maps out the level of suffering held in groups, communities, and nations. Context allows history and data to both inform what is it I am not seeing. How do I get beyond my blind spots to truly see systems anew so improving livelihoods and protecting earth can both happen? What are the places of resistance that slow change making? What are the enablers/attractors that can positively bring transformation? Understanding how resistant or enabling factors link to socio-political-economic context is critical in growing effective leadership and trust.

The sector, I am working in, brings innovation, sustainability, and economic growth together to improve local livelihoods and respect for the planet. The interconnectedness of these issues is central to how I lead and work within complex systems. I am always aware that I will never have all the data to make a perfect decision but I have the opportunity to advance solutions that may be imperfect but effectively bring people, profit, purpose, and planet to align with the best data I have at each stage.

THE ENABLING POWER OF CULTURE

The idea that culture eats strategy for breakfast keeps me focused on understanding the contexts in which I am working. Understanding culture is primary to any task where leading with trust is intended. How change processes are designed, addressed, and implemented need a strong foundation of listening, observing, and seeing patterns that create cultures.

Beginner's mind is critical to leading in different cultures. Asking questions, even ones that feel stupid but are asked to illuminate my own ignorance while respecting others skills and capacity is the best way I know to lead in different cultures. Cultivating engagement across cultures creates learning environments where people feel safe to ask questions, share failures, and find solutions collectively. Beyond all the places where I feel uncertain, the other stands ready to help as long as I show up equally holding my strengths, vulnerabilities, passion, and capacity to vision/co-create with others.

What surprises me most is how little attention is given to culture in international development and how often power dynamics are not explored and dismantled. The search for silver bullets often causes leadership to neglect the power of culture to shape context and enable or prevent change from occurring. This quick fix grounded in patriarchal heroic leadership that accepts implicit violence in the classic image of a silver bullet is the polar opposite of a culture of empathy and caring grounded in partnership as voiced by Riane Eisler in all her writings.

BUILDING ON MY MOTHER'S LEADERSHIP IN SUSTAINABLE DEVELOPMENT

Growing up on three continents exposed me to different ways of living on this earth. What has stayed with me through the years has been the amazing ways my mother ran our family farm in rural Rwanda and ensured nothing was wasted, whatever could be composted nurtured the soil and whatever could be reused was done so respectfully at a time where garbage collection was not available. She introduced me to recycling decades before I had access in Europe or North America to a blue recycling bin. Now more than a decade after her passing, whether I am advising a government, NGO, or private sector organization on climate resilient pathways, I remember the lessons I learned through watching my mother, nothing is too ugly to be wasted, even pain, even anger when shared with vulnerability and compassion can fertilize what seemed sterile and dead. My mother lived with a deep responsibility for cleanliness not only inside our home but also in taking responsibility for what we put out in the environment. There was no difference for her between our home and the soil that nurtured the crops we grew; each needed intentional nurturing and conscious choices to uphold this nurturing. I have realized that taking responsibility for a clean mind and heart was find ways to air my frustrations in ways that built bonds and did not engage in character assassination. I learned to let go where the resistance to the changes I believed in and the valued I held were not shared. Sustainable development for me is an alignment of purpose, people, and the planet. As a scientist, I know that innovation is not the limiting factor to humanity intentionally living with purpose and respect for the earth. According to Jungian therapist Luke (1962), "the true light never hides the darkness but is born out of the very center of it, transforming and redeeming. So to the darkness we must return, each of us individually accepting his ignorance and loneliness, his sin and weakness, and, most difficult of all, consenting to wait in the dark and even to love the waiting." The leadership work I want most to engage in is being able to nurture the light that hides in darkness that will allow when ignited all human kind to live in dignity and safety and nurture mother earth. What I have come to understand in my leadership work is that growing the needed compassion for all of us to care as much about the planet, people we don't know in the ways we care about the people and things we love is our limiting factor. Sustainable development requires expanding our definition of "we" so policies, businesses, and social programs globally work together to create sustainable livelihoods for all and allow a healthy livable planet for generations to come.

The 17 UN Sustainable Development Goals (SDGs) represent a higher plane of consciousness compared to the millennium development goals. What the SDGs reinforces for me is that respect for environment/emotional space/built space/design are critical to humanity's thriving in ways that do not hurt the planet. The SDGs have made things that were seen as "soft stuff" take on more importance today and give my leadership greater credibility. I am not seen as a soft feminine leader but as a leader who believes in the interconnectedness of all. Qualitative data are given a space where only quantitative data were used in the past. New avenues of work that bring the whole to the table instead of dismantled parts are creating spaces where my leadership can be of greater service to sustainable development. Fierce feminist leadership's time is now. My hope is that everyone will get a seat at the table, that equity for all will become a reality we can tangibly say we are building and for that equity not only include humankind but also mother earth. Ultimately, she has birthed us all and caring for her is definitely leadership my own mother would cheer for.

REFERENCES

Buchanan, L. (2013). What a Leader Needs Now: 7 'Feminine' Qualities. Retrieved from https://www.inc.com/magazine/201306/leigh-buchanan/what-leaders-need-to-know.html

Jironet, K. (2011). *Female leadership: Management, Jungian psychology, spirituality and the global journey through purgatory*. New York, NY: Routledge.

Luke, H. (1962). Parabola: The search for meaning. Retrieved from http://parabola-magazine.tumblr.com/post/19984421502/the-true-light-never-hides-the-darkness-but-is

5

EMBRACING MODERN LEADERSHIP AMIDST CULTURAL TRADITIONS – THE NICHE TO FORGE AHEAD

Keba T. Modisane

In the past, leadership in Botswana was greatly influenced by culture, traditions, and values, which sometimes evoked unpleasant storms that subjected one's leadership skills to a litmus test. Nonetheless, as one surmounted these stormy challenges in order to lead successfully, one had to view the often conflicting moments between modern leadership and cultural traditions as learning curves. It is from the convergence of these learning curves that I share my leadership experiences.

In Botswana, in the past, it was unthinkable that women could hold positions of leadership. Batswana knew that;

ga di ke di etelelwa pele ke manamagadi, di wele ka lengope

The literal translation of this Setswana proverb is that female cows could not lead oxen in a trail-path as they would all fall into a ditch.

The above-mentioned proverb implied that women should not, and could not, be given positions of leadership as this portended disastrous consequences for all. Proverbs such as the one above influenced societal perception and, more importantly, held women back from exerting themselves vigorously to become influential team players and leaders in the society. It is largely on this account (or mind set) that women continuously took a back-seat approach in socioeconomic development at both community and national level. Recent developments, however, prove that women too can successfully hold positions of leadership in organizations and institutions in Botswana. Currently, women's visibility is clearly seen in social and economic development. In fact, the position of women in Botswana has improved considerably over the years since women, like men, receive high education opportunities and hold positions of power over a broad spectrum of both public and private institutions. Statistics show that in Botswana in 2009, women accounted for 45% of senior management positions in the public service, up from 37% in 2005. During the same period, middle management in almost all public departments was predominantly women (Ministry of Labor and Home Affairs, 2008).

SETSWANA LANGUAGE: A SYMBOLIC ICON OF CULTURE

It should be noted that the Setswana language is peppered with idioms, proverbs, and allegories, which in the past influenced cultural and societal values and expectations of how women should be viewed. Throughout this chapter, I use some of these proverbs to provide a glimpse of how women were viewed through the lens of Setswana culture, customs, and traditions. In Setswana, a woman is called *mosadi*. Among Batswana, a woman's worth was measured from the domestic chores she performed. Batswana stated that,

> *mosadi tshwene o jewa mabogo*

The proverb holds that a woman's worth was assessed from the domestic roles of feeding and caring for the family and not from her physical appearance, hence the metaphorical comparison to a baboon was seen as fitting. Notwithstanding that, Batswana also stated that

> *mosadi ke thari ya sechaba*

The literal translation of this proverb is that a woman is the cradle of the nation, thus implying that the nation's growth rested upon women's shoulders. It was the responsibility of women to feed, clothe, and care for the family; thus translating to caring for the whole nation.

This chapter concentrates on my leadership experiences in relationship to gender. Throughout the chapter, Setswana cultural practices and views are discussed in relation to gender perspective. National sustainability is also discussed from the perspective of sustainable development goals (SDG). I have also taken the opportunity to highlight my leadership experiences during my employment as Chief Human Resources (HR) Officer at Rural Industries Promotions Company (Botswana) (RIPCO (B)) and as Manager – School of Graduate Studies and Research at BA ISAGO University. Besides these, I have captured my experiences while I developed and coordinated an HIV/AIDS program for the workplace at RIPCO (B) through support of the Swedish International Development Association (SIDA); during my role as Vice Chairperson of the District Productivity Improvement Forum for the Southern District (in Botswana) and also while I performed roles of trainer for the National Food Technology Research Center (NFTRC) and the Botswana Technology Center (BOTEC). After reading this chapter, readers are left to determine from these experiences whether women will inevitably lead the nation into ditches or are capable of demonstrating leadership potential that could be nurtured and strengthened for the betterment of their communities and the nation.

WELCOME TO LEADERSHIP: SPONGE

I arrived at Rural Industries Innovation Center (RIIC) in Kanye to take up the position of HR Officer having previously worked as a teacher for five years. Upon arrival, I realized that the work environment was completely different from my previous work environment – it was like moving from the Tropic of Capricorn to the Equator if such difference in climatic conditions are anything to go by today. Despite the differences, I was thrilled to move to a dynamic work environment that offered challenges that were multi-faceted. I arrived into an HR function that was thinly staffed; there were only three officers; my immediate supervisor and two young men who were on a one-year National Service program that was called *Tirelo Sechaba*. Examination of the HR department unearthed that I was moving into an HR function whose records were ill-kept; policy documents were archaic and needed review; performance appraisals were a yearly monotonous ritual and to ice the cake, the majority of employees had resigned themselves to the ineptitude of the HR function – they felt that the HR function was hopeless. Despite the hopeless image portrayed of the near nonexisting HR function, members of staff at RIIC appeared relaxed, content, and joked about HR malfunctions as if they were discussing a naughty shepherd boy who always cried wolf when in fact there was none. Despite these disturbing truths, I immediately liked the new workplace partly because of my determination to make the best of my new job opportunity and partly because employees displayed warmth and welcomed me as one of their own. I developed cordial working relations with the employees and little did I imagine I would serve these employees for the next 16 years.

I decided to take one step at a time to learn more about the new organization while I also learned the new job. I reasoned that as much as I grew in experience and knowledge of HR processes and practices, the HR department would also develop for the better. I immersed myself in my new work roles. One of my key strength is learning and absorbing new information and new experiences like a sponge. This helped me hone my skills on issues of employee relations, training and development, occupational health and safety, and performance management among others. My willingness to accept my limitations, my willingness to learn, and my willingness to seek advice from others laid a good foundation for my career advancement. I also realized that networking and communicating with HR practitioners in other organizations afforded me the opportunity to build a good working relationship with others and learn from their experiences. After a short while, I developed a list of networking professional colleagues in the public service, parastatal organizations, and private institutions which readily provided guidance and support on HR issues in Botswana.

GETTING BAPTIZED INTO THE WORLD OF HUMAN RESOURCES AND TAKING THE BULL BY THE HORNS

Every organization is unique and offers unique experiences and challenges; so was RIIC – the operational arm of RIPCO (B). One morning, during my first month of employment, I received an internal phone call that I shall never forget; it is as if it happened yesterday, probably because it sounded scary; hence it terrified and chilled my little HR novice spine. The caller asked,

"Is that the HR Officer?"

I replied, "Yes. This is the HR Officer."

The caller then shouted, "I am going to kill someone here!"

I was startled with disbelief but chose to remain calm. After composing myself, I said in response, "Go ahead kill the person; at least you informed someone who would later act as a witness in court."

The caller hung up. That was terrifying information and I had also responded carelessly. I was worried but remained calm, though threatening to kill someone is not a joking matter notwithstanding my flippant response. Many questions flooded my mind. I asked myself, who is the caller? Why on earth would he want to kill someone? Still puzzled, I enquired from the reception about the caller. After getting sufficient information about the caller, I called his office and asked him if he had already done anything stupid yet or if he was prepared to discuss the issue. Inexplicably, he now sounded a bit calm. He opened up and poured his heart out. I listened. For hours, he lamented about how his age pitted him against younger employees. As days went by we discussed the issues in-depth in order to find solutions to the problems he raised. Finally, we invited the culprit who was nearly turned into toast. It turned out that the officer was the head of the section. He had joined RIPCO (B) the previous year after completing his engineering degree from the UK. He was a tall guy who walked with long strides. As he entered my office he looked relaxed and was happy to see the complainant. He was clueless that he was the course of this impromptu meeting. Talk about miscommunication and misunderstanding! As we talked the supervisor looked and sounded surprised. He was clueless that he had wronged anyone let alone offended the elderly employee who had now roped HR to his rescue. As we discussed issues raised by the elderly officer, I asked the "young" supervisor to examine and reconsider issues from the viewpoint of the complainant. The "young" supervisor (I prefer to call him "the toast" because he nearly met his demise) apologized for his insensitivity and seemingly offensive approach in his communication to the older officer and promised to approach issues more caringly in future.

Cases like this one show that age is very important in workplaces in Botswana. Batswana respect the elderly irrespective of their position in society hence a thoughtless comment by a "younger supervisor" can set tempers flaring. As an HR practitioner, I also realized that listening to employees afforded them the opportunity to voice their problems, and also created a platform for discussion and finding solutions to old problems. As I continued interacting with all employees, both employees and management, I unearthed their problems, their fears, and potentials. In return, I created a platform for information sharing and open communication with a view to bringing everyone on board. I sincerely believe that solutions to most emotional problems in the workplace do not lie outside the organization but rest squarely within. I also believe that open communication and discussion quell differences and pave way for harmonious working relations. Sincere discussions between antagonistic parties, I realized, calmed heavy hearts and paved way to cordial working relations – a work environment desired by all. As an HR practitioner and scholar, I believe that it is the responsibility of everyone in the organization to help create a conducive work environment to the extent they possibly can by mutually identifying and quelling inconceivably storms of personal differences and misinformation among others for the benefit of all.

RESIDE AND SUSTAIN THE PLANET OR MOVE TO MARS! LEADING OPTIMISTICALLY WITH HOPE

"We don't have plan B because there is no planet B" is the often quoted assertion by the former United Nations Secretary-General Ban Ki-moon that has largely informed the SDGs whose themes focus on the rights of the human family to healthy and sustainable development in dimensions of the environment, economics, and society. Effective and efficient leadership should subscribe to all the 17 SDG goals. I believe that good health and well-being of employees, their families, and the community lays a foundation for a happy employee. Furthermore, issues of gender equality; quality education; decent work and economic growth; industry innovation and infrastructure development; peace, justice and strong institutions; and partnerships for the goals are critically important to leadership. These goals call leadership to think globally, while acting locally, by ensuring that national policies and programs dignify human lives by moving people out of abject poverty, poor sanitation, and contaminated water. In Botswana, leadership at the national level has created poverty eradication programs to move Batswana out of abject poverty. Furthermore, leadership at the national level has reviewed laws and enacted new ones in order to create opportunities for including gender equality and uplifting women's economic well-being.

SDGs should thus be viewed as a scale that determines commitment to the well-being of employees and society. At this point, I would like to discuss in-depth my efforts in sensitizing employees on HIV/AIDS in the workplace. Why did I embark on the development and implementation of an HIV/AIDS educational program and policy? The answer rests in that workplaces in Botswana have not been spared of the HIV/AIDS scourge. Since the beginning of the epidemic in 1985, Botswana's workplaces continue being depleted of many productive adults who developed AIDS and were not able to work.

Statistics show that Botswana has experienced the most severe HIV/AIDS epidemic in the world. According to the US State Department (2008), between 1999 and 2005, Botswana lost approximately 17% of its healthcare workforce due to AIDS. The HIV prevalence rate of 24.8% makes Botswana the highest country in the world affected by the scourge of HIV/AIDS behind Lesotho and Swaziland (Avert International, 2018).

As an HR practitioner, I decided not to sit around helplessly, but rather to try to help in as small a way as I possibly could. Between 1999 and 2001, with support from the SIDA, I focused on a project whose outcome was the development of an HIV/AIDS workplace educational program and implementation of an HIV/AIDS workplace policy and procedure that championed principles of shared confidentiality. In order to undertake the project, I decided to use the participatory approach of involving all members of staff – both management and employees. After presenting the HIV/AIDS project proposal to top management, one of them remarked that "you always offer good training programs but now I have a problem with you offering this program because you now want to enter our bedrooms."

That did not sound right, but I knew that I did not initiate the HIV/AIDS educational program for the workplace to evade anyone's privacy. Initially, I felt dejected since all I desired was for RIPCO (B) to openly dialogue on issues of HIV/AIDS in order to find a common ground for addressing issues of discrimination and stigmatization. Furthermore, I designed this program to sensitize employees on HIV/AIDS as I could see that we were all pained by the prevailing situation – we were all directly or indirectly affected or infected. I devised a new strategy. I invited the then Ministry of Health (now called Ministry of Health and Wellness) senior officials including retired nurses who had previously worked in HIV/AIDS programs to conduct the training. The training program involved a number of sessions that would be conducted over a period of time. I assumed the role of training program evaluator. The results were amazing – both management and employees appreciated the information that they received. Everyone appeared comfortable in discussing issues of sexuality, a topic that was previously considered taboo and could not be discussed openly in Botswana. Perhaps, employees' comfort with discussing issues of sexuality and HIV/AIDS emanated from the fact that program conveners and instructors were highly experienced and older people from the health sector. As the educational program gained momentum, employees had different avenues to reach out to for counseling, testing, and family support. I believe that helping others, displaying love, and caring for them in a small way (during their darkest hour) is a God-given gift we can all display no matter what our position is in the organization hierarchy and in the society.

Through this project, I realized that there are times when the custodian of a program has to step back and allow others to handle issues. Involvement of relevant stakeholders shows that SDGs are not an individual issue but call for partnerships and collaborations. Support from officials from the Ministry of Health ensured that the training program objectives were realized. It was also through this project that I realized that the development of collaborative long-lasting partnerships with people from different fields and backgrounds is important for work efficiency and effectiveness. More importantly, the quest to help others encouraged me to move out of my comfort zone.

MEASURING PERFORMANCE: IT DOES NOT START FROM THE WORKPLACE

When I was growing up, my siblings and I did all the household chores. Work was equally shared between all of us; there was no segregation of boy child and girl child chores. We fetched fire wood, fetched water, pounded corn to make sorghum meal, and took turns to cook. The principle was simple – we all worked to have a plate of food on the table. My mother loathed laziness of any kind and resented seeing us hanging out with children from the neighborhood. In her mind, hanging out with children from the neighborhood bred indiscipline through bad association. We stayed at home.

The same principle of assigning out chores should apply to organizational work roles – work should be divided equitably mindful of employee's position, competence, and capabilities. Though it sounds doable, workplaces have people who take credit at the end without exerting effort to attain the outcome and this should be discouraged.

THE INDUCTION PROCESS: THE FIRST STEP INTO GUIDING PERFORMANCE

New employees should be welcomed into the work environment so that they can quickly settle into their work roles. Too often, organizations leave new employees to find their own way around in the workplace. While working at RIPCO (B), I introduced an induction process that ensured that new employees were introduced to the new work culture and environment. I believed that through the induction, RIPCO (B) affirmed to the new employees that the organization valued them and wanted to keep them.

Together with the Chief Quality Assurance Officer, we developed the initial stage induction program that provided an overview of the work environment, quality policy manual requirements, performance management processes, and requirements of the RIPCO (B) policies. Even though supervisors performed the second stage induction, one of the things which I found missing in the induction process was mentoring and peer-training programs that could have benefited the new job entrants especially those who had recently completed from tertiary college.

Besides induction training, I also conducted in-house training programs to sensitize employees, middle management, and top management about the Employment Act, issues of workplace health and safety, labor relations issues, and other HR-related practices and processes. By conducting such training programs, I realized that as the organization learned, I also learned. I knew that failure of employees, line managers, and top management to implement HR policies and procedures mirrored the failure of HR Department to communicate and guide the implementation of HR policies and procedures organization-wide. Did I achieve effective implementation of HR policies, practices, and processes at RIPCO (B)? Impossible. When the environment is turbulent, chances of succeeding in work roles is limited but that does not mean there were no notable successes – a lot of positive developments were made, for example, training of employees to achieve their competencies was done on a large scale, record keeping and policy and procedures were well documented. Employee wellness programs were implemented including knowledge of HR processes was disseminated using rightful forums including using the staff information sharing meetings. But a lot could have been achieved had rightful climatic conditions and support been created by those in leadership. I sincerely believe that through sound and effective leadership support HR could have performed better and produced more tangible results.

BOTSWANA'S SOCIOECONOMIC JOURNEY

Botswana's socioeconomic growth journey can be traced from 1966, the time when Botswana gained independence from British colonial rule. The journey is firmly imprinted in the faces of the now old men and women who inherited only one thing from their forefathers' – land. Beaming with pride and happiness many of these men continued working in South African mines and farms while others remained home to till the soil and rear cattle and goats. The discovery of diamonds changed the socioeconomic landscape. It is from the discovery of diamonds that tarred roads, telecommunications, health services, and employment opportunities surged in the country. More importantly, through the economic boom from the diamond revenues, Batswana children now had the opportunity to receive government-sponsored tertiary education in different fields including education, law, social work, nursing, medicine, and agriculture among others resulting in notable human resources development and national sustainability. I also benefited from government-funded training programs.

One realizes that though culturally it was unthinkable for women to hold positions of leadership in society back then, now women hold positions of leadership in the judiciary, banks, insurance companies, public administration, and many more different workplaces. Botswana, it should be noted, is a signatory to a number of international human rights treaties and their protocols, in particular gender and human rights. These include the International Convention on Civil and Political Rights (ICPPR); the

Convention on the Elimination of all forms of Discrimination Against Women (CEDAW); the Beijing Declaration and Platform for Action; the African Charter on Human Rights and People's Rights and Protocols; the International Conference on Population and Development; and the Protocol to Prevent, Suppress and Punish Trafficking in Persons, especially Women and Children; and the Solemn Declaration on Gender Equality (Botswana Country Report on the Implementation of the Beijing Platform for Action (Beijing Plus 20 Years) June 2014 (Gender Affairs Department, Ministry of Labor and Home Affairs, p. 15).

As a country, Botswana has performed well in promoting women's economic empowerment, and in ensuring that women participate at community and national level in decision-making in the public service, private, and civil society. Perhaps this can be attributed to the fact that Botswana has never been involved in any armed conflict that could prevent the country from implementing all the signed treaties. In fact, Setswana culture is one that promotes dialogue and upholding peace and development. In Setswana, it is said that;

Ntwakgolo ke ya molomo

The literal translation of this proverb is that the biggest war is fought through dialogue. This proverb means that differences between people can only be settled by talking about them, not through physical fighting. Women in Botswana have used rightful platforms to communicate their desires and have been heard. Botswana has eradicated cultural prejudices and stereotypes of women and girls. Women now participate in socioeconomic development of the country and in national building programs.

I grew up as the youngest sibling of seven children; I had three older brothers and three older sisters. My mother, born in 1930, had the responsibility of raising us after my father returned to his homeland in South Africa. My mother assumed the responsibility with vigor, determination, and self-drive that ensured that all of us went through high school, completed tertiary education and fended for ourselves even though she had never been to school herself. Even though my father returned to Qumbu in South Africa to assume family responsibilities as the eldest son, he always sent money for school fees every year. I remember that one particular year school fees for two of my older brothers (twins) did not arrive on time. My mother was dejected since students who did not have school fees were returned home.

One day, she heard from the school administration that there was something called "bursary" that could assist her in getting her two sons into school. I remember that she went knocking on one door to another looking for "bursary" until she got it. Her story of leaving no stone unturned in her quest to educate her children is not unique, but it is a story that portrays her generation in Botswana who felt that what they did not achieve in their lives their children should achieve. As I grew up, I saw my mother as a symbol of resilience and hope that life around the bend will turn out right. Her daily struggles in life to raise her children translated to the strength and resilience that I have. Yes, women worked hard and continue to work hard as they shape the outcomes of the generation coming behind them.

INGENUITY TO LEAD WITH HONESTY, HUMILITY, FAIRNESS, AND INTEGRITY

Among Batswana it is said that;

moremogolo go betlwa wa taola wa motho a ipetla

The literal meaning of this proverb is that a traditional doctor shapes his bones of divination but an individual shapes his destiny. This Setswana proverb means that each one of us can shape our destiny unlike divination bones that are shaped by the user hence I have never looked at myself as a hapless endangered female who expects the world to bend over because I am a woman. I believe we all choose to become the ultimate person we want to be. I have chosen to let my upbringing, work experiences, failures, achievements, and challenges to shape me for the better.

I believe that the biggest mistake in leading is to assume airs of "I know it all, I have the power." I believe as human beings we have limitations, but our limitations should be a strength through which we gain opportunities to ask others to "fill up the gaps" where we are lacking. When I confer with others I take such moments as humbling periods that help me achieve important goals that benefit all. As a leader, I continuously enquire from others to get more information and weigh possible options; this I believe legitimizes one's role in leadership.

Leadership strategies and tactics differ with context and desired goals that are expected. I believe that the context of leading staff to learn a new process is different from chairing a disciplinary hearing and is equally different from conducting a training program and even from functioning as an arbitrator. However, throughout these differing hats, dealing with others with honesty, sincerity, fairness, and integrity made me leave the workplace each day feeling satisfied. I have always believed that bending over rules to satisfy certain groups of people at the expense of fulfilling laid down rules and regulations has a catch-22 at the end; either you lead using shortcuts or you lead with candor, honesty, fairness, and integrity. Others will surely hate you but the equally honest and sincere people will respect you for your strength of character and candor.

PURSUIT OF HAPPINESS AND SPIRITUAL FULFILLMENT

The work environment is pressured with continuous requirements of fulfilling demands of customer and stakeholders' expectations. But, as one absorbs these pressures, at the same time, one should have room to pursue happiness, which is a foundation of a good life. We all strive to attain that – at least some of us. My pursuit of happiness, therefore, compels me to refuse to be swallowed up by pressures of the workplace, politics of the workforce or even negativity of those around me. Though I acknowledge negative experiences and behaviors existing in the world, I distance myself from such a world by focusing on social relationships and interactions that are characterized by compassion, honesty, humility, love, integrity, and respect. Even in the workplace, I believe my interaction with others should bring happiness to all of us as we spend a good portion of our time in the workplace instead of at our homes. I believe that in the workplace we can fend off organizational toxins by building bridges of communication and dialogue and cultivating a culture of maintaining good ethical behaviors and practices.

My spirituality remains a sustaining pillar for my happiness and peace of mind. In my spare time, I interact with friends during leisure time. My belief is that we owe it to ourselves to surround ourselves with happy people and relax and rewind after a busy work schedule. In Setswana, it is often said;

mosadi ga a inama o a bo a ikantse mosese wa ko morago

The literal translation of this proverb is that a woman bends forward with assurance derived from a petticoat. This proverb means that one takes

decisions when they know that they are fully supported by tangible information. Though I say that my spirituality is my pillar to happiness I am aware
that some people may say that physical exercise, leisure reading, partying,
and drinking with friends or going for holidays in exotic places give them
peace of mind ... each to their own story. Well, there goes a reflection on
modernity in leadership amidst cows trailing into ditches, hardworking
baboons, nation's cradles, and petticoats that give assurance ... basadi! ...
... Adieu.

REFERENCES

Avert International (2018). Avert Global Information and Education on
HIV/AIDS. HIV and AIDS in Botswana. Retrieved from http:// www.avert.
org.proffesional/ hiv-around-world/

Gender Affairs Department, Ministry of Labor and Home Affairs. (June,
2014). *Botswana Country Report on the Implementation of the Beijing
Platform for Action (Beijing Plus 20 Years)*.

US State Department. (2008). 2007 Country Profile: Botswana. Retrieved
from www.pepfar.gov/documents/organization/101652.pdf

Women Affairs Department, Ministry of Labour and Home Affairs. (2008).
Implementation of the Convention of the Elimination of all Forms of
Discrimination Against Women, Botswana Report.

PART 2: LEADERSHIP FOR WOMEN'S EMPOWERMENT AND EQUITY

Women's role in developing economies and the importance of their empowerment and equity to improving the well-being of countries was only highlighted as an important issue in the late 1960s, when female development professionals noted the critical role African women played in agriculture. Women in Development (WID) became an effort to more purposefully target development projects on women's issues. However, WID was soon replaced by Gender and Development (GAD) as it was realized that both men's and women's issues needed to be dealt with simultaneously. Still, women's place in development was overall sidelined and played a marginal role, generally relegated to subsistence agriculture, health, and education. Women were not viewed as significant private sector actors.

Amanda Ellis spent much of her career pushing for the inclusion of women as key actors in private sector development, as she recounts in Chapter 6. Exemplifying passion and perseverance, Ellis successfully argued for the provision of private sector finance for women in diverse roles while a diplomat in the New Zealand Foreign Ministry and later as Deputy Secretary and head of the Development Agency, as inaugural National Manager, Women in Business for Westpac Banking Corporation, founder of the Global Gender Unit at the International Finance Corporation, and Lead Specialist for the GAD Group in the World Bank. Ellis's career-long leadership in changing the policies and practice of major development organizations vis-à-vis women has resulted in some of the most significant changes in international development since its inception post-World War II.

Ellis describes in great detail the leadership approach she employed to establish new policies vis-à-vis financing women private sector entrepreneurs in the New Zealand Foreign Ministry, the World Bank, and Westpac Banking Corporation. Her system change model, mentioned also, in the volume Introduction has far-reaching implications not only for gender considerations but also for international development in general. From her experience, she catalogs leadership lessons, which are summarized below:

- *Be brave. Call out gender discrimination for what it is.* Find relevant analogies to help those in power recognize why it is unacceptable.

- *Be strategic: make the business case for positive change.* What might be the motivation for the other party to actually shift behavior? An important element for progress in gender equality in the context of international development is recognizing the importance of the data-driven dimension of leadership, providing an evidence base that creates a desire for change.

- *Make the economic case for change to move gender discrimination from marginal to mainstream.* While the percentage of macroeconomic growth foregone can of course only ever be a proxy, it frames the issue of gender discrimination in the context of economic as well as rights-based arguments.

- *Be smart about access.* Befriend the gatekeepers and remember the most powerful allies for change are not always the most obvious. Leadership for systemic change involves befriending gatekeepers and creating allies across all levels of an organization, all dimensions of society.

- *Engage the CEO (or key leader) as both ally and advocate.* The tone is set at the top and is especially important in hierarchical, command and control organizations.

- *Embrace key influencers as champions for change.*

- *Be inclusive.* Create networks of support to maintain momentum and prevent scapegoating.

- *Listen!* What are the different stakeholders' lived experiences? What is the context? How have they attempted to address problematic issues in the past? What worked? What didn't? Where are the roadblocks?

- *Engage your teams in system design.* They are the ones most able to create innovative solutions and being part of the design encourages ownership and compliance.

- *Lead from behind and co-create.* How can solutions to development problems be jointly crafted with the key stakeholders to work in the specific cultural context, taking constraints into account

- *Take a holistic approach.* An interdisciplinary approach provides insights into gender issues that need addressing in a holistic way if we are to co-create lasting solutions, as opposed to "quick fixes" that will end when the donor money ends.

- *Create a pilot project to innovate and test.*

- *Support internal organizational cultural change to underpin business aspirations.* Carefully tailor approaches to target audience, from transformational at the top, through business case at managerial level to demonstration and compliance at the front line.

- *Accurate benchmark data is critical.* If you don't know where you are starting or how you compare to others it's impossible to measure progress and figure out what is working and what's not.

- *Measure results to demonstrate success and share these widely*: impact and outcomes matter most even if much harder to measure than inputs and outputs.

- *Engage partners to scale up.* Recognize your development model needs to evolve to increase impact; use partnership models to replicate and scale.

- *Tackle adaptive leadership problems by "getting on the balcony"* to gain a broad perspective before you get "back on the dance floor."

- *Learning journeys create a multiplier effect for change.* Providing an organized forum to capture and share lessons for positive change helps members implement new approaches and incubates innovative partnerships.

- *Gain recognition of results.* Recognition spurs leaders to accelerate action! Powerful leaders are spurred by competition and create a "race to the top."

- *"Both and."* General and dedicated focus on gender equality! Both matter!

- *Patience! Persistence! Resilience!*

Anne Spear, the author of Chapter 7, determined from years of experience in the field that economic empowerment of women is key to their advancement as well as to the advancement of their countries. Economic empowerment needs to be accompanied by both political and social empowerment. Spear introduces the notion of building "trusting mutual" relationships in international development as the most important first step before any real change or progress can be made. This is a central theme carried throughout this volume and one that has been given far too little attention to in international development. She also highlights the importance of local leadership of women as key to female empowerment. Spear also introduces the notion of power in international development, also a key concept that leaders often do not systematically assess and develop approaches to. Based on her years of observing development professionals and their many mishaps and often arrogant and patronizing behavior, Spear introduces a new model of development built on "empowerment of women and facilitation" as leadership approaches. These concepts are more fully developed in Chapters 7 and 8. Spear argues that "the first shift that is required for developing and implementing a new model is making it a priority to access, get to know, and empower local women leaders. The second shift that is required for this new model is for development organizations to act as facilitators as they empower and support local women leaders, rather than implementing their own solutions."

Nila Wardani and Kate Mangino continue the theme of women's empowerment through developing close relationships and employing facilitation as a leadership approach in Chapter 8. Having worked with Indonesian rural women for several decades, Wardani and Mangino have discovered that Appreciative Inquiry and Participatory Rural Appraisal are the most impactful approaches to facilitate the development of women's self-consciousness and their recognition that gender stereotypes and their marginalized, dependent role in society are socialized not inherent. Amazing opportunities for self-determination open-up for women who achieve this awareness. Leadership for Wardani and Mangino involves "stepping back" and allowing women to progressively fill the space of leadership and creativity where they discover opportunities they never before imagined. The women dream and then realize that their dreams are achievable.

Ashley Lackovich-Van Gorp recounts in Chapter 9, how she "fell in love" with working with adolescent girls living in very difficult cultural environments. She "quickly learned that being a leader is far more complex: being a leader is an identity, a persona that one must embody." She spent many years to gain credibility as a leader in her own eyes by her self-assessment. Lackovich-Gorp has dedicated much of her career on ending child marriage and hence has come face-to-face with cultural barriers and also do-gooders who feel that her focus on adolescent girls at the expense of adolescent boys is futile. She employs participatory action research and positive deviance[1] to partner with women from communities who have passed through the marriage abduction risk age without getting married who serve as "positive deviants."

Lackovich-Van Gorp has discovered by "moving from context to context … [that] perceptions of me and my leadership change according to the culture and situation. This constant shift in perception has taught me that my struggle is not me, but the context and so I mold my response to these challenging perceptions to the specific situation."

She has also made the disappointing recognition, as have Spear, Obasanjo, and Ubalijoro, that not everyone in development shares her passion and dedication. She recognizes that "international development emerged from colonialism and these roots remain embedded in the field." She recounts that she has had "colleagues who maintain that colonial mindset of 'saving the natives' who are perceived as too primitive to save themselves, while they indulge in a life of luxury." She bemoans the reality that "it is difficult to navigate the toxicity that comes from some of the attitudes and selfish actions in this field, and even more difficult when a person in a leadership role is oblivious to those attitudes."

Lackovich-Van Gorp raises for the first time the issue of "burnout" which is a very real but heretofore taboo subject among development leaders. She relies on adaptive leadership "for the ambiguous challenges that arise when I challenge gender roles and expectations amid uncertain and complex situations such as wars, extreme poverty, and political and social unrest." A leader comes face-to-face with almost unbearable trauma in such situations, a point Mashzhu-Makota touched on, and the reality of burnout resulting from empathy is a real condition leaders need to recognize and cope with.

Lackovich-Van Gorp concludes that "my passion is a constant leadership tactic and I strive to be a transformational leader so that others can share in this passion. In this sense, I aim to create visions for change and inspire others to work toward creating a more just and inclusive society for girls.

My vision is for adolescent girls to lead safe, dignified, and empowered lives regardless of their situation, but this is a tough concept to grasp."

NOTE

1. Positive deviance (PD) is strength-based approach based on the assumption that communities are the best experts to design and implement their own behavioral and social change approach by employing their collective intelligence. The "positive deviants" in communities who have discovered more successful cultural and coping behaviors and solutions to commonly-held challenges serve as internal change agents by "acting their way to change" and modeling the new, more effective way by their behavior.

6

FROM MARGINAL TO MAINSTREAM: LEADERSHIP IN INTEGRATING GENDER INTO PRIVATE SECTOR DEVELOPMENT

Amanda Ellis

"An interesting proposition, Ms Ellis ... but what on earth have gender issues and women got to do with private sector development? Shouldn't you rather be focusing on health and education issues if you want to make any real impact for women in developing countries?" The World Bank Vice President (VP) was skeptical that the heavily pregnant woman in his office pitching the importance of the Bank including a gender perspective in private sector advisory work had any idea what she was talking about. But he was polite. And he was fair: "I am not sure I understand exactly what this might look like, but I'll do you a deal. I see you have a track record in the private sector promoting access to finance for women in Australia – half a billion annual turnover is pretty impressive in just three years – so I am willing to give this a shot. If you can prove the business case to me in six months I'll find you funding and staff to scale up."

As I waddled out of the VP's Washington, DC, office in 2003, I was both perplexed and delighted. Perplexed that despite the theory on the merits of gender inclusion in international development, it seemed the Bank's perspective in the private sector context was rather traditional to say the least. Delighted I had a chance to prove the relevance of an integrated approach and to demonstrate I believed there could be a win–win, where practical

support for women's economic empowerment could significantly contribute
to the development agenda in developing countries.

THE PERSONAL INFORMS THE POLITICAL

The personal has definitely informed the political, with my own experiences
facing gender barriers in a relatively enlightened country – the first where
women won the right to vote (in 1893), for example – shaping my advocacy
for the integration of gendered analysis and design across the suite of development interventions. My career in international development has been a
varied one in terms of the central role that gender has played both as a crucial tenet of good development policy and as a woman leader myself trying
to lead and create change.

Full of youthful passion and purpose, including a rather misplaced opti-
mism in my self-confidence that I would of course change the world for the
better in short order and surely solve global poverty in just a couple of years,
I joined the New Zealand Foreign Ministry as a young diplomatic trainee in
1988. I was alternately shocked, disbelieving, and despondent when just a
couple of months into my service I was summarily "uninvited" to a meeting
where I was to have taken notes on Asia Pacific economic cooperation issues,
the lead up to the Asia-Pacific Economic Cooperation (APEC), due to its
being held at the Wellington Club. Still a bastion of male-only membership,
the Wellington Club was a favorite meeting place for local diplomats and as
the Americans had requested the venue I was told "not to rock the boat" as
all the senior management in the Foreign Ministry belonged. My boss point-
edly remarked that while I may have passed the entrance exam, I was still a
diplomatic trainee on probation. Senior men held the power and they would
not view kindly an upstart young woman disturbing the status quo.

WRESTLING WITH VALUES VERSUS PAYCHECK

I had joined the Foreign Ministry to help solve global poverty and change
the world for the better, especially for women, but it seemed just the fact of
being a woman was going to preclude me even getting into the meetings
where any important business was done. Extraordinary, in 1988! Finally,
I decided I needed to be true to my values and saw no other choice but to

resign. I plucked up courage to request an exit interview with the Secretary of the Foreign Ministry and when his executive assistant told me this would be unorthodox I confided to her the reason.

"I think in this case, Ms. Ellis, I will make my first exception. I suggest you hold on your resignation and just explain what has happened to the Secretary."

I did so, asking if I had been Maori (New Zealand's indigenous people), would it have been acceptable to exclude me on those grounds? A long pause ensued. After studying the ceiling for what seemed to be an interminable length of time the Secretary looked back at me.

"I propose to write to the Wellington Club pointing out that in 1988 women are entering the work force in greater numbers and if they don't get with the times they will lose much needed revenues. Will that be satisfactory Ms. Ellis?"

I didn't think it was satisfactory at all, but it was certainly better than nothing so I thanked him and as I left he suggested I might like to discuss the issue with some of the senior women in the Ministry and seek their views. That idea hadn't dawned on me, given the hierarchies in place, but I was both surprised and delighted by the incredible support senior women provided, along with a proposal to start a women's network to deal with just such issues as a collective group. Despite a number of senior men muttering under their breath "it's the bra-burning lesbian feminist brigade plotting against us again" whenever they saw more than two of us together in the Ministry's foyer, members of the Ministry women's network subsequently took great delight in lunching together the following year at the newly gender equitable Wellington Club.

TURNING POINT: STEPPING UP TO LEADERSHIP

This incident was truly a turning point for me, and the leadership lessons I learned have remained with me throughout my career. Not only did I not resign — which would have left me with no influence for change internally — but I was able to ignite a positive shift both by directly engaging at the top of the totem pole and subsequently becoming part of a network of colleagues who became much stronger allies for change as part of an organized collective. In my later career at the World Bank, where I had the privilege of managing the WB President's Global Private Sector Leaders CEO Forum, I realized again the incredible influence set by the "tone at the top" as some of the world's most powerful business leaders turned their attention to the issue of women's economic empowerment and helped create systemic change in their own organizations and those they did business with through their direct influence.

GENDER BARRIERS IN INTERNATIONAL DEVELOPMENT

My first direct, as opposed to theoretical, experience of the importance of including a gender perspective in international development projects was in Vietnam in the mid-1990s. I was assigned a rotational role to manage New Zealand's Official Development Assistance (ODA) to Vietnam, Laos, and Cambodia. On my familiarization visit with the local team, I was introduced to a woman in a small village in Vietnam who had a vision of small business and job creation through raising silk worms. She explained why as a woman she had been unable to secure the US$20 loan she needed to buy the worms to get started. Although she and her husband owned land together, only his name appeared on the title deed and hence she was unable to apply for this small loan to get her business started. So we agreed to provide this modest start-up capital as a grant. A year later, I returned to find a thriving micro-enterprise that was providing jobs and income for four others. This experience prompted my special interest in the gender dimensions of access to finance in particular and the underlying systemic constraints. It led first to a job in a private sector bank dealing with women entrepreneur clients, Westpac Banking Corporation in Australia, where I became a founding member of the Global Banking Alliance for Women (GBA) and then to the World Bank Group where I led the creation of the first ever lines of credit for women small and medium-size enterprises (SME) in Africa, as opposed to grassroots microfinance programs.

GENDER BARRIERS IN ACCESS TO FINANCE

The leadership lessons I had learned in the Foreign Ministry stood me in good stead at Westpac Banking Corporation as I worked to improve access to finance for women customers. I knew I needed to quickly make the business case, engage the CEO as both ally and advocate, and create a network of powerful influencers across the company who would support the new Women in Business program. There was initial resistance, as there always is when leading a significant cultural change initiative, but within three years we went from anonymous calls asking "Why are you running a lesbian business unit, Ellis?" to friendly business bankers who called to ask if new women clients running multimillion dollar businesses might be featured in our company *Women of Westpac* newsletter. Being included as a founding member of the GBA was a godsend to me as the inaugural National Manager for Women in Business at Westpac. The other founders, who were from the US, Canada, and Ireland, were already very experienced in running initiatives that addressed the discrimination women customers complained of, designing relevant products and generating significant revenues for their banks. I was able to accelerate rapidly by learning from their programs, without having to actually find too many things out the hard way.

Support from the very top of the organization was critical to Westpac becoming the "bank of choice for women." The CEO himself championed the initiative and went on record in the public marketing brochures to say it was not "just an add-on, but rather an integral part of the long-term business strategy." In my experience, creating systemic change to promote women's economic empowerment is nigh impossible without support and active advocacy from senior management. The tone is very definitely set at the top.

But the rest of the organization also needs to get on board for successful change to occur. Our internal cultural change program differed across the organization depending on the target group: The senior leadership team held a two-day offsite designed to create emotional buy in to the commitment of becoming bank of choice for women; for business bankers, practical workshops outlined the business case; and for the 29,000 front-line staff, compulsory customer service video training in teams was backed up by mystery shopping. So the three approaches varied significantly based on a social cognitive model of change. At the most senior levels, a *transformational* deep dive approach to expose unconscious bias was essential to help all the executive team become role models and visible advocates for their own teams. At the mid–level, the focus was on the *business case* and how better servicing the women's market would help business banking managers to meet their targets. At the front-line level, demonstration video training – what does providing excellent service to women as well as men actually look like? – was backed up with mystery shopping so the approach was one of *compliance*.

Without direct positional power, I had to develop a collaborative, strategic approach to engage those with power at the top of the organization to "own" the agenda and then use *their* directive power to create change through the hierarchy. At the same time, change agents who truly believed in the transformational value of becoming the bank of choice for women were pivotal as passionate and tireless advocates across the organization at all levels.

Finally, measuring results helped drive a positive cycle of change. My talented team of state Women in Business managers created significant revenue streams for the bank, going from a standing start to an annualized turnover of US$504 million in just three years. For bankers driven by bottom-line success, this powerful demonstration effect shifted attitudes significantly and today Westpac is still at the forefront of the women's market in Australia and through active international engagement with the GBA.

TRANSFERRING AND ADAPTING LESSONS LEARNED: CONTEXT IS CRITICAL

The issues facing women accessing finance in developed countries were almost all attitudinal in the experience of the GBA founding member banks, although there was a lack of relevant provisions for loan holidays in Australia where no paid maternity leave existed at the time. In contrast, when I subsequently moved to Washington DC to work at the World Bank Group with a focus on developing countries, I discovered a whole raft of legislative and regulatory barriers. In many countries, women were – and are – still legal minors. They often don't have property ownership rights, and even if they do in theory, in many cases, custom law prevails, preventing women from being able to take out loans for business due to lack of collateral. This directly impacts their ability to contribute to, and benefit from, international development initiatives.

I documented barriers that impacted women's ability to be economically active in a range of developing countries and duly presented them to the VP for Private Sector Development who had asked me to make the case, including the example of land titling certificates in Vietnam I had come across a decade prior. Once presented with the research and evidence, he realized the enormous constraints women were dealing with as they attempted to engage in formal sector economic activity. I was provided a multimillion dollar budget and five staff positions to create the first private sector gender initiative for the World Bank Group, a new global "Gender Entrepreneurship Markets" (GEM) program.

GEM AND GENDER AND GROWTH ASSESSMENTS

The initial focus was on making the business case to client country Ministers and to engage women's business networks as catalysts for change. We created a new multidisciplinary tool called a "Gender and Growth Assessment" which correlated macroeconomic performance losses to institutionalized gender inequality. Building on an institutional economic framework, practical recommendations were made for gender issues to be incorporated into national private sector development strategies. The first was in Uganda, with a special request from the Minister of Finance, prompted by the Director of the Investment Authority, Dr Maggie Kigozi, now Uganda's United Nation (UN) Sustainable Development Goal 5 Ambassador to promote gender equality for women and girls. "Dr Maggie" is not only an outstanding leader in her own right, but also the one who is always supportive of others and a powerful gatekeeper. She is an expert at "leading from behind" and I learned so much working alongside her. It was critical not just to infer what women were experiencing in Uganda by consulting with experts; we needed to hear directly from a diverse group of women with business interests. This fundamental tenet of sound international development practice is for me the most important dimension of leadership in the field. What is the lived experience of the people we are trying to empower? How can deep listening help frame the issues? How are women's perspectives different from those of men? What insights can a gendered diagnostic provide? How can solutions be jointly crafted that will work in the specific cultural context and gain momentum beyond that provided by ODA dollars and input?

We worked with groups of local women entrepreneurs and lawyers to reveal the issues that needed to be addressed and the gains Uganda could make toward its Poverty Eradication Action Plan growth targets as a result. The biggest problems for businesswomen in Uganda related to access to finance to be able to grow their enterprises. This was related to the kind of bank loans available, which was largely collateral-based, and to the widespread practice of custom law preventing women access to land ownership. It logically followed that few women were able to access business banking loans. It was also from first-hand accounts that cultural mores negatively impacted the attitudes of predominantly clear male bankers toward women entrepreneur. Women had lower levels of education than their male counterparts, less financial and business experience, and fewer contacts and networks. So the barriers were threefold: at the macro-level, legal, and regulatory barriers; at the meso-level institutional discrimination in terms of access to finance as a key input for business growth; and at the micro-level lack of basic business skills and access to markets.

INNOVATE, REPLICATE ... NEXT STEPS AND THE PERSONAL IMPACT

The Gender and Growth Assessment prototype was well received and subsequent requests came in from Kenya, Tanzania, and Ghana, from the Middle East, Asia, and the Pacific. In fact, there were so many requests it was difficult to handle them. This had significant implications for me personally as a mother with a young son, despite having a very supportive husband. My boss was naturally keen to capitalize on the growing interest and that I accept a request from the governments of Lao, Cambodia, and Vietnam to cover all three in the same time block. My husband was traveling during the same period as my proposed travel. My inability to find someone to care for our son while I was away helped me realize I couldn't do it all myself. How could I engage partners? How could I train others to lead Gender and Growth Assessments? The UK Development agency, the Department for International Development (DFID), and the Canadian Development Agency both came on board as financial supporters and partners to help scale up our work, with DFID replicating the approach itself in Brazil and in India. A number of civil society groups also approached us to partner.

PRACTICAL IMPLICATIONS: FROM ASSESSMENT TO ACTION

The analytical model was proving successful, but there needed to be practical solutions to the lack of access to finance. Local currency lines of credit from local banks to local women entrepreneurs had emerged from our consultations as the logical solution. But how to persuade them to take the risk on a market previously underserved for all the reasons outlined?

Drawing on the useful lessons learned from the Global Banking Alliance collective, I invited in private sector bank representatives to speak to colleagues at the International Finance Corporation on the potential of the women's market in developing countries. There was much skepticism among male colleagues who had not previously focused on women as an entrepreneurial target group in the development context. They were, however, persuaded by the evidence base of barriers uncovered by the Gender and Growth Assessments and reassured by the results of the GBA banks in developed countries. IFC took on the Secretariat of the GBA to learn the lessons and translate those into a developing country context, bringing new banks on board as members. Finally, colleagues were prepared to let me give it a shot and provide a direct line of credit targeting women entrepreneurs as long as we could find a local client bank and get World Bank Executive Board support.

The powerful lesson I had learned about key champions across an organization materialized again as two extraordinary women leaders joined forces to persuade senior management a focus on women in private sector development was absolutely key to poverty reduction and economic growth in developing countries. Ngozi Okonjo-Iweala, who had been Nigeria's Finance Minister, connected us to access Bank in Nigeria where a US$30 million line of credit was requested, along with training in how best to serve the women's market. Given property collateral challenges, we innovated and used gold jewelry instead. Jan Piercy, then the Executive Director of the United States to the World Bank, helped persuade the Board this was a worthwhile endeavor, although skeptical IFC colleagues cut the line to US$15 million, unconvinced there would be enough SME businesswomen to use up the credit line.

These successes had a knock-on effect. Today, the IFC has over a billion dollars invested in lines of credit for women clients and the specific focus on women is fully mainstreamed across its access to finance work. A mentor of mine, Laura Liswood, who founded the Council of Women World Leaders, neatly encapsulates the road to change: "first the idea is unthinkable, then it is impossible, then it is INEVITABLE."

SYSTEMIC CHANGE: CAPTURING SEX-DISAGGREGATED DATA AND MAINSTREAMING GENDER ISSUES INTO PREVIOUSLY GENDER-BLIND DEVELOPMENT MODELS

The broader World Bank Group began to be persuaded of the role women could — and were — playing in economic development as actors, not just beneficiaries. Efforts to secure sex-disaggregated data in survey tools were finally successful! Women business owners were included in the enterprise surveys and IFC clients were asked to sex-disaggregate their own client bases. The next step was to persuade the lead of the World Bank *Doing Business* project that annually ranks business regulations and their enforcement to include a gender component.

With the active engagement of both the World Bank country economists and the Economist Intelligence Unit (EIU) economists to proxy implementation, we adopted the *Doing Business* practice of country rankings. Both the letter of the law and the economists' averaged estimation of implementation were included. This of course stood to change the original *Doing Business* rankings significantly for those countries with legal and regulatory regimes that discriminated against women.

ACTIVE OPPOSITION TO CHANGE

There was huge resistance from a number of countries on the World Bank Executive Board. A prominent and powerful Middle Eastern country in particular did all they could to stop the work, claiming I should be fired for bringing in a focus on what they argued were cultural rather than economic issues and therefore outside the remit of the World Bank's work.

I thought I had prepared the ground so carefully, engaging other relevant institutions such as the IMF, the International Labor Organization, and OECD's Development Assistance Committee. I had enrolled a powerhouse advisory committee to help with the design of the work, including then Chief Economist of Goldman Sachs, Jim O'Neill, and Harvard Director of the Center for International Development, Ricardo Hausmann. I had painstakingly consulted across the World Bank Group. But I had not thought to engage the Executive Board up front, and at a technical briefing, the roadblock suddenly emerged. I was devastated. I had organized the team with a lot of hard work, and we were all passionate about the importance of this groundbreaking new work. Given the realpolitik at the time in the form of World Bank capital raising I was advised to put the work on hold for a year, during which time I was sent to Harvard's Kennedy School of Government to participate in a wonderfully appropriate course called "Leadership on the Line: Staying Alive Through the Dangers of Leading" with Marty Linsky and Ron Heifetz.

LEADERSHIP ON THE LINE

The course delivered by Linksy and Heifetz focused on "adaptive leadership," with a couple of very helpful metaphors that helped me step back and get perspective on what the real roadblocks were and how best to adapt my approach. The first, "getting on the balcony" involves figuring out what the values of the stakeholder groups are and how best to figure out a way through the adaptive challenge. The second, "getting on the dance floor" refers to then being able to step back into the fray and take practical steps forward. While I was immensely frustrated by the situation created by the Saudi opposition, it was an excellent lesson in patience and adapting strategy to situation – neither natural traits for me, but both so important for successful development outcomes.

MANY MINDS: THERE IS ALWAYS ANOTHER WAY

My issue was chosen as a case study to work through with the entire group of participants to help devise a range of strategic options that could enable the work to continue. After many twists and turns including an exploratory undercover visit to Saudi Arabia with the Council on Foreign Relations, we decided to award the copyright to the EIU as an independent research brand to maintain the integrity of the model and the data. The EIU released our joint work as a complementary and separate publication that retained the country rankings and was called the *Women's Economic Opportunity Index.*

This long and complicated story helped me to learn two other critical leadership lessons: resilience and persistence in finding another approach. My team and I were grateful to be guided to find other outlets to disseminate the material we had chronicled. The adaptive leadership course at

Harvard was just what I had needed to regain perspective. It helped me shift from taking the issue personally to recognizing the opportunity to "get on the balcony" before I got back "on the dance floor." A workable solution emerged.

Rather than allowing this important work to be set aside and banished from the World Bank's research agenda, we shifted focus to the strict letter of the law, reverting to merely collating and documenting countries' legislation as it related to women's economic empowerment. The *Women, Business and the Law* project is ongoing, providing regularly updated data on all the laws that impact women's ability to be economically active in the formal sector. It also tracks reforms and provides recognition for positive progress, although at time of writing, over 90% of countries still have gender discriminatory laws that negatively impact women's ability to be economically active in the formal sector. Hopefully, the time will come when a set of indicators can again be developed and country rankings deduced.

ENGAGING PRIVATE SECTOR LEADERS

The importance of the private sector's leadership in women's economic empowerment in developing countries and emerging markets was recognized by former World Bank President Zoellick in 2007 and held up as a development model. He decided that for the first time, the IBRD should actively engage with and learn from CEOs who had enormous power for transformative change through their business operations. To demonstrate the importance he accorded this new initiative, Zoellick determined he would lead the Global Private Sector Leaders CEO Forum himself. "Gender equality is smart economics" was deliberately crafted as the tagline of the Gender Action Plan (GAP) to shift perceptions from the idea that women's engagement in private sector development was merely marginal to a mainstream development intervention. Zoellick embraced this approach wholeheartedly and made it part of his own personal leadership brand as well as that of the Bank. He went on record in the GAP brochure with:

> Gender equality in business is smart economics. Enlightened private
> sector companies recognize that. Gender and women's
> empowerment are also at the core of what we need to do in

development. It is not just a women's issue. Improved economic opportunities for women lead to better outcomes for families, societies and countries.

The World Bank president actively championing gender equality as smart economics was a signal to all the Bank staff that this was an issue clearly shifting from marginal to mainstream. The ambition was to create and integrate a mainstream agenda with enlightened private sector companies serving both as leaders and as role models for others. Each year the carefully geographically and gender balanced group of 23 member CEOs[1] would meet either in the margins of the World Economic Forum at Davos or the World Bank Annual Meetings. They shared their insights and progress in developing countries through both good practices and lessons learned around three key areas of focus: corporate diversity and inclusion, philanthropy and community engagement, and an integrated business approach.

Members like global accounting and services firms Price Waterhouse Cooper and Ernst and Young and engineering firm Boeing were especially concerned about the war for talent and the significant costs of women employees leaving, as well as the business benefits of a diverse workforce. Their contributions were focused on strategies to best retain and promote women as well as men through diversity and inclusion. Members like Cisco and Goldman Sachs focused on corporate social responsibility and community engagement. Cisco championed a Networking Academy to teach IT skills to over half a million students a year, ensuring the involvement of women and girls. Goldman Sachs *10,000 Women* program committed US$100 million over five years to train 10,000 women in developing countries in a mini-MBA in business, linking developed and developing country business schools together for both knowledge exchange and delivery. Of course, these were also investments in brand equity and staff engagement, too, at a time financial services firms were not the most popular, to say the least. Tupperware, Belcorps, and Standard Chartered Bank addressed the "women's market" as a core business proposition.

Other members, such as the Indian arm of fast-moving consumer goods company Unilever, combined both philanthropic and market goals. Hindustan Lever devised a win-win partnership with rural women who became central to the company's distribution model. The *Shakti* ("empowerment" in Hindi) Women Entrepreneurs program trains women who live

below the poverty line in rural villages to become distributors, often dou-
bling their household income.

LEARNING JOURNEYS IN GENDER EQUALITY AND WOMEN'S ECONOMIC EMPOWERMENT

Each member took a turn in hosting a "learning journey" to share good
practices and these were also captured in written format.[2] Members became
active disseminators of each other's material and, as Zoellick had hoped,
often added elements of other members' approaches to their own. As relationships strengthened, innovative partnerships among members emerged
and the engagement model shifted from a "hub and spokes" with the World
Bank at the center to more of a multiplex ring including developing country
governments and civil society groups. Building on the Paris Declaration, the
Accra Agenda for Action (OECD, 2008) encouraged, *inter alia*, more focus
on both inclusive partnerships and capacity development, which engaged private sector commitment and resources. We saw this play out.

Around this time, the UN Global Compact had been working hard on
developing the Women's Empowerment Principles: equality means business
(http://www.weprinciples.org/), and approached us to see if members of the
Private Sector Leaders Forum would be willing to sign on. The PSLF CEOs
were unanimous in supporting the development and launch of the UN
Women's Empowerment Principles in 2010, and it is very heartening to see
they continue to gain momentum.

FULL CIRCLE ... BACK TO NEW ZEALAND TO LEAD THE AID PROGRAM

In 2010, I returned to New Zealand as Deputy Secretary for International
Development in the Foreign Ministry and the first woman to lead the New
Zealand Aid Program. I was concerned I was also the only woman on the
Foreign Ministry Senior Leadership team and the only woman with a young
child to have ever served as Deputy Secretary.

I was thrilled to find a team with a genuine passion for international
development, including mainstreaming issues of gender equality, but I soon
discovered there were significant relationship difficulties. Staff told me they

had heard the Minister was concerned he had inherited in the New Zealand Aid Program a "group of tree-hugging sandal-wearing hippies." Staff engagement was at a low 13%. I soon discovered the Minister wanted to set a new direction, save significant money from administrative overhead cuts and staff downsizing. He was frustrated he wasn't getting the data he wanted. Data was indeed a problem, I discovered, including the fact that it was not sex-disaggregated and hence we had no systematic picture of the impact of New Zealand's ODA on women in developing countries. I set about gathering baseline data, including through survey tools and focus groups as well as traditional reporting mechanisms.

It struck me that despite the fractious relationships and the seeming disparities, both the Minister and the committed development professionals running New Zealand's ODA actually wanted the same thing: to deliver high-quality ODA with maximum impact for the poorest and most disadvantaged in the developing countries we served. After engaging all staff in workshops around how we could improve processes and efficiencies, some of the great ideas that emerged were collated, and teams organized to work on creating improvements. The results were amazing. The staff themselves rationalized more than 2,000 pages of guidance down to simple one and two page templates with flow charts; administrative overheads were cut by close to 15% with annual cost savings resulting of US$10.2 million.

But there were still real challenges with measuring the actual impact and outcomes of New Zealand's ODA. When I asked about results, staff would respond with how much money had been spent. Measurement had been all about budget expenditure. Having had input/output/outcome/impact relentlessly drilled into me at the World Bank, we set about changing our templates to capture these concepts and included sex-disaggregated data as the norm. It was a long, laborious process but once people began to internalize the concepts and the way they helped them better measure progress and outcomes the shift occurred! We knew we had succeeded when local NGOs wrote to say they had initially really not wanted to make the change, but now they appreciated having a much more accurate picture of how they were making a practical positive difference for partners on the ground.

Finally, everyone agreed it was essential to have a dedicated focus on gender equality and women's empowerment – and the selection team opted for a male gender advisor who was a passionate advocate and champion. From my perspective, this helped take things to the next level, modeling the need for gender equality to be just that and not merely a "women's issue." The role was pivotal in not only mainstreaming gender issues throughout our work, but in developing key relationships with partners like the Australian Aid Agency and UN Women. This led to active engagement with the inaugural Australian Ambassador for Women and Girls, the Director General of UN Women, and the office of then-US Secretary of State Hillary Clinton in support of the Pacific Island Forum's work to create the Pacific Leaders Gender Equality Declaration in 2012. Known as the Rarotonga Declaration, it reinvigorated commitments to progress gender equality in the Pacific region, which had a poor track record, second only to sub-Saharan Africa, and helped set the stage for active Pacific debate in the UN 2030 Development Agenda.

It was subsequently very gratifying to be part of the advocacy for a stand-alone sustainable development goal on gender during my tenure as New Zealand Head of Mission, Ambassador to the United Nations and Specialized Agencies in Geneva (2013-16). In addition to a mainstreamed gender approach throughout all 17 UN Sustainable Development Goals (SDGs), the agreement on UN SDG 5 to achieve gender equality and empower all women and girls was proof to me that gender issues had indeed moved from marginal to mainstream, not just in the private sector development but in the broader context of an integrated approach to global international development.

NOTES

1. http://siteresources.worldbank.org/INTGENDER/Resources/336003-1232650627030/WB_GPSLBrochure.pdf

2. https://issuu.com/jcutura/docs/pslfcasestudybelcorp

REFERENCES

OECD. (2008). Accra Agenda for Action. Retrieved from https://www.oecd.org/dac/effectiveness/45827311

7

WHAT ABOUT THE GRASSROOTS LEADERS? A MODEL FOR CULTURALLY APPROPRIATE LEADERSHIP THROUGH EMPOWERING LOCAL WOMEN

Anne M. Spear

"No one is listening to me!" Principal Ouedraogo[1] told me in a hot, dusty street in a suburb in Ouagadougou, Burkina Faso. "I have an idea that works, but I have no funding to train other schools. So what can I do?" She was speaking about an alternative to corporal punishment in primary schools, in which she applies the tenets of Marshall Rosenberg's (2015) famous nonviolent communication to her primary school protocols to train teachers on an effective form of classroom management.

When I met Ms Ouedraogo, I had already spent two months listening to similar stories from other women who were active leaders in their communities, and so, I was not shocked by the lack of support that her novel approach was receiving. Multiple international nongovernmental organizations' (INGOs) development agencies had gotten funding from foreign governments and international institutions, such as the World Bank, to address the same issue of corporal punishment and were busy applying their own programs, yet local leaders like Ms Ouedraogo were getting little sustainable support for implementation of innovative, local programs. While some female teachers have viable solutions to problems they experienced as students and educators as I will demonstrate in this chapter, they are ignored despite the international rhetoric branding teachers as change agents.

In this chapter, I reflect on my own experience as part of an international development organization and researcher in Burkina Faso and as an observer of other INGOs in action. I call for a reformulation of the concept of culturally appropriate leadership and the role of grassroots, local, female leadership. I make the argument for reconsidering the appropriate influence of expatriate workers and leaders in the international development community.[2] I argue that the contribution by local leadership is a valuable and sustainable resource that is often misunderstood and overlooked in meaningful ways by development professionals. This fact is particularly true with regard to the leadership within marginalized groups.

IT TAKES ONE TO KNOW ONE: PERSONAL LESSONS LEARNED

Entering into Peace Corps service in Burkina Faso in the sector of girls' education and empowerment, I believed that the field of international development presented the means to address global inequality and poverty. In just the first six months in my host village, before learning the local language or culture, I started to form my own nonprofit organization with the goal of solving problems around girls' lack of access to secondary schooling. I left the village to travel to the city in order to attend meetings and access resources to develop needed documents. I went so far as to schedule a trip back to the United States in order to start raising money for projects. I initially got the feeling that the villagers did not appreciate my efforts and I started to realize that I was not integrating into the community as authentically as I wished. One day, with not much "work" to do, I sat and shelled peanuts with some women. One of the women turned to me and expressed how pleased she and the others were that I was sitting with them and practicing Moore, the local language. I started to do this more often and began to see the development from their view of the world: white SUVs that drove by to talk to the most privileged *male* politician in the village; money and projects, which never touched their lives; new buildings remaining empty; women who stood in the hot sun to watch celebrations honoring foreign guests that were seated in the shade of a tent; and women walking home as the wealthy guests and local *male* leaders went to a private reception with chicken and soda. This is what development looked like to these women. I soon realized that spending my time with them was what they valued most of all in order to build relationships. For them, whether it is business or other types of development, it all starts with a trusting, mutual relationship. Through building these types of relationships within the community, I was able to conduct projects with them, such as school gardens, and to have important personal conversations, such as how to support their children in school and manage their money through small income-generating activities. Without starting by developing relationships, I would be alone in implementing programs in *their* community.

I decided not to proceed with the NGO. Through developing relationships instead of a new organization, I learned that my friends and colleagues had better solutions to the issues around girls' education; they just did not have a space to implement them. I lead from behind, often learning more than leading. Instead of claiming knowledge beyond those that have lived the experience, I worked and continue to work to support *their* associations and projects.

In the next section, I highlight three failures of the traditional approach of the international development community in Burkina Faso, as I have observed in my experience. Following that section are three case studies of women leaders who were in different spaces of recognized leadership when I met them. The final section draws on my experience described earlier to introduce a new approach that I argue would serve the international community to better identify and support local leadership to achieve the sustainable development goals (SDGs) for quality education (SDG 4) and gender equality (SDG 5).

WHAT IS WRONG WITH THE TRADITIONAL?

This section demonstrates three ways I have observed that the traditional approach to international development has failed, within the context of power and privilege: (1) The failure to build relationships creates missed opportunities; (2) development leaders fail to become skilled at "playing" with and around power, and (3) development organizations themselves are unwilling to concede power and influence, refusing to challenge harmful power dynamics, particularly regarding gender inequalities. My discussion about the exercise and negotiation of power by the international development community in Burkina Faso draws on the three forms of power, outlined by Gaventa (2006): visible power, hidden power, and invisible power. The visible form of power is observable influence such as a law or formal structures and procedures. Policymakers and those in positions of power have visible power. An example of visible power is the national government laws or the SDGs developed by the international development community. Hidden power sets the priorities through influence. Lobbyists hold hidden power. They are not the policymakers, but they have influence on what gets prioritized and on the agenda. In the development world, agencies such as the World Bank hold a lot of hidden power within governments. Invisible power dictates the meaning, beliefs, and values of the group. Gaventa (2006) explains this power as "influencing how individuals think about their place in the world … shapes people's beliefs, sense of self, and acceptance of the status quo even their own superiority and inferiority" (p. 29). Religion institutions and other groups that contribute to socialization hold invisible power. The development organizations' approach to media campaigns aims to use invisible power to influence social change.

Development organizations, such as INGOs working in Burkina Faso, both contribute to and contend with all of these forms of power when implementing development projects. First, I address the visible and hidden powers of the development community to build my first point. As stated earlier, development organizations implement their own projects while working with the national government rather than supporting local projects. This practice gives organizations both visible and hidden powers to influence development goals for the country, outside funding, and what strategies to prioritize, rather than focusing on integrating into the local culture, developing relationships, or learning about local solutions. This visible power is most obvious through the global agenda of the millennium development goals (MDGs) in the 1990s and the current SDGs. These goals are developed by outside development experts, most of who have been trained in the West. This elite group draws up the development priorities as well indicators that are used to measure progress. Once there is agreement within this group, the goals and indicators are drawn up as international development goals, such as the SDGs. All governmental and nongovernmental organizations that focus on development start to implement projects to address these goals. Countries' local leaders are not involved and have no influence on what the development goals should be for their communities, nor do they have a voice in how progress should be measured.

The traditional approach of larger INGOs is to use hidden and visible power to develop projects for countries such as Burkina Faso. This is done through obtaining outside funding and striving to achieve invisible power that influences how people think, believe, and act. In order to achieve this invisible power of influence, rather than focusing on relationship building, the development community traditionally relies on media campaigns, policy reform, and formalized trainings. This can be seen as the development community gives attention to ending corporal punishment in schools by putting up billboard ads in the regional capitals in Burkina Faso. The political pressure led to the Government of Burkina Faso outlawing corporal punishment. Foreign organizations, such as Plan International and US Agency for Development (USAID), developed teacher trainings on classroom management to persuade teachers to avoid using corporal punishment in classrooms. These approaches are well intended and perhaps needed as part of a solution to ending corporal punishment. However, they do not address the cultural norms in Burkina Faso. Many parents and teachers do not see corporal punishment as violence and often see the practice as beneficial for students' learning.

Notably, powerful international agencies such as the World Bank and the International Monetary Fund (IMF) used national loans and grants as visible and hidden powers to influence the government of Burkina Faso to decentralize as a means of cutting government spending, advocated as an opportunity to increase community involvement. In the education sector, a result of decentralization was the creation of parent associations (APE) and mothers associations (AME) in each public school. However, these groups were implemented in a top-down fashion that is often the traditional development approach of dictating rather than facilitating solutions and failed to establish these community groups as functioning and influential entities because the development workers did not *go into the communities and develop relationships* with the local members to support the functions of the APEs and AMEs. In turn, they failed to empower the members, some whom had never had space to participate in the past (see Spear, n.d.).

Not only do foreign development leaders carry power and influence but they also must contend with the dynamics of all forms of power that exist throughout Burkina Faso. To be culturally appropriate, it is essential for foreign guests, who form the majority of the development community, to recognize individuals that hold power and privilege, nationally and locally. I do not advocate that development workers go against this cultural practice, as it would be inappropriate and offensive and is likely to block access to other members of society. Nevertheless, by blindly following and supporting the visible decision makers, who hold hidden and invisible powers, foreign development organizations can work against their own objectives as well as disrupt communities (particularly in the case of SDG 5: "Empowering Women and Girls"). I have personally witnessed how INGO workers contribute to the support of harmful power dynamics at a local level, often unknowingly. Many people desire to work with development organizations because there is usually an exchange of money, resources, and power. Thus, many corrupt leaders become opportunists and make themselves quickly visible to development organizations in order to be part of projects. These leaders do not have the right motives and are often not trusted by their communities. The foreign workers do not know this, at least in the beginning, and they inadvertently contribute to the power and influence of a negative leader as well as set up local implementation of projects to suffer.

My approach to breaking from traditional ways of leading as a development worker – to include more of an emphasis on grassroots approaches and a reconceptualization of the role of local female leaders – stems from my personal experiences, the cultural context of Burkina Faso, and my knowledge of working around the patriarchal system. Women hold knowledge and solutions, and thus far, the international community has struggled to unleash the potential of women leaders.

CASE STUDIES: WOMEN LEADERS IN BURKINA FASO

Women in Burkina Faso may not have access to traditional leadership roles or positions, but some have the courage to use their voices, the knowledge to disrupt the status quo, and the passion developed from their personal experiences of discrimination to create solutions to improve their society. The following section connects three case studies to my own development as a leader. In each case, I outline the process of seeking allies, accessing knowledge, and challenging harmful norms.

Principal Ouedraogo

Principal Ouedraogo was introduced at the beginning of this chapter. When I inquired about her motivations to find a successful method of classroom management, she listed two realities: (1) That teachers need a skill other than corporal punishment and (2) that as the first female principal of the school, she needed to demonstrate her abilities. The men in the community, school, and ministry were constantly challenging and doubting her. Uniquely, Principal Ouedraogo did not use allies at first to gain confidence to stand up to the sexist attitudes at work. Instead, she sought out knowledge, in this case, the nonviolent communication program, and taught it to her teachers. She found her allies in funders, specifically the Ashoka Foundation.[3] Becoming an Ashoka Fellow, she was able to develop her training program, which has been working, anecdotally, at her school. Despite this recognition, Principal Ouedraogo has not been able to further her program. Up until the summer of 2016, no other organization had contacted her and she said she received no additional funding, in spite of the fact that there are about a dozen INGOs in the area with their own programs to address violence in schools. I left the meeting with Principal Ouedraogo impressed at her innovation; she is a fierce woman leader. She left the meeting visibly frustrated. She had hoped that I was connected to an organization that would help her implement the program, and she was no closer to her goal.

The Association for the Promotion of Women and Girls

The Association for the Promotion of Women and Girls (APEFF) is a local association consisting of a group of female school teachers who became allies. These women were educated in a school system where they were sexually abused and harassed, enduring verbal and corporal punishments. As teachers, they saw the same thing happening to school girls. They knew the pain of such encounters, and so, they decided they had to help protect and support the girls. Informally, they started to talk and work with the girls and to report incidences to the school administration. Because most adults turn a blind eye to violence and abuse, the girls soon began coming to them for help. The members sought out training on girls' education and gender equality, and after gaining a reputation, as well as increased threats for working with a taboo issue, they formed the small organization.

This case study provides an example of what can happen when women leaders are supported. A large INGO, the Forum of African Women Educators (FAWE),[4] partnered with APEFF. FAWE had selected one of the schools in the area where some members taught, to implement a girl-friendly program. In 2010, the two organizations did a week-long awareness campaign, which, in turn, got the attention of Peace Corps volunteers in the area, who then offered training to the APEFF members (see Forsyth-Queen, Gonzalez, & Meehan, 2015). In 2016, I asked Peace Corps staff how they were working with APEFF at that time, particularly after Michelle Obama's Let Girls Learn initiative[5] was introduced. Staff told me there was no current partnership. When I met with four of the members, they confirmed that they were not working with any partners and while they still helped girls, they did little formal programming. Where did the momentum go? What about all the knowledge and experience they hold as individual teachers and gained through trainings? As the international development community develops programs to combat violence in schools, what solutions do these women already hold that would surely be more culturally appropriate than those being developed in Washington, DC, and London?

Madame Diallo

I include Madame Diallo, a retired primary school teacher, as a representative of all the untapped female leaders in Burkina Faso. Ms Diallo has never formed an organization or implemented a development program but she is an example of a revolutionary woman of Burkina Faso. Like me, she was raised in an environment that told her that as a girl she was not as smart as boys. Unlike me, she was barred from school. However, luck was on her side when a French expatriate convinced the men of her village to send one of their daughters to school.

Madame Diallo is the only literate, educated child in her immediate family. She went on to become a teacher and experienced discrimination as a student and teacher. Breaking cultural conventions, she left an abusive husband and raised her six children on her own. Like my story, education and access to knowledge allowed Ms. Diallo to challenge negative practices. In her story, as in mine and in all of the women highlighted in this chapter, there is a community of support. Ms Diallo received help from international members of her religious community, and this support allowed her to care for her children and remove them from the presence of an abusive man.

Leaders do not simply materialize. These case studies, along with my own experience, make pertinent the importance of supportive allies. In each case, the allies looked different and provided different modes of support. The women of the APEFF came together as their own allies. Economic allies helped Principal Ouedraogo and Madame Diallo take action to be change agents in their communities. Personally, people who could confirm my experience and show me solidarity and truth bolstered me. Each of the women in this chapter sought out knowledge and applied the knowledge she obtained, whether from formal schooling, training, or other means, to confront gender discrimination.

It is curious that there seems to be such a limited capacity in the development world to build on local, grassroots knowledge. Having worked in Burkina Faso for a decade, I have found dozens of women who have been able and willing to bravely take a stand as these women have done. However, if development leaders are not adept at maneuvering around power in Burkina Faso, it is unlikely they will have access or ability to partner with a modest association of women.

A NEW MODEL

Goldenberg (2008) found similar themes in his case studies examining women's political participation through women's groups in Uganda, Kenya, and Russia. Women groups can self-organize, as did the APEFF, and confront issues by creating and claiming their own space in order to work with local authorities. Building on Goldenberg's (2008) and Gaventa's (2006) analyses of invited and created spaces and incorporating the process of empowerment outlined by Stromquist (2015), I lay out an alternative method of leadership for the development communities in Burkina Faso (see Table 1). To be clear, my proposed model for development organizations in Burkina Faso is to support the work of women and other marginalized groups, such as those highlighted in this chapter, as facilitators. Facilitation can be a variety of actions, such as providing resources, assisting with networking or fundraising, exchanging ideas, giving trainings for capacity building, and so on. Women leaders do not lack solutions nor do they lack drive and motivation, but in these stories, the realities of gender inequality in

---

Table 1. Comparison of the Traditional and Alternative Development Models.

Traditional Development Model	New Alternative Development Model
Business approach toward development: aligned with outside cultural practices	*Relationship-based approach* toward development: aligned with local cultural practices
Top-down approach to decision-making: draws on hierarchal leadership structure to influence development goals and projects	*Bottom-up approach to decision-making:* drawing on local knowledge to influence development goals and projects
Focus on *transfer of material resources* or one-way exchange of information	Focus on *comprehensive empowerment*
Reproduction of power: working within privilege and power dynamics	*Redistribution of power:* challenging harmful power dynamics
Working with visible *traditional (male) leaders* to assist in implementing *outside solutions*	Identifying *grassroots (female) leaders* who are implementing *organic solutions*
'Elite' development community prioritizing development goals and projects	Including *community participation,* particularly local women, when establishing development goals and projects
Development community *leading in front*	Development community *leading from behind*

Source: Author.

Burkina Faso block women from spaces that would make their ideas heard and themselves visible. The lack of economic and political power keeps women and their knowledge hidden and unused. Developments leaders have the opportunities to step around the power structures in Burkina Faso to build meaningful relationships with women leaders and provide space for their work.

The first shift that is required for developing and implementing a new model is making it a priority to access, get to know, and empower local women leaders. Stromquist (1995) makes a clear argument for way the development world should focus on working with women. She states,

> *Empowerment is a process which should center on adult women*
> *for two central reasons: First, their adult lives have produced many*

experiences of subordination and thus they know this problem very well, although they have not labeled it as such, and second, the transformation of these women is fundamental to breaking the integrational reproduction of patriarchal authority. (p. 14)

Often by default, due to the historical and current gender inequalities, development organizations have more access to, and therefore engage more frequently with men. In Burkina Faso, men hold positions of power and influence, often have more education, and certainly have more freedom of movement and time than women. In most of my projects in Burkina Faso, I have worked with male counterparts, among them school directors, leaders of organizations, community leaders, and students. I have had to make concerted efforts to develop relationships with women in the country. I learned a local language, which allowed me to form relationships with poorer, often illiterate women who constitute a large percentage of the female population in Burkina Faso. This is ultimately how I got to know the country. I did not stay in the space prescribed to me; I sought out women, knowing that they hold solutions to gender issues in their country; and I was humble. Development leaders need to follow these same efforts. There is potential for successful results in getting closer to the SDGs if development organizations start to work with women who demonstrate the same resilience, passion for, and local knowledge about girls' education as Madame Diallo has shown.

The second shift that is required for this new model is for development organizations to act as facilitators as they empower and support local women leaders, rather than implementing their own solutions. This shift will require development organizations to challenge power, including their own, at a visible level by using hidden power to prioritize the women's grassroots solutions. For example, development workers can spend time with a community, before choosing a liaison. Beyond attending organized meetings and meeting with the visible leaders, in which the more privilege are able to attend, development workers can visit with community members in their homes, places of worship, local markets, and shops. They can visit schools and talk with parents, teachers, and students.

A clear understanding of the process of empowerment will help development leaders to determine what type of support is needed for each female leader or group. I am employing Stromquist's (2015) categories of empowerment: psychological, knowledge, economic, and political. These four categories address different areas of need for women to gain access to a variety of resources. Psychological empowerment gives women the self-confidence to take action and enter public spaces, traditionally only reserved for men. Knowledge empowerment includes access to knowledge either from formal and nonformal education. Economic empowerment includes access to material goods, financial resources, and economic rights. Examples of economic empowerment include legal protection to own land and get bank loans, as well as to access economic markets and enter the labor force. Political empowerment comes from women's ability to use their voices in their community, often in local politics or community organizations. This extends to the right to participate in politics and have political representation (Stromquist, 2015). I provide examples from the case studies that highlight how these four different categories help empower the women.

By listening to women, development leaders are likely to learn that the women of Burkina Faso can be empowered into action and self-organization, as the nation as a whole demonstrated with the 2014 revolution that ousted President Blaise Compaore. For example, Principal Ouedraogo and the APEFF displayed psychological empowerment by confidently taking action and organizing. All of the women sought knowledge empowerment through formal education, training, and informal learning. However, they vocalize the limits of their work and influence due to their economic and political disempowerment. Development organizations have an important role to play in creating space for economic and political empowerment for women leaders, as Stromquist (2015) states, "women's movement in the global South could not exist without international support" (p. 318). INGOs have the power to invite women groups into spaces that are often inaccessible to them and to support them as they create and claim space for their work (Gaventa, 2006).

Some practical steps toward this new development leadership model that leaders of INGOs in Burkina Faso can do, without challenging the whole structure of the development world, include: (1) funding local language learning for nonlocal staff; (2) creating opportunities to spend unstructured time in communities, sitting with community members in different spaces; (3) being creative about how to apply for funding; and (4) bringing in local women leaders to conferences and events. The first recommendation is easy, though can be met with resistance, particularly as staff is struggling to get along in French. However, whether in the country for one, two, or five years, learning a local language will allow for more authentic integration into the culture as well as the ability to do better work. I have encountered countless situations where knowledge of the local language Moore has served me, beyond the obvious advantage of being able to communicate with more people, particularly women. One example is when a group of INGO workers was working with a community leader. When they thought the leader was translating to the local group, he was instead issuing directives and contradictions to what he communicated to INGO workers, in Moore. Clearly, this man was neither honest nor respectful of his followers but without understanding Moore, there was no way for the foreigners to know what he was doing. Nobody in the local group had an opportunity to go against their boss and speak up.

The only way to identify women and other marginalized leaders is to go into the communities and get to know the people. The only way to get to know the people and form relationships in Burkina Faso is to spend time with them. Therefore, I recommend that development workers in the country incorporate unstructured community time into their strategies and work time. Although sitting aimlessly in a village can be uncomfortable, it will have numerous benefits, as I have recounted in the beginning of this chapter.

There is a reality about development work. In order for an organization to survive, they must get funding and promise to implement a project within the parameters defined by the funders. However, development leaders can be creative in how they design projects within the required goals and parameters, and in the people they bring in to do the work. Particularly with the focus on sustainability and capacity building, organizations can start to work with and fund women leaders and organizations through their own project funding. However, this will only happen if relationships are built and development organizations recognize the knowledge of local leaders.

Finally, a simple strategy that development leaders can develop is to bring local leaders into spaces of power and privilege. This could include space for women leaders, such as Principal Ouedraogo or the APEFF, to present at conferences or attend trainings. Networking events within the development world would allow women leaders the opportunity to access political spaces that could lead to economic opportunities to enhance their work.

INGOs and development leaders can achieve their goals, particularly SDGs 4 (Quality Education) and 5 (Empowering Women and Girls), by supporting local women leaders. We know that local solutions to local problems are often the best, but we continue to fail to provide space and empowerment for those solutions to be seen and applied. Development leaders do not need to create local leaders or groups; they exist. Instead, new strategies are needed to access them.

CONCLUSION

Throughout this chapter, I have shared my experience and three case studies that demonstrate how women were empowered to organize and take action as well as the continued barriers they face to implement change. I call on development workers to acknowledge the failures that have prevented us from successfully acknowledging and working with local women's groups. By recognizing these failures, organizations can revise their approaches and find meaningful ways to engage with women. In this chapter, I offer modest suggestions that development leaders can consider implementing to be more successful at achieving their goals. I have demonstrated how the strategies have benefited my own work in Burkina Faso. These local leaders are waiting for a space to bring forth their solutions.

NOTES

1. Pseudonyms have been used in place of real names

2. For the purpose of this chapter, I define the development community as all foreign government agencies, embassies, and INGOs that conduct programs in Burkina Faso using outside money. These organizations may use locally registered associations to implement their own programs. Those employed by these organizations, referred to as development leaders/workers in this chapter, can be local or foreign nationals.

3. The Ashoka Foundation is an INGO that provides funding for the implementation of a community member's innovative project that addresses community development. An Ashoka Fellow is chosen after demonstrating that their project has transformational potential. A Fellow is given financial support for a year to start their project.

4. FAWE is an African INGO that was developed by several African female educators. FAWE operates in several African countries.

5. Michele Obama developed The Let Girls Learn initiative in 2015 to support girls in schools through the world. Burkina Faso was chosen as a pilot country for the initiative. The program ended in July 2017.

REFERENCES

Forsyth-Queen, E., Gonzalez, L., & Meehan, S. (2015). Doorways: Preventing and responding to school-related, gender-based violence in West Africa. In S.L. Stacki & S. Baily (Eds.), *Educating Adolescent Girls around the Globe: Challenges and Opportunities* (pp. 96–117). New York: Routledge.

Gaventa, J. (2006). Finding the spaces for change: A power analysis. *Institute of Development Studies Bulletin, 37*(6), 23–33.

Goldenberg, D. (2008). Grassroots women's leadership and "deepening democracy": The Huairou Commission's Local to Local Dialogue replication. *Gender & Development, 16*(3), 443–456.

Rosenberg, M. (2015). *Nonviolent communication: A language of life: Life-changing tools for healthy relationships*. Encitas, CA: Puddle Dancer Press.

Spear, A. (n.d.). Implementing theory in northern Burkina Faso: A case study of a gender and education initiative. Manuscript under revision.

Stromquist, N. P. (1995). The theoretical and practical bases for empowerment. In C. Medel-anonuevo (Ed.), *Women, Education and Empowerment: Pathways toward Autonomy* (pp. 13–22). Hamburg: UNESCO Institute for Education.

Stromquist, N. P. (2015). Women's empowerment and education: Linking knowledge to transformative action. *European Journal of Education, 50*(3), 307–324.

8

LEADERSHIP THROUGH EMPOWERMENT

Nila Wardani and Kathryn B. Mangino

INTRODUCTION

The term "leadership" often brings to mind thoughts of powerful politicians or business CEOs, and when the world gathers to celebrate women leaders, we tend to applaud those who are already accomplished and newsworthy. This chapter, however, asks for the attention of the grassroots woman; the unrecognized every day leader who is brave enough to question traditional gender norms and works for gender equality in small ways in her household and community. We highlight our role in development as motivators working to bring out the leader in the everyday rural woman. We believe in leadership through encouragement, support, networking, and valuing others. We believe that true, sustainable leadership comes from acts of humility and trust; humility in the recognition that we "development professionals" do not have all the answers, and trust in a belief that all women have the capacity to lead if given the appropriate context, tools, skills, and network.

The "we" in this chapter refer to Nila and Kate, colleagues, and friends who share the common interest of leadership through empowerment. We chose to use the case of Indonesia (Nila's home country) and hope that by contextualizing this chapter in this local environment lessons can be applied globally because the low status of rural women in Indonesia will resonate with their status in many parts of the world.

Leadership can be a vague and, frankly, unreachable concept for marginalized, rural women. But once women become aware of broad leadership principles they realize that they are already leaders in their domestic space. This realization can be empowering and makes leadership feel more attainable. Now women can identify the real functions of leadership – influencing others, protecting those who need protection, making hard decisions, and directing others to a better future. Women realize that leaders can also be good followers and good listeners, which opens them up to dialogue and a variety of ideas and opinions.

Emerging women leaders learn to be comfortable with themselves. They learn to respect and acknowledge one's own ideas. In the simplest words, they become confident simply for being themselves. Over time women (not all, but many) find that with a newfound network, skills, and supportive environment, they are able to achieve more than they ever thought possible.

Neither Appreciative Inquiry (AI) nor Participatory Rural Appraisal (PRA) is new. Both tools are decades old and well tested. We choose to write about them here not because they are cutting edge, but in the hopes that they are not forgotten. In an era defined by big targets and efficient investment and an emphasis on technology, we hope that some development leaders still attest to the power in classic, community-based development tools that truly support sustainable change at the grassroots level. We hope students of development continue to learn about how true community-led development happens. And we hope donors still find these programs worth funding.

WOMEN'S EMPOWERMENT AND THE SUSTAINABLE DEVELOPMENT GOALS

The theory of women's empowerment is not new in development. The phrase was used throughout the 1970s with women's groups working in South-East Asia (Batliwala, 2007) and perhaps made famous by Caroline Moser's publications in the 1980s (Moser, 1989). The term "women's empowerment" is now more widely interpreted to mean any development project that targets women (CARE International, 2009). But at its core, experts agree that women's empowerment is instead to be a methodology to bring groups of women together for the end goal of increased self-awareness, increased self-esteem, and increased skills. Empowerment is achieved by simply working with the same group of women over a period of time to:

(1) realize their role in a gendered society;

(2) assist group members to set goals; and

(3) support the group in reaching set goals.

The United Nations (UN) Sustainable Development Goals (SDG) illustrate that the global community believes in the importance of women's empowerment. SDG 5 calls for the world to "achieve gender equality and empower all women and girls." To make this enormous and daunting goal more palatable, the UN breaks SDG 5 down into nine targets, which include the end of gender discrimination and gender-based violence, as well as the fostering of equal political participation, universal access to sexual and reproductive health, enhanced use of technology, and strengthened policies. All of these targets are founded on empowerment. When women's confidence is improved; when women better understand their gendered context; and when women have the skills to set and reach goals, then they are able to run for local government. Then are they able to advocate for reproductive health. Then they are able to stand up against gender-based violence and protect one another.

The work of Nila and Kate has not changed since the SDGs were written. We worked in women's empowerment long before the SDGs were promulgated. However, the SDGs act as an effective framework that allows us to more easily communicate the importance of women's empowerment to others and validates the resources used to conduct empowerment programs.

The SDGs however do not specifically outline how to achieve the results they promulgate. That is left up to national and international donors and implementers and by testing and retesting a variety of methods. Through our combined work, we have found that both PRA and AI are reliable tools with which to achieve successful results in women's empowerment. We have used these methods throughout Java Island ourselves. In the following pages, we will describe how each of these methods is used and then give examples of how these methods have brought about results for us in Indonesia.

INDONESIA OVERVIEW

The majority of rural women in Indonesia have little decision-making power; they are socialized to lack any personal interest or future aspirations. As societal subordinates, their positions are always represented by men, who do

acknowledge women's' reproductive roles, but do not recognize their productive roles. Rural women in Indonesia are typically defined in terms of
family and motherhood. To be a good and successful woman is to be a supportive wife and mother. Although there are more progressive voices in
modern Indonesia, generally speaking a woman's role in Indonesian society
is to preserve family harmony. Although many rural women work out of
economic necessity, the societal ideal of family harmony derives from a
sexual division of labor – men work for income, and women tend the home.

Many traditionalists argue that this family framework is not degrading to
women. They claim that men's work and women's work are equally important to the health of the nation, but that those forms of work are distinctly
separate. Men are tasked with work for the country, through government or
business, while women are asked to manage the home and care for children
and the elderly. Women have the duty of controlling the family budget,
which does allow women considerable power inside the home. However,
men are given control of the social, religious, and political realms outside the
home. This results in a general domestication of Indonesian women that
frames Indonesian culture. This culture is then reinforced by policies
throughout government, business, education, and religious institutions.
Though some women of the business or elite classes have broken through
the glass ceiling to gain power (such as Sri Rismaharini, who has served as
mayor of Surabaya since 2010), the average rural woman is considered successful only when she tends the home, refrains from decision-making duties,
and accepts her husband and/or father as the leader of the household.

In the eyes of Indonesian law, women technically have equal access to
nearly all of economic resources. But they have far less control over the
country's major economic resources such as land, natural resources, large
animals, and agricultural equipment (Geertz, 1961). Wives are said to share
equal status in the household decision-making process according to the saying that men might be the head of the house, but women are the neck – sug-
gesting that the silent or informal partner shares equal status. However, until
women can have transparent decision-making power in the public sphere,
their small exercises in power are stifled. Many families are dependent on
women's financial inputs. However, Nila has found that it is typically the
man who is always described as the breadwinner, and his salary is always
discussed as the primary source of income, even if it amounts to less than his
wife's. Women's income is always described as "extra" or "supplementary."

Indonesians do not like to admit that it is often a woman's salary that holds a family together. The fact that these truths are kept hidden is an indication of the power imbalance between men and women, and how gender norms and stereotypes can alter one's perception of reality.

According to the traditional perspective, only men are active in community decision-making processes. Therefore, in practice, women are rarely present during formal village meetings for annual development planning and budgeting. This reality illustrates that although women have financial power in the home, they have little to no financial power when it comes to government expenditures. Because men make community plans, men see to it that these plans are implemented. Through this cycle of experience, men gain knowledge and understanding of local government despite their lack of a formal education. Women, however, are rarely part of this cycle. They are left out and so lack new experiences that might otherwise introduce them to the world of local government and development. As a result, over time, women become far less likely to express their ideas or opinions publicly or even privately.

APPRECIATIVE INQUIRY

AI was born from Case Western University's department of Organizational Behavior. The first time the theory was presented broadly was in David Cooperrider's dissertation, where in 1986, the concept of problem-solving was challenged. Cooperrider argued that instead of an expert diagnosing an institution's flaws and forcing members to focus on the negative, members of the institution would experience far more success and positive change by focusing on their own assets, and nurture what was positive and life-giving within their collective traits and organization (Cooperrider & Srivastva, 1987).

The basis of this assets-based approach is brilliant in its simplicity. A group of people, be it 5 or 500, can be led through a facilitation process to identify a vision and goals and forge a path to reach these. Cooperrider referred this process as the 4-D's, namely "Discover," "Dream," "Design," and "Deliver." Further, AI welcomes all voices in the room irrespective of position or role. Opinions of low-ranking personnel are just as valuable as those in leadership. Therefore, a true inquiry could include the president and the janitor, the finance team and the receptionist, and human resources director and the driver. Everyone's perspective to an institution is important and valued and should not be ignored (Watkins & Bernard, 2001).

AI has proven to be successful in a wide range of institutions including private and government sectors. But we think that AI is especially suited for work with marginalized women who have had unequal access to resources. Many Indonesian women we work with have only a few years of formal or informal education and no job history and face many challenges in their everyday lives. Going into these communities with a problem-based methodology adds to their challenges and can frankly be depressing. An empowerment group can spend days discussing the confines of poverty, the lack of opportunities, the harsh realities of an early marriage, poor health care, and the barriers to resources and the disinterest of local government. Nothing could be more disheartening, and after spending days making an exhaustive list of "what is wrong" we can't imagine anyone mustering the energy to find a way to do something right.

Because AI is an assets-based approach, women have the opportunity to instead focus on what is going well. AI does not ignore problems, but simply opens participants up to pathways around them, which can lead to creative and innovative solutions. An AI methodology helps empowerment groups answer questions such as: What do you love? Where are you when you are happiest? What are your wildest dreams? How can we work toward making those dreams a reality?

Earlier in this chapter, we discussed how Indonesian women are socialized to not have personal dreams or aspirations. They instead focus their time and attention to their husbands, children, parents, and communities. Therefore, AI is often quite difficult at first to use. Women have a hard time allowing themselves to dream and an even harder time in expressing their opinions in a clear way. Facilitating meetings that help them to work through deep social norms takes months, if not years. However, once women start to learn how to articulate their opinions, they tend to wholly embrace AI. Imagine the power of being asked, for the first time in your life … how do you feel? What do you like? What do you want to do? How can I help you? Then the power of the positive is limitless. In application, we repeatedly move through the 4-D cycle during our time with an empowerment group. Whereas an American institution might only lead participants through an inquiry once during a strategic planning phase, women's groups we work with in Indonesia follow an AI loop that constantly helps push them to better understand their role in society, set new goals, and work toward those new goals.

AI EXAMPLES FROM KATE

Facilitating is not easy. Many people assume because they are skilled speakers or presenters, they can facilitate. But the skill set is actually quite different. Facilitators lead from behind by asking a series of well-crafted questions; facilitators don't lecture on the truth, they help others to find the truth for themselves. Facilitation can be frustrating – group participants sometimes come to conclusions not shared by the facilitator. But if true sustainability comes from the empowerment of those who were previously vulnerable, we must be open to the risk of allowing people to come to their own conclusions.

As a facilitator of a group going through an appreciative process, Nila and I have to establish group cohesion. First, we must establish a safe space, both physically and emotionally, conducive to an environment of openness and honestly by allowing the group members to set the date, time, and place of the meeting. The facilitator always follows the lead of the women, instead of creating her own environment. For example, if the women participants sit in a circle, so do we. If the women are eating, we join in. If they bring children, we welcome the kids and bring toys. The facilitator cannot dive straight into planned dialogue, but take the time to greet everyone individually and answer all of their questions before we start in with our own.

We must help participants decide on group norms – what is to be allowed, and what isn't – focusing on mutual respect and encouraging group members to not judge each other. A good facilitator makes every participant feel as though they have something important to share. This is critical to my style of leading through facilitation – every woman needs to have the opportunity to become a leader, and I must recognize that some women will need more help than others. Therefore, I like to start with a common tactic for facilitators, which is starting with an easy discussion. I choose a topic of which everyone is an expert – their own lives. Through this process, we encourage everyone to participate by slowly going around the circle and asking that everyone add a thought. This ensures that even the shyest participants share something. A facilitator is not a teacher, calling those out by name who aren't paying attention. A facilitator gently ensures there is opportunity for everyone to share, for everyone to participate, and for everyone to add value to the group.

We discuss leadership theory, without ever calling it as such. We ask the women what they most appreciate in their leaders, and then encourage them to strive for those attributes. We ask questions to help them think through new concepts – such as, do you think a leader looks weak when he or she admit they are uncertain or something? Do you think leaders are ever followers? Conversations about leadership continue throughout the group meetings, spanning several months or even a year.

As soon as possible, we try to realign the power imbalance. At the first session, we, as the facilitators cannot help but to hold most of the power. Everyone in the room knows that the outsiders have more formal education and more professional experience. Women tend to look up to us, ask about our opinions, and our experiences. But for true empowerment to proceed, this cannot remain, and it is necessary for women to start recognizing power that exists inside of them. So slowly we shift power back to the group, usually by electing group leaders, motivators, secretaries, and financial managers.

The AI process then helps participants envision the dreams they have for themselves and for their children. Experience has shown me that usually, women do not ask for much. Men leery of women's empowerment tell me they fear that if given the chance, women will divorce their husbands and take over the political economy. But I have never seen this to be true. In all the groups I have ever worked with, I have found that women simply want to be able to educate their children (girls as well as boys), pave a way to earn income for themselves, have respect in the community, and be treated with dignity.

The role of facilitator does not fit into traditional models of leadership, and I can understand why some would argue that the two concepts are not compatible. But I have come to believe that facilitating is one of the best forms of leadership, because facilitators have the power and the opportunity to inspire new leaders.

PARTICIPATORY RURAL APPRAISAL

The genesis of PRA starts with Paulo Freire, a Brazilian economist of the twentieth century. Although Freire never used the term "empowerment" in his work, he described the process in his most famous book, *Pedagogy of the Oppressed*, by insisting that minority groups could gain power and a political voice through education and knowledge (Parpart, 2002). Freire spoke to educational (formal and informal) tools for communities to use to enable them to become active participants in the Brazilian political economy. Robert Chambers, working as a fellow at the Institute of Development Studies in the United Kingdom, coined the term Rapid Rural Appraisal. Crediting Freire for his inspiration, Chambers designed several tools to be used by the community to help with development planning. In the 1990s, Chambers rebranded the term PRA with new case studies from Africa and India, and a renewed emphasis on community involvement and ownership (Chambers, 1994).

Like AI, the benefit of PRA is that it allows people control over their own situation – and makes them less dependent on outside expertise. PRA uses visual tools with little to no writing, so that even illiterate participants, and/or those without a formal education, are capable to participate in the discussion and reflection. When Chambers first published a description of PRA tools, it was considered shocking to think that rural women had the capacity to take on serious issues such as infrastructure, resource management, or agriculture. The development world assumed that in order to complete a community diagnosis there needed to be an NGO or donor-led intervention. But then Chambers tested and reported impressive results in the field the development community took PRA tools seriously.

PRA can be especially helpful in work with women and girls. As with AI, PRA gives women's groups a framework from which to start. PRA presents a range of activities that local populations can use to better understand themselves and their context in society (linking back to the first step of women's empowerment). PRA puts the power of information into the hands of community members themselves and builds trust that they have the knowledge and skills necessary to pinpoint their own area of needs and create a way to achieve those needs. Instead of locating root problems (which can lead to finger-pointing among friends and family members), PRA gives communities tools to empower themselves and build upon their strengths.

For example, women often appreciate participatory resource mapping to understand where community resources are, who has control over them, and who benefits (and doesn't benefit) from those resources. Women appreciate exercises that identify the sexual division labor, and help explain which daily activities are done due to biology and which daily activities are done due to gendered expectations.

PRA EXAMPLES FROM NILA

In Java, PRA results are quite enlightening to women, who never before saw how marginalized they were simply because they were born female. The rural communities where I work reveal that many people are guided by customary law — women's rights are essentially the same as men's with respect to marriage, divorce, inheritance, and property rights. Villagers emphasize the concept of complementarity, saying that men and women have different but equally valuable roles. However, I would like to remind our readers that *complementarity* does not equal *parity*.

In Java, women are free to participate in most activities, but not in spirituality. Men are considered to be more spiritually powerful. Women are defined by their reproductive role as mothers and wives, and men are defined by their productive role in the spiritual and economic spheres. Men are not at all expected to take part in domestic tasks, as this is not seen as their natural domain. Time is made available for men to be involved in the civic and public activities that are closely associated with status and power, while women must grapple with household responsibilities before they can take on other tasks. Villagers rarely question this arrangement, as it is the social structure that has existed for generations.

The magic of PRA comes when rural women start to realize that they work hand-in-hand with men in almost all reproductive *and productive* work. Through applying PRA tools, women realize that they may not have land rights, but they make a significant contribution to agricultural outputs. They might not own the herd, but they put in the same time as their husbands in rearing the animals. They do all this while at the same time maintaining responsibility for all household chores and duties.

If I came into a rural meeting and announced this finding to a women's group that has not engaged in PRA, I would be laughed at and told to leave. The power in PRA is that women make this discovery for themselves. I never push or lead them to any one conclusion. I simply ask them to complete the activities as presented by PRA and they come to these conclusions themselves. *Why is it that we don't have any collateral for a loan, but put in a longer day's work than any man they know?* Aha! Good question! It is only after this discovery that empowerment can take place.

But allow me to reflect back on a previous statement – that economic empowerment is *the* entry point for women and girls. I say this because, as determined by the World Bank, a woman's income is the family's income. No matter how much a woman brings to the household, that money will be invested in education, food, and healthcare for her children, enabling a stronger and more viable family unit. I have witnessed that each woman that starts a small business, and each group that decides to generate income, invests that money back into her children, her family, and/or her community.

However it is very difficult for rural women to grow their economic pursuits. Women's contributions are less likely to be counted and more likely to remain small. For example, though a woman works side-by-side with her husband, when agricultural products are sold, it is he who claims the income. Her income from small economic pursuits (such as selling snacks to friends and neighbors) is micro scale, and cannot grow because women lack access to credit facilities. Over time, this barrier also creates a psychological barrier, and women come to truly believe that are dependent on men.

So I have taken to incorporating economic empowerment into all group work, which has become the mission of my organization called Ruang Mitra Perempuan (RUMPUN). Translated as *A Space for Women's Friendship*, RUMPUN works to help form and facilitate groups through the empowerment process, using PRA tools as a guide. Once a group has been well established, RUMPUN facilitates a discussion on economic issues such as income generation, savings, and loans. As Caroline Moser writes, we development professionals do not want to add to the triple burden of women. Likewise, I do not want the women's program to add to the long list of responsibilities for a rural Javanese woman. I therefore use a local agricultural calendar, and the women determine for themselves when they have time to turn their energy to economic pursuits, and how to best incorporate them into their daily lives.

A STORY OF SUCCESS – BY NILA

I would like to close with the story of a women called Ms Tuti, who I hope will illustrate for our readers how empowerment can produce the strongest of women leaders. Tuti was born in 1987. She was married at the age of 20 and over the next 10 years had three children. She lives in the village of Makmur[1] with her husband, just a few kilometers from where she grew up. Makmur is dry, which makes agriculture difficult; thus it is also very poor. Girls tend to drop out of school around the age of 12 and many local women go abroad as domestic migrant workers. Too often they become statistics of human trafficking.

Thankfully, Tuti had another option. In 2008, RUMPUN initiated a women's empowerment group in Makmur, and Tuti took advantage of an opportunity when she saw it. Through RUMPUN, I ensured this group had access to a range of capacity building activities, including organizational development, gender empowerment, financial management, and leadership. She also chose to participate in a RUMPUN savings and loan program, and the group produced some small food products for added income. Tuti is a quiet person; when she did speak, she used a local dialect and said as few words as possible. But she was smart and hardworking, and slowly her confidence grew.

In 2011, Tuti become frustrated with her group's leadership, and so asked permission to start her own empowerment group. I agreed, and RUMPUN delivered the same package of services to Tuti's new women's group. She began with 15 women who immediately adopted a savings and credit scheme, with a small coffee production enterprise on the side for income generation. The group made only a few dollars a week, but slowly they saved and turned extra pennies into a sum big enough to offer small loans to members who had cash flow issues. The most common loans were to cover annual school fees or buy seeds and fertilizer during planting season.

Six years later, Tuti's group has grown to over 100 members with an annual budget of over US$10,000. Along with the group's business pursuits, Tuti initiated a simple welfare program for group members that provides food staples to families during hard times. Tuti remains the group leader and manager and has gained the confidence and trust of the entire village in the process. Now when there is a local dispute, people turn to Tuti for advice. She now attends local government meetings and isn't shy about voicing her opinion; people listen to her and respect her ideas and perspective. Still quiet, Tuti doesn't say much. But what she does say is highly valued in Makmur.

I could not be prouder of Tuti. She not only manages the group, but she manages people. She has earned the respect of farmers and government workers alike due to her contribution to local development. She is truly a leader in every sense of the word, and she has done this through women's empowerment and through facilitation. No one hired Tuti. No one gave her a salary or elected her to a board. Through the power of appreciative tools she slowly realized her own potential, and gained the confidence to dream big. When I visit Tuti, now she always has a big smile on her face and is eager to explain her next pursuit and future plans. Her group is currently saving money to fund a new community well so that residents don't have to walk the long way to the river twice a day.

I am also proud of Tuti's group members. I could write stories on so many of them; they have been loyal followers and hard workers. Many of them have benefitted from Tuti's group and now have new aspirations of their own. True empowerment is contagious; every woman can indeed be a leader when given the opportunity.

KATE AND NILA'S LESSONS FOR THE NEXT GENERATION OF DEVELOPMENT LEADERS

- Lead by example.

- Start with a simple case; you don't need to change the world overnight.

- Always consider and respect other people's values and beliefs.

- Keep an open mind and welcome unanticipated solutions.

- Be humble.

- All leaders make mistakes, and good leaders admit when they make a mistake. Simply apologize, and move on.

- Don't be threatened by other leaders. In international development, we're all trying to do the same thing — we're all working toward the same goal. There's no need for competition. Instead, embrace other people's leadership qualities and work together.

NOTE

1. Tuti's name and the village name have been changed to protect this woman's identity.

REFERENCES

Batliwala, S. (2007). Taking the power out of empowerment – An experiential account. *Development in Practice, 17*(4–5), 557–565.

CARE International. (2009). *Strategic Impact Inquiry on Women's Empowerment*. Retrieved from http://www.care.org/sites/default/files/documents/Women%27s%20Empowerment%20Overview%20Brief%202009.pdf

Chambers, R. (1994). Participatory rural appraisal (PRA): Challenges, potentials and paradigm. *World Development, 22*(10), 1437–1453.

Cooperrider, D. L., & Srivastva, S. (1987). Appreciative inquiry in organizational life. In R. W. Woodman & W. A. Pasmore (Eds.), *Research in organizational change and development* (Vol. 1, pp. 129–169). Stamford, CT: JAI Press.

Geertz, H. (1961). *The Javanese family: A study of Kinship and socialization*. Prospect Heights, IL: Waveland Press, Inc.

Moser, C. (1989). Gender planning in the Third World: Meeting practical and strategic gender needs. *World Development, 17*(11), 1799–1825.

Parpart, J. L. (2002). Rethinking em(power)ment, gender and development. In J. Parpart M. Shirin M. Rai, & K. Staudt (Eds.), *Rethinking empowerment: Gender and development in a global/local world* (pp. 165–181). London: Routledge.

Watkins, J. M., & Bernard, J. M. (2001). *Appreciative inquiry: Change at the speed of imagination*. San Francisco, CA: Jossey-Bass/Pfeiffer.

9

LEADING WITH GIRLS

Ashley N. Lackovich-Van Gorp

NEEDING TO LEAD

I started working in humanitarian response after the 2004 Indian Ocean earthquake and tsunami. I didn't plan this career. At that time, I was teaching English. Yet I had several friends from Southeast Asia whose lives were impacted by the disaster. Walking them through their own loss and trauma, I felt compelled to act in solidarity with them and humanity as a whole. After exploring many opportunities, I ended up volunteering in Indonesia. This experience led to work in Israel and Palestine where I first worked with children's education and then later with women's rights programs. During this time I neither saw myself as an emerging leader nor emerging "expert" on any aspect of the work that I happened to be doing. At this point, my career was indeed just happenstance. I was not even convinced that I would be doing this work long-term and still planned to return to teaching. I simply felt that I was contributing to a more just and equitable global society while I was young and travel was easy and that was enough for me at the time. "At most," I remember telling my family and friends, "I'll do this for five years."

My feelings shifted in Ethiopia when I found myself working with adolescent girls aged 11–19. Instantly, I was fascinated by adolescence, horrified by the impact of gender norms and expectations and fervent about girls' rights to lead safe, dignified, and empowered lives. Although it may seem odd, I can only describe my feelings for my work as falling in love. At first, I was overwhelmed by my unbridled and undirected passion. *What are the priorities and needs of adolescent girls? How can I contribute my knowledge, experience, and privilege to ensuring that they thrive? What is my role in this sector, and how do I most effectively exercise that role?*

Gaining knowledge and experience in the adolescent girl sector happened quickly, as I immersed myself into the work and became engulfed by an ever-growing snowball of learning and practice. I soon realized that my passion was also a talent. I grasped girls' realities quicker than my colleagues and I was able to think quickly and yet carefully to respond to the needs and opportunities facing girls. For example, once I remember advocating for tackling school dropout by teaching girls life skills rather than school success skills. At first, my colleagues thought this was ridiculous. After all, my colleagues argued, girls need to learn to study, not how to make decisions. Eventually, I persuaded them to agree on a pilot project. Monitoring this project, we saw girls stay in school, articulate their desire to continue their education to their parents, and succeed in the classroom, all because they had the life skills to reflect on their education, identify and articulate their desires, and set goals and work toward achieving those goals. Teaching girls life skills for school success turned out to be the basis for some of the most successful projects we ran.

This is the point where I decided to pursue leadership. At first, I thought that my experience and talent alone would enable me to lead, whether formally or informally, by providing recognizable knowledge and insights that others valued. Leadership, I thought, would be a natural evolution. Yet I quickly learned that being a leader is far more complex. Being a leader is an identity, a persona that one must embody. Still, I felt that I had this identity. I certainly felt like a leader. I saw myself as a leader. I took on leadership roles and responsibilities. And yet, there was something limiting my effectiveness. Eventually, I realized that something was others' perception of me – a young, petite woman with long hair and bangle bracelets – as more of a token woman in a leadership role than an actual leader. I felt like a leader and by this point, I had taken on leadership roles for designing and implementing programs for girls, yet others doubted my ability.

I experienced a clear discrepancy between how I was seen as a woman and the qualities and experiences people tend to associate with leaders. This gender bias is sometimes quite conscious and other times more latent. In my experience, it caused people to doubt my competency and question my judgment in emergencies and discredit my knowledge, experience, and practice with adolescent girls to "maternal instincts" rather than hard-earned expertise.

I became aware of how my gender impacts others' perceptions of me the first time I sat at a table filled with men. About half of the crowd was from Ethiopia and the other half from various countries in the Global North. All of the men were smartly dressed, and all were older and all engaged in familiar banter as they settled in the room. Then, there was me: a 30 year old director of a program for girls, a young, female leader trying to find a space for my voice at a working group meeting on access to education. Acting as if I had not noticed the gender ratio, I engaged and deliberated and hoped that I would be treated the same as each man. "This used to be a man's world," someone said jokingly as we all introduced ourselves, "now it's a man's world with an immigrant." Some laughed sincerely, others laughed uncomfortably, and I sat there grappling with how to navigate this environment.

Although colleagues reassured me that my legitimacy would increase to some extent with time and age, I was determined to create legitimacy for myself to navigate a sexist field. Searching for a strategic way forward, I noticed that the few female leaders in my field were not just practitioners, but scholar–practitioner who researched, published, and presented their work. This merging of theory and practice provided them with credibility as well as a highly effective set of knowledge and skills. Seeing that I could both increase my legitimacy and improve my practice, I pursued a PhD. Already having a BA and MA, I enrolled in Antioch University's Graduate School of Leadership and Change and spent four years theorizing my practice on leading change for adolescent girls. This program challenged and inspired me to push my practice beyond what I had previously considered my limits. Wanting to develop a specific skill set in line with my scholarship, I began my own consulting agency, Enhancing Girlhood, in which I advised UN agencies and international organizations on rights-based approaches to reaching and engaging girls. I focused on rights-based approaches that, based on international human rights standards, address an unbalance of power and empower girls to access their rights. It's not charity, but an active strategy for engaging girls to identify, articulate, and access what they need to lead safe, dignified, and empowered lives in their particular context and circumstance.

Together, my academic program and focused technical consultancies provided me the knowledge, experience, and scholar–practitioner platform to take a tremendous risk in my dissertation. I piloted a new child marriage prevention strategy in a rural community in Ethiopia with high rates of child abduction for marriage. I used a form of participatory action research, positive deviance, to partner with women from a community I knew to identify older girls who had passed through the abduction risk age without getting married. This iterative action research process was filled with ambiguity and took over a year. After identifying these girls, we went on to determine how they – and their families – kept them safe from abductors, ultimately providing at-risk girls and their mothers with actionable, culturally appropriate, and effective strategies to stop marriage by abduction. This process enabled me to apply academic knowledge to my practice, helping me to find a creative solution to a seemingly intractable challenge to both create social change and demonstrate my ability to lead.

Today, my knowledge, experience, and education together help me counter the norms, stereotypes, and expectations that delegitimize my leadership. Yet I still struggle. I still become frustrated when judged by such arbitrary traits like the length of my hair or pattern of my voice, and I still fight entrenched sexism, whether blatant or in the form of micro-aggressions or unconscious bias. Although much research indicates that women lead differently than men, I do not believe that I do. I think that leadership is more individualized than it is gendered, but cultures perceive and label women's leadership differently due to norms, stereotypes, and expectations. Moving from context to context, I witness perceptions of me and my leadership change according to the culture and situation. This constant shift in perception has taught me that my struggle is not me, but the context and so I mold my response to these challenging perceptions to the specific situation. For example, sometimes I need to listen more and talk less, or vice versa. Sometimes I develop personal relationships with colleagues, other times I recognize a need to keep relationships professional in order to be respected. There are times I need to be assertive, times I need to be passive. Over time, I have learned to be perceptive and gain insights into how I am viewed to select specifically how I can best affirm my voice and make a powerful, lasting impact on the lives of girls.

LEARNING TO LEAD

Learning to lead is a lifelong process. From the start, my biggest mistake has been believing that everyone working in international development has positive intentions. In reality, it is like any other field. Some people choose this work because their heart is in the cause; others elect it for more self-serving reasons. Further, international development emerged from colonialism and these roots remain embedded in the field. I have had colleagues who maintain that colonial mindset of "saving the natives" who are perceived as too primitive to save themselves, while they indulge in a life of luxury. It is hard for me to believe that these patronizing attitudes, paternalistic efforts, and imperialist goals are still seen as acceptable, but I encounter them in each and every country in which I work repeatedly and consistently. It is difficult to navigate the toxicity that comes from some of the attitudes and selfish actions in this field, and even more difficult when a person in a leadership role is oblivious to those attitudes. Once a colleague from the Global North actually said, "the problem is the Ethiopians cannot think for themselves." I was so shocked and appalled by this comment that I could not gather my thoughts fast enough to respond. I should have recognized this man's racism long before this comment, but I was naïve and embedded in my own privilege, not realizing his level of bias because his bias did not directly impact me. I still assume positive intentions among my colleagues, but with caution and awareness that I may not be seeing their authentic selves. I remember that I am allotted certain privileges as a white, well-educated, and financially well-compensated individual from the Global North and need be acutely aware of imbalances of power. I pay attention to micro-aggressions and I seek feedback from national staff and project participants to ensure that my privileged position is not obscuring my perceptions. There is no room for any hierarchy on my teams, especially not one founded on discrimination and prejudice. I strive to create an environment with an equitable balance of power, where all team members participate in decision-making, where local knowledge is valued as guiding knowledge and we truly see, understand, and respect each other.

Burnout has been another challenge. When I am working directly in conflict zones or resource poor environments, I guard myself against burnout, vigilantly focusing on self-care and managing stress. But in environments where stress is less obvious, burnout creeps up on me like a stress fracture.

In 2016, I spent six months leading a technical project in the Syria response. When I was undertaking this work, I did not realize I was struggling. After all, my project was going well and I spent most of my time in an air-conditioned office in Amman, Jordan. I counted myself as fortunate and never entertained the thought the situation may be creating excessive and damaging stress. But I was working on child marriage prevention and response, every day grappling with the reality that more and more girls were being wed to adult men, more and more girls were, in many if not most cases, entering a life of obedience, dependence, and servitude. I applied appropriate, technical terms to address their rape and abuse, masking my own emotions in the name of professionalism and effectiveness and denying myself any compassion because I, after all, was not in Syria, was not in the refugee camps, and was working from a safe, stable place. I did not realize the emotional toil it took until the project was finished and I returned to the United States, tired, emotionally battered and exhausted. Removing myself from the situation helped me to recover, but I also realize that the burnout hindered my effectiveness while working on the project and harmed my emotional wellbeing.

Learning to understand intentions and manage burnout are two of the tangible challenges I face whereas others are less defined. Given this complexity, I rely on adaptive leadership for the ambiguous challenges that arise when I challenge gender roles and expectations amid uncertain and complex situations such as wars, extreme poverty, and political and social unrest. There is no handbook response to mitigating the trauma of trafficking and all of the research and best practices in the world cannot prepare me to work under extremists like Boko Haram or ISIS. Each country, each community, each program, and each individual project presents a new set of obstacles that cannot be overcome through a predetermined solution. In response, I continuously learn in each new situation, making mistakes and sometimes failing as a way to understand how to move forward. My leadership is an evolving and reiterative practice in which I observe, learn, and interpret the situation and then mold my style, strategy, and tactics accordingly.

Over the course of my career, most of my work has been in the Middle East and Ethiopia where I work on designing, implementing, and evaluating girl-centered programs. In 2016, I took on a new role and developed guidance on child marriage prevention and response in the Syria crisis for the United Nations Refugee Agency (UNHCR). This presented a new challenge.

Instead of designing a program for girls, I was tasked with designing guidance to support and inform UNHCR staff and partners on preventing and responding to child marriage in one of the most devastating conflicts of our time. The process entailed working with UNHCR team members in Syria, Jordan, Lebanon, Egypt, and Turkey to determine the most effective prevention and response strategies as well as seeking input from global experts such as those at Girls Not Brides, the convener of a global partnership of organizations committed to ending child marriage. This task was neither small nor easy. Based in Amman, Jordan, I engaged a virtual team of individuals working in very stressful situations on an intangible and ambiguous project that they had not previously heard about. I drew on all of my knowledge and skills to engage, inspire, and motivate. I was organized and attentive, creative, and intentional. Yet I was not achieving the intended results, as my colleagues engaged superficially and marginally. Finally, I had a revelation. These individuals were overworked and overburdened and they truly had very little more to give. For the first time in my career, I shifted the paradigm of my expectations and instead of asking for maximum effort I asked for the minimum. This seems counter-intuitive, as I have always believed that people either rise or fall to the occasion, but in this case, I saw a need to meet my colleagues exactly where they were. I realized that creativity and technology were not going to motivate those whose schedules and stressors required them to focus on exactly what needed to be done in the most direct, effective, and fastest way possible in that very moment. I learned that 10 concentrated minutes of time were more effective than 30 distracted minutes. Once I realized the power of 10 minutes, I asked for 10 again and again, and received it again and again. Together, the knowledge in those minutes became knowledge in hours, and I was able to combine their insights with mine to create a document that represents all that we collectively know about preventing and responding to child marriage.

Currently, I'm working with Mercy Corps to establish a Middle East and North Africa regional knowledge center on girls. The initiative is based on the premise that adolescent girls are the only true experts regarding their own wellbeing and that practitioners can more effectively reach and engage girls if we put them in the lead to research, design, implement, and evaluate their own programs. For instance, we are currently operating a USAID Youth Power project through Making Cents International, an NGO that trains adolescent girls as researchers so that they can investigate the issues that impact their lives to help practitioners truly understand issues as seen and experienced by girls. The girl researchers in this project are investigating what makes a public space safe for girls, who will help practitioners, policy-makers, and governments better respond to their needs. This model completely shifts the paradigm regarding the role of adolescent girls in pro-grams from participant to leader. This shift is especially powerful in commu-nities where adolescent girls have decreased freedom and mobility, such as in communities impacted by the Syria crisis.

Regardless of the specific program I am leading, my passion is a constant leadership tactic and I strive to be a transformational leader so that others can share in this passion. In this sense, I aim to create visions for change and inspire others to work toward creating a more just and inclusive society for girls. My vision is for adolescent girls to lead safe, dignified, and empowered lives regardless of their situation, but this is a tough concept to grasp. *How can a 14-year-old girl married to an adult man live a safe, dignified, and empowered life? A 16-year-old survivor of trafficking? A 13-year-old domes-tic worker? A girl refugee who lost her family and her home?* In these situa-tions, many people jump to return to fundamentals and focus solely on girls' basic physical, mental, and social needs because they cannot grasp the possi-bility of girls in such circumstances as being empowered. But my unwavering belief in the power of adolescent girls to identify and solve their greatest challenges helps inspire others to think beyond basic wellbeing. Girls deserve more, and we cannot give them more unless we believe that they are capable of receiving more.

LEADING ACROSS CULTURES

Some leaders become geographic experts, centering their practice in one country of location. My practice is centered on my sector, which means that I need to adapt my experience and knowledge to various contexts, countries, and cultures. The global scale of the adolescent girl sector relates to its precision. My sector is a small, relatively new, and not a universally recognized sub-sector of child protection and gender-based violence. Given that my sector is novel and rather fringe, I feel that I need to be more per-sistent and vocal than colleagues working in more established, recognized, and dominant sectors. My leadership both within my organization and among the greater relief and development community entails advocating for some of the most vulnerable, marginalized segments of the girl population, including married girls, survivors of all forms of gender-based violence including trafficking, out-of-school girls, and girls with disabilities. These girls tend to fall through the cracks of even the most inclusive programming, with some of my colleagues in other sectors neither understanding nor even recognizing the need for girl-centered programs. It is an uphill battle, and I have learned that it is not enough to identify and articulate issues facing adolescent girls. Lack of attention on and understanding of the complex lives of marginalized girls among UN agencies, development organizations, governments, and donors requires determined, strategic, and consistent advocacy. I tailor my message to the audience, with some needing to engage with facts and figures, others needing to understand strategy and outcomes, and still others needing to empathize with them. To be an effective leader working with and for adolescent girls means to take on a 24/7 role, to be known as a girl advocate and to have my presence itself spark meaningful conversations on girls. It's a high visibility, and often highly contested, leadership role that has become synonymous with my own sense of self.

Still, the lack of understanding is difficult. There are some colleagues and partners who will not be swayed, as they simply do not believe that girls face unique challenges or, if they do, they believe that it is their role in life to undertake these challenges. For instance, in one situation, I needed to collaborate closely with a woman who did not believe in girl-focused programming. She believed that all young people should have access to the same resources and that particular attention to girls would only increase tensions and hostilities among boys and girls. After getting to know her and her position, I realized that there was nothing I could do to sway her opinion. Instead, I sought to find common ground where there were opportunities for us to collaborate in a more neutral zone; where my work with girls could translate to work with boys; where I could work with girls within her program to complement existing efforts with boys. Further, I often sought her advice in my work, recognizing that she had meaningful experience with youth programming and that I could indeed learn from her. My openness, respect, and willingness to engage made her more open to learn from me. Together, we were able to acknowledge that we could support each other without being in complete agreement.

Given that I switch geographic locations often, I am constantly relearning leadership. One of the first aspects of leadership I need to question is how to present my work in a specific cultural context. Although my vision of adolescent girls living dignified, equitable, and empowered lives does not change, I do change how I can convey and work toward that vision and customize my message and its delivery to the specific audience. For example, in most places in the Middle East, preference for sons and the culture of masculinity make it very challenging to speak about the needs of girls without acknowledging the needs of boys. "What about our sons!?!" one male community member asked during a discussion on the unique needs of refugee girls who are prone to child marriage. Noting in my head that the mere act of asking about sons in a workshop on girls indicated the gender imbalance, I quickly addressed the challenges facing boys. Acknowledging that this culture is more open to equality than equity, I have integrated messaging about adolescent boys into my presentations on girls as a way to make the audience more receptive of girl-centered messaging. I am seen as being a very "balanced leader" who "treats boys and girls the same." Thus, I am able to have deep, meaningful, and intentional conversations about girls with some of the most gender-blind audiences. For another example, in Ethiopia, I can speak directly about girls' empowerment because there is widespread acceptance that girls should be able to participate in society and make decisions. However, I cannot talk about a girls' right to control her body because there is a widespread belief that girls do not have control over their bodies, as their bodies ultimately belong to their current or future husbands. Instead, I have learned to talk about girls' decision-making and reproductive health separately within the same conversation, a subversive way of letting like-minded individuals know where I stand while still respecting the cultural norm. Working in the DR Congo, where the role of women and girls is very rigid and culturally confined to caregiving roles, I learned that speaking out for women and girls before establishing a relationship with partners was detrimental. There, where personal relationships are valued over professional roles, I am able to convey my message most effectively when speaking privately to colleagues who trust me. Each culture has different gender norms and expectations and my leadership is most effective when I work within that cultural framework while not sacrificing my vision. When I mold my message, I can undertake my work, whether designing, implementing, or evaluating programs, with success.

The tension between international human rights and national govern-ments' views of women's rights can be debilitating. In the DR Congo, for instance, married girls and women cannot access contraception without the permission of their husbands and unmarried girls and women cannot access it at all. Pregnancy and childbirth are leading causes of death for adolescent girls globally, which makes this restriction outright dangerous for the girls I serve, especially married girls who have very limited control over their bodies and very limited access to health services. These situa-tions are daunting. I do my best to work within the existing framework and to respect the government regulations. At the same time, I recognize that women and girls carry the burden of a culture created by patriarchy and legislated by mostly male governments. Ultimately, I am there as an ally to girls, which makes it difficult — and in some cases impossible — to remain balanced and adapt. Not all laws are just, and I am accountable to girls above all.

Still, often I am surprised by how fluid and adaptable culture can be. When I first begin to work in a new culture, I always seem to perceive gender stereotypes and expectations as intractable, entrenched, and insurmountable. The work seems daunting because, for instance, I'm not sure I can ever get a community in rural Ethiopia — where the majority of girls are out — of-school and married — to see the value of sending girls to school. But I've learned that all people can grapple with their culture when they have reason to, and often the most seemingly stubborn individuals are the ones who initi-ate change. It's a beautiful lesson in the power of our humanity.

But the question is how. How do I get a community to value education for girls? How do I get parents, who may neither have nor see no other options for their daughters, to stop their plan to marry them off? How do I work with female university students in the DR Congo to inspire them to find the courage to work after marriage? The answer is that I do not do any of this alone. I work with local community members, mostly girls and women, who know these issues, who live this reality, who have identified these challenges and who are the only true experts able to propose sustain-able, effective, and culturally appropriate solutions. My leadership is never unilateral, but always in a partnership. I recognize that I bring a specific leadership skill set to the table, and at the same time, the participants in my programs bring an intricate knowledge of the issues impacting their lives and what they need to change in their reality.

LEADING FOR THE FUTURE

There is nothing I want more than to be out of work.

The longer I work with adolescent girls, the more my leadership changes. I no longer see my role as helping girls by providing them with the resources I think they need; instead, I see my role as helping girls identify and articulate what they need and ensuring that they have access to those resources. Now and then, I become influenced by mainstream narratives that stereotype girls as passive victims, which takes my work in a hierarchical direction in which I do not want to go. In these moments, I pause and remember adolescent girl leaders to help me reorient my thinking. In particular, I look up to Malala Yousafzai and Nujood Ali. Malala, the Pakistani girl who was shot in the head by the Taliban for speaking up for girls' right to education, reminds me of the inherent bravery in girls. Nujood, a Yemeni girl who was married to an adult man when she was nine years old and who used her market money to buy a bus ticket to the capital where she found the courthouse and asked for a divorce, reminds me that girls can navigate challenges and overcome just about anything.

UN agencies, governments, and international organizations are recognizing that the wellbeing of girls is connected to the well-being of us all. The UN acknowledges that not a single one of the Sustainable Development Goals (SDGs) can be achieved without the full participation of girls and women. The SDGs sparked my own reflection on how girls can contribute to each goal. For instance, I had not previously considered the link between girls and climate change. I even worked with girls in Ethiopia who were displaced by floods caused by climate change, and yet I never connected the two until the SDGs broadened my perspective. Climate change further impacts girls, for instance, by causing water shortages in places like Ethiopia, where girls are responsible for fetching water in communities that do not have wells. Less water means girls need to walk farther to find a water source, which reduces the time that they can spend in school and increases their risk for gender-based violence as they travel longer distances from their home. In this sense, the SDGs prompted me to use systems thinking and ultimately made me a more informed leader because I recognize that girls' wellbeing is intertwined into the wellbeing of the community, the state, and the world.

Still, these are daunting times with reduced budgets for supporting girls. So, I have to do more with less funding and navigate a cultural climate that discourages my work. The small silver lining is that I now have a new, more progressive framework for programs: I foster girls' leadership so that they can empower their peers without me, my programs, or any outside resources. If I am not directly working on leadership and life skills programs, I am providing girls with the support and resources to design their own programs, as with Mercy Corps' Center for Girls. I can no longer be certain that some donors will fund programs for girls, I am no longer sure that there is another organization to pick up where mine left often. So, when I end my project, the girls must begin their own projects. They are tasked with being leaders and peer mentors to create change in their communities. It's daring and daunting, but my experience has shown me again and again that adolescent girls are resilient, resourceful, and brave beyond measure. It's their leadership, and not mine, that matters the most.

PART 3: SPIRIT-FILLED GRASSROOTS LEADERSHIP

Leadership for the authors of Chapters 10, 11, and 12 is synonymous with "service" derived from a higher calling from God. These leaders introduce the concepts of principles and values as the foundations of the leader repertoire. Leadership for them also entails ministering to the whole person, including the spiritual as well as material aspects of one's life.

Debby Thomas, author of Chapter 10, titles her leadership approach "Holistic Community Development." She devoted 18 years working in a community in Rwanda, motivated by the belief that spiritual life cannot be enhanced without including the economic and social realities of one's lived experience. Thomas challenges Rwandan cultural expectations of the leader to be autocratic and directive, a "culture-challenging" process that required a great deal of effort to establish her credibility as a collaborative leader. As an American individualist, she also wrestles with the collectivist culture of her community, learning that the community expects her to work with the collective, not with individuals, and applies collective discipline to her when they think that she has made affronts to their value system. Thomas learns that positive change only occurs when she helps to change the mindset of the community and of individuals. Once their mindset is changed, the community takes over the life-enhancing process and uses their own creativity and talents to push innovations through that improve their well-being and give them hope for the future. Relationship-building, Thomas discovers, is key to development. Thomas's experience also illustrates that long-term dedication may be required for sustainable development, a time commitment that most development professionals do not provide.

Josh Armstrong, the author of Chapter 11, has led student groups to the same community of Zambezi in Zambia for 12 years. Although the intention of the program is to "provide a transformational opportunity for students to develop ... culturally intelligent leadership, a greater sense of self awareness and critical engagement of culturally intelligent leadership," they also "come alongside" and serve the community and intentionally assist the community in their own development through projects such as bee-keeping and honey, building a library, literacy, engineering, health education, and computer projects. Armstrong argues that the experience of the students has implications for international development leaders. Students practice "accompaniment," the act of being with and doing with, walking together in solidarity on the same path, which a community defines and which mobilizes the work of the community rather than giving them solutions or pointing the way. The leader "reflects on ways to take the work off her shoulders and place it into the various factions within the organization to work on the problem together."

The accompaniment is based on relationship and humility and vulnerability. The role of the accompanying leader "seeks to inspire hope and be part of a positive process of transformation." Leaders listen to and share stories, based on the recognition that "personal narrative gives us a unique window into experiences, needs, and potential ways forward." Armstrong contends that "the most successful international development leaders are those who have become skilled empathetic listeners." Further, leadership begins with guiding principles and values. Servant-leadership combines with accompaniment, Armstrong argues, and facilitates true change that builds partnerships.

In Chapter 12, author Gordon Zook, initially establishes the principles and values upon which he leads, driven by a vision to see "communities living in right relationship with God, one another, and creation ... by sharing God's love and compassion for all by responding to basic human needs and working for peace and justice ... within improved relationships." Zook has helped communities build economic opportunities while ministering to their whole person and has practiced servant leadership based upon his faith's teachings. Servant leaders "look out primarily for the welfare of those they are leading rather than focusing on their own position, privileges, or level of respect." Zook's work has focused largely on community empowerment through the process of conscientization, an approach initiated by Paolo Freire, applied in the areas of agriculture, irrigation, small business development, and community reconstruction. This approach forms community groups whose members "discuss common problems, analyze their root causes, and develop a plan of action to address them."

A critical job of leadership is to help develop other leaders through serving them, Zook writes, but one must be cognizant of and careful about not abrogating cultural norms in so doing. Leading requires credibility, legitimacy, and trust also, Zook reflects. It also requires leading from a firm foundation of both academic knowledge and field-based practice. Zook is a highly self-reflective leader and he has recognized his introversion, his particular personality traits, as well as his personal comfort level vis-à-vis relating to others and has modeled an effective leadership style derivative of these. Active listening and management by walking around have been key components of this style.

10

HOLISTIC COMMUNITY DEVELOPMENT IN RWANDA

Debby Thomas

When I left the United States to live in Rwanda, Africa, I had a nine-month-old baby, and I was pregnant. I knew I wanted to help the Rwandan people but wasn't sure how. The first challenging years included learning French in Belgium (where my son was born) then learning Kinyarwanda (the language of Rwanda) from French. Living in Rwanda while learning language with children was incredibly taxing, difficult, and dangerous.

As I started to work with my organization – The Friends Church of Rwanda – I was deeply disturbed to discover that spirituality and the physical life were not linked. Many of the people in our churches attended church on Sunday full of excitement and hope but would return to a poverty-stricken home with broken marriages, scarce food, and where babies died of diarrhea. Spirituality was not consistently linked with the physical realities of poverty that Rwandans faced on a daily basis. I could not tolerate being a leader in an organization that encouraged spirituality that had little or no effect on the physical lives of Rwandans. My sincere conviction is that true spirituality transforms every aspect of life; I see our spiritual and physical lives as inexorably intertwined.

It was from this underlying sense of frustration and discomfort that I began to arise as a leader. Although I had an official position of leadership at the national level of the organization, my true leadership presence only emerged when I set my mind on bringing about change. I wanted to address the physical problems that Rwandans faced and advocate spirituality that effects whole life transformation. This conviction led me on a three-year journey of trying various approaches, many of which outright failed or had a limited impact. I learned through personal experience some leading causes of development failure.

I had several failures or semi-failures around fuel efficient cooking, farming, animal husbandry, small businesses, and other projects. I was perplexed about why my solutions did not take root. I learned that I needed to spend more time and energy in relationship with people, helping them to change their thinking and beliefs around dependency and fatalism. I needed to help them walk through the process of identifying problems, finding solutions, and implementing these solutions on their own. I was still taking too much initiative and trying to find the answers for them. When they identified their own problems, and found and implemented their own solutions, it stuck. Not only did it stick, but their solutions were richer, deeper, and more applicable then mine. Helping them become problem solvers meant that they became capable of solving every problem they ever encounter. That is infinitely more powerful than me using my resources to solve a few problems for them.

This powerful way of engaging in development is called *Discipling for Development* where the discipleship (spiritual) and the development (physical) aspects of working in communities are intertwined. I was trained by the Navigators in these innovative and empowering ways of doing holistic community development which gave me the tools to facilitate the holistic community development that I dreamed of. I found that once Rwandans understood, accepted, and implemented this way of doing development, they became capable of driving their own development indefinitely and they have the ability to help others engage in this process as well.

I have an entrepreneurial spirit. When I see a problem, I become obsessed with finding solutions, doing research, implementing, failing, learning, designing, teaching, and training until I come up with a solution. This process is how I found my calling as a leader — not out of a desire to lead, but out of a desire to find answers, to solve hard problems, and to have a lasting impact. Holding an official role as leader was less powerful for me than leading organizational change. Once I had a vision, and faced opposition, my inner leader arose. Even then I didn't lead change through my official position, but rather I led by example and through relationship.

THE THREE ELEMENTS TO DETERMINE LEADERSHIP STYLE

In determining the style, strategy, and tactics to create, grow, and lead sustainable development, there are three main factors that I considered, and each of these comes with a question. (1) The cultural context in general and cultural norms for leadership. Do I know the culture deeply, can I operate in that culture, and have I identified the cultural expectations of leadership? (2) The desired outcome of sustainable development. What kind of leadership will produce sustainable development among these particular people? How can my leadership help them own the development process and make it sustainable over time?, and (3) My own personality and leadership preferences. What kind of leadership works for me? What kind of a leader am I willing and able to become to help these people in this context to attain sustainable development? Throughout this chapter, you will see how I navigated these three factors, how I answered these questions, and what kind of leadership I found to be most effective in producing sustainable development in the Rwandan context.

Leadership and Culture

In my 18 years in Rwanda, I found that the preferred leadership style leaned toward the authoritative and paternalistic models of leadership. Rwandans wanted a strong leader who would provide for them, and they would in turn honor and respect that leader. It is easy for development workers to fall into a paternalistic relationship. For example, Americans tend to have a "can do" attitude. We believe we can make a difference, solve the problem, and initiate change. Many Rwandans, on the other hand, tend to have a fatalistic and dependent attitude in which they believe they cannot affect their circumstances, and they are entirely dependent on others to provide for their needs. These two beliefs come together in a paternalistic leadership style; each party gets to keep their dominant belief system, and each gets what they need from the other. However, I had seen the crippling effects of dependency resulting from paternalistic styles of leadership and I wanted to find a different way to lead. I was looking for a form of leadership that would empower people to affect their own transformation rather than trap them in a dependent relationship.

Although the communities where I worked expected and preferred paternalistic leadership, I resisted implementing this form of leadership. The paternalistic style of leadership repelled me; it didn't fit with my egalitarian values, or the results that I desired. I found it difficult and complicated to break out of this culturally acceptable form of leadership. When starting to work in a community, I spent three to five months building relationships, doing skits and discussions exploring and describing an alternative relationship to dependency and paternalism. My goal was to walk alongside Rwandans, helping to build their confidence, helping them recognize the resources they have, identify their own problems, and learn the problem-solving process to pull themselves out of poverty.

It was hard going. I spent long days in communities experiencing the extreme poverty of the community members. I didn't help them or do anything for them. I built relationships and tried to convince them there is another way to work together. I worked toward a relationship that would allow empowerment to happen. Although it took a long time, and much effort, they came around. They started taking responsibility. They started identifying their resources and greatest points of poverty. We worked together to find solutions to the problems that they perceived to be the most pressing. And when they succeeded in some small way, they gained confidence and tackled another issue. The most important aspect of this kind of leadership is that Rwandans themselves provided not only the solutions, but also identified what they perceived as their biggest problems. There was ownership from the beginning. It took us a long time to gain momentum, but once we did, it was sustainable.

I consistently struggled to find balance between leading in a way that is an authentic expression of who I am, leading in a way that provided what the people needed, while being culturally appropriate. Empowering leadership fits well with who I am, I felt comfortable and authentic leading in this way. I resisted paternalistic leadership which was the expected and acceptable form of leadership because I found that empowering leadership was the most effective for producing lasting change and sustainable development.

RWANDA'S HISTORY AND CONTEXT

The development work I did was deeply affected by the culture and context of Rwanda. The recent genocide, the political realities, and working with government officials in the process of doing development affected my work.

I speak Kinyarwanda fluently so I understand many of the nuances of culture and the larger political and environmental context as I heard it explained by the people I worked with. The work of empowering community members to find creative solutions to their problems necessitated taking into consideration the many complexities of culture and context in Rwanda.

Rwanda's history of genocide in 1994 stands out as a distinguishing factor affecting how I led in Rwanda. When I arrived in Rwanda in 1997, the country and the people were still devastated from war. I found that listening was an important part of leading in this context, for example, listening to people's stories, their experiences, their hurts, and their dreams, also, listening to their struggles and how they perceive their own poverty and difficulties. This required knowing the language, which was a significant investment of time and energy on my part. I also had to develop the ability to distance myself from the hurt and devastation as well as their formidable expectations of me and what I could provide for them. It threatened to drown me at times. Many people told me their stories of hardship and misery, and wanted me to help. At times, it was more than I could manage.

The default for a development worker arriving in a country like Rwanda is to plan and implement activities immediately. This relief activity is necessary after a disaster, but is not ideal to produce long-term stability and economic growth within the population. True help, true change, doesn't happen this way. It took me many years to learn that my role was to help Rwandans assume responsibility and ownership over their own life circumstances. The economic realities were dire, and my desire to offer immediate help was understandable. However, I set my sights on a form of development that would be sustainable in the long run rather than expedient in the moment.

GAINING LEGITIMACY AS A LEADER

I found it hard to develop my legitimacy as a leader since people wanted me to be a paternalistic leader. Their first reaction was to brush me off, thinking that I was not a real leader, that I didn't know how to lead, or that I didn't have anything of value to offer. It was the consistency of relationship, my commitment to understand and honor their language and culture, and the consistent message through my leadership style and actions that I wanted to empower them, not provide for them that eventually won them over.

I had some fierce opponents; my entrepreneurial spirit and penchant for trying new things were not always appreciated. There were a few leaders in my organization who were loud and publicly declared my inability to lead, discounting the kind of development I wanted to enact. They thought I was crazy to experiment with a different approach to development and declared that it would never work.

Instead of reacting or quitting, I kept my head down and kept up my work in the communities. I trained like-minded Rwandans who more readily accepted my leadership style and were open to my new ideas on development. I also garnered the grace of one or two top leaders to move ahead with my projects; they acted as protectors for me to move forward even under opposition. After three or four years, the first community that I worked in had some profound and dramatic changes moving them out of poverty.

As I worked with the community, they identified farming and animal husbandry as two areas of difficulty for them. We learned about different ways to farm, ways to combat some of the problems they identified. Some of the farmers in the community tried out a few of the techniques. One of the leaders in this community, Ugiriwabo, was a farmer and he tried out some of the techniques we discussed. When we started, he had one small field and would get 2–3 bags of beans and corn from his field each season. After a couple of years, he was getting around 20 bags of beans and corn from his field. Soon he had enough money to buy another field. Later, he was growing seed corn for the government that was sold to other farmers. Another man in this community, Bosco, described himself as the poorest of the poor. He says he used to beg from the beggars. After a couple of years in our community development group he was growing better crops, raising pigs, chickens, rabbits, and even had a cow (a cow is a sign of wealth in Rwanda). In fact, he stood out as having an outstanding household and was hired by an international non-governmental organization to train people in other communities. He went from being the poorest of the poor to having a salaried job, which was unheard of in this rural community.

Community members also grew spiritually and that impacted the development efforts. Together we studied stories from the Bible highlighting God's love for people and gift of grace for empowering people. This helped form a foundation of self-acceptance, value for every person in the community, and a sense of purpose and stewardship of their resources. Understanding that

God cares for every aspect of their lives built a foundation of hope and empowerment from which to take initiative and improve their lives.

The stories of whole life transformation are too many to describe here. Family after family has improved their livelihood by leaps and bounds. Many significantly increased their crops, raised animals successfully, became healthier as they ate more vegetables and drank clean water, and started small businesses for increased income. They spent six months discussing how to improve their marriages so as to further improve their livelihood. They also spent time learning how to budget – how to use the income they now had for the first time in their lives. Women became fully engaged in the community, respected, and listened to. The best part is that since we didn't do this for them, we didn't give them anything, once they learned how to change their lives they kept on growing and changing long after we left. They are still hard at work today; most recently, they built a primary school for their village.

When the success of the community development efforts became public, the leaders who had opposed me started asking questions. It wasn't long until they were convinced that this community was seeing profound changes and they wanted help doing the same work in their own communities. Soon, there were so many requests to work in various regions of Rwanda that we did not have the staff to cover the needs.

I had to earn legitimacy. With some, it was through consistently building relationships based on empowerment. With others, I needed to prove that my way of approaching development as well as my way of doing leadership was legitimate and that it worked. I went through some hard years with significant criticism and pushback. But now, those are the people who are continuing this work because they experienced the results. Establishing legitimacy doesn't happen in a day or a month or a year. For me, it happened over a longer period, especially since my leadership style is different than the cultural expectations.

During this time, I held an official position of leadership. Yet, I didn't choose to use that positional leadership to enforce my ideas. Rather, I focused on proving that what I was doing had merit. My goal was not to tell people what they ought to do, but rather to effect change in the organization. I wanted to affect profound change, not enforce my ideas through positional leadership.

INDIVIDUALISM/COLLECTIVISM

I lived and worked in a culture that was dissimilar to mine in many ways. Collectivism and high power distance are aspects of the Rwandan culture that I found to be different from my own culture. I discovered that although I did not choose to embody their preferred leadership style, it was important to be intentionally knowledgeable and respectful of their culture.

My personality and ways of being are influenced in many ways by the individualistic values in the American culture. I love getting things done, accomplishments are important to me, and tasks matter. In my mind, being different is desirable and thinking outside the box is a strength. My default is to challenge the status quo, try new things, voice my opinion, and find ways to solve problems. I see change as good and seek to create a better solution. The low power distance ideals in my culture also shape me. I desire to respect everyone equally and give others voice when possible. I am not drawn to a leadership style that enforces power, but rather one that shares power. These personal characteristics, rooted in my cultural values, created tension in the collectivist and high power distance environment. My Rwandan friends cared deeply about community, about being like others, fitting in, and honoring the "status quo." At times my actions were perceived as strange, threatening, and inappropriate. It was a constant struggle for me to decide when to embrace their cultural norms, and when to challenge them.

In many instances, I worked hard to do things their way. When working with Rwandans I often took their cues as to how to get something done, how long to discuss an issue, when to get permission from superiors, and so on. Protocol is important in Rwanda and doing things the prescribed way is important to being successful. Breaching protocol is a serious misdemeanor, and yet understanding the expectations of protocol was often baffling to me even though I spoke the language. I developed an ability to watch and learn, follow the flow of others, and ask questions so that I could "get it right." My effort in this area helped my Rwandan colleagues become more comfortable with me. It helped me build trust with them. However, there were times when I missed the cultural cues, and there were other times when I chose to go against protocol. I chose when to go against the cultural norm, most of the time choosing to do things their way as much as possible. Big issues such as how to lead, breaking the cycle of dependency in development, melding the spiritual, and physical aspects of development were areas where I intentionally chose to differ from cultural norms and expectations.

When I did not meet role expectations or personality expectations, I found that my colleagues, friends, and neighbors would deal with this in a collectivistic way. When I was perceived as having "deviant" behavior, they would act under the collectivistic assumption that I desired to fit in and to meet the community's expectations of me. Thus, their main form of correction was to start talking about my actions among themselves, as a way of informing me that I was acting as a deviant and as incentive for me to change my ways. This was the respectful and appropriate way to deal with social deviancy.

This form of cultural discipline would backfire on them since I did not respond well to this behavior. First, the rumors often didn't reach me since I didn't involve myself in those activities. Also, rather than hearing the rumors and changing my ways I would either feel confused and hurt or I would resolutely continue in my ways (if I had purposely chosen to do something outside of cultural norms). This form of social discipline was effective for Rwandans and appropriate in their culture but highly ineffective on their American colleagues.

During the times when these tactics were most rigorously used, I would long for an environment where I could be authentically me and use my strengths and gifts freely. I longed for an environment where I was appreciated, respected (according to my cultural norms), and understood. The expectations were overwhelming and strong, and the dissatisfaction with me being different was difficult. I felt it was a constant struggle to use my gifts and strengths; there was constant push back. In the long run, all of this made me stronger, but at the time it made already difficult and taxing work all the more challenging.

Because of my individualistic bent, my proclivity was to work with one or two families in a community and then let them be an example for other community members. However, in a collectivist society, this is counterproductive. When one or two families start to rise above the others, the community is shamed by their success, and they may sabotage those families. Thus, I adopted the methodology of working with whole communities instead, honoring their value to remain on the same level as their peers. In this way, the whole community would experience significant improvements in their lives. If a family or two didn't experience improvements, they were seen as deviant to the community standard and were pressured to meet the new status quo. In this way, the cultural norms worked toward sustainable development rather than against it.

The difficult question is: What do you strive to change and challenge about the culture and what do you strive to honor, respect, and incorporate into the development effort? For me, this was a question I faced moment by moment every day.

Gender Issues

I am a woman who founded and led a grassroot-level holistic community development movement that is active and growing today. As a formal leader, I often did not fit the social norms and expectations of me. Most of the leaders in my organization were men, but there were a few of us women leaders. In the language of Kinyarwanda, there is a word that is used to praise a woman, or to praise a man for the kind of wife he has – *witonze*. *Witonze* means a woman who is calm, reserved, obedient, and mild mannered. This word is used to praise children as well. I did not fit into this category of a praiseworthy woman.

The preferred role of women was also well established. Since this was a church organization, a woman who preached with great enthusiasm or prayed often and prayed in public was acceptable and even praised. Furthermore, White women were expected to take on traditional roles like leading children's ministry, teaching Sunday school, or leading women's Bible studies. None of these activities fit my personality, strengths, or desires. There was a sense of tension between my community and me due to the mismatch between their expectations of me and my unwillingness and inability to meet those expectations.

One distinct advantage that I had as a woman is my proclivity toward empowerment and collaboration. It was easier in some ways to convince people that I was not the "White person who has come to save them" since I was a woman. I came across to them as having less authority. They were more comfortable learning to discuss issues with me rather than having me be in charge. Empowerment and collaboration seemed natural to me. I was drawn to collaborate, and to empower others to take on their own development, both spiritual and physical.

In one community, when I started working with them the women came to the meetings, but they sat silently. They would not look at me, talk to me, or participate in any way. Only the men spoke. It took years of work, but today, in those communities, the women are animated and fully involved, they teach, they discuss, and they are full members of the community.

WHAT I AM MOST PROUD OF

Go to the people,
Live among them,
Learn from them,
Love them.
Start with what they know,
Build on what they have:
But of the best leaders, When their task is done,
The people will remark, "We have done it ourselves."
[Chinese Proverb]

I am most proud that the people in the communities where I worked are accomplishing bigger and better transformation now than they did when I was with them. I am proud that I helped them change their way of thinking, to learn to be less dependent, to think for themselves, and to take on full responsibility for their own transformation and growth. I helped them to become problem solvers. I helped them to appreciate what they have and to change what wasn't going well. I gave them something that they will use for the rest of their lives. This gift is much bigger than any amount of money I could have given them. Now they have what they need to continue their own journey of development, to teach their children to do the same, and they are reaching out to neighbors and other communities to help them as well. And in all of this, they look around and say, "We have done this ourselves!" that is what I am most proud of as a leader.

I had been working in one impoverished rural community for several years. One day on my long, hot, and bumpy journey into the village I noticed some new houses by the side of the road. My heart sunk. Was there a non-governmental organization here building houses for them? I had worked so hard for them to take ownership of their own development and I feared a recurrence of the dependent mindset through an organization providing houses for them. During our community meeting, I sheepishly asked them about the new houses. They looked at me and said, "Those are our houses." "Oh," I responded, "How so?" They proceeded to explain to me that none of them had ever owned houses, and the hovels they rented were not satisfactory, and they were fed up with that fate. So, 16 families got together to build themselves houses. They were all too poor to build their own house, but all 16 families had enough pooled resources to complete one house. Once they completed the first house, they built another one. They had built eight houses so far. Furthermore, they shared, three of the families consisted of widows and children whom they included in the group even though they lacked the resources to contribute on the level of other families. I was dumbfounded. My initial thoughts were: Why hadn't they thought to tell me this? They had been working for months, and it never came up in our weekly meetings. They didn't ask for my help, or my thoughts, or seem to need me in any way as they proceed to build 16 houses.

After a few moments of reflection, I realized they were empowered. They were taking responsibility for their problems and finding local, sustainable solutions. They were taking community development in their own hands. They were in charge; they were empowered, they didn't need me. It is at this moment when I knew that I had succeeded in this community. I went to the people, I lived with them, I learned from them, I loved them, and I started with what they knew and built with what they had. But I knew I had succeeded when the people said: "We have done this ourselves."

ADVICE TO THE NEXT GENERATION OF LEADERS

You cannot do development for people; they must do that for themselves. What you can do is help them to change their way of thinking. You can help them gain confidence in themselves, to grow their belief in their ability to affect their world. You can help them recognize their resources, identify what holds them in poverty, and teach them how to solve their own problems with their own resources. When you do this, you unleash an unimaginable power. The community becomes an unstoppable force of change. Innovation, solutions to problems, teamwork – the community becomes alive with the energy of breaking the bonds of poverty.

I heard a story once about the slums of Kenya. A rich man walked through a slum and had pity on the people who lived there. He worked with local government and funded development for the community. He had piped in water brought onto every plot, provided electricity, and proper roads. He went back to his home country content that he had changed the face of poverty in this one Kenyan slum. A few years later, he visited the community to see their progress. To his dismay, they weren't there! He found that the poor had sold their plots of land to the middle class who built beautiful houses to go with the amenities of the area. The poor community was now further from the city and in a worse situation than they were before the man found them.

You cannot change the environment and think you are effecting change – you are not. You must start with the mind, endure through the long and painful relational process of worldview change from dependency and fatalism to a belief that they are valuable, and have power over their own lives. This mental change will, with time, move into a sincere heart and values change. This value shift will change the way people interact with each other and the way they live in the world, leading to them changing the world around them. They will embark on development, and it will be sustainable development that will last. They will own it, believe it, live it, and it will stay with them forever, transforming communities for generations.

11

ACCOMPANIMENT: FACILITATING TRANSFORMATIVE CHANGE IN THE WORLD

Josh P. Armstrong

I saw it first in their eyes: a handful of Zambian leaders "switched on" when working alongside Gonzaga University engineering students to build a more effective and sustainable cooking stove in Zambezi, a rural African town. After three lessons on heat generation from our students, our Zambian partners were ready to get their hands dirty. Using bricks and other locally sourced materials, we developed a stove together. Then something *really* interesting occurred. One day while we were out gathering new materials, the Zambian leaders made another, improved stove. When we stepped aside, they used their new knowledge and took ownership of the project. With each additional iteration, the stove and our global relationship improved.

For the past 12 years, I have taught and directed a study abroad course for Gonzaga University students who have traveled to Zambezi, a community in the southern central African nation of Zambia. Gonzaga-in-Zambezi provides a transformational opportunity for students to develop leadership skills and immerse themselves in another culture. Students return home with a deeper understanding of culturally intelligent leadership, a greater sense of self-awareness, and critical engagement with intercultural competencies. Essential to this learning is student involvement in international community development projects, including leadership development/capacity-building training, literacy projects in local schools, engineering projects, health education partnerships, and basic computer education (Gonzaga University, 2016). The essence of the program is rooted in accompaniment – meaning that, while in Zambezi, students generate opportunities *to receive* in the places they are serving, become mutually indebted to the community, and develop meaningful relationships that assist them in operating at eye-level within this community (Ausland, 2005).

My experience watching students partner with Zambians to improve their stoves was a lesson in *accompaniment,* and I believe it has implications for the ways that we function as leaders around the world and drives our commitment to gender, context, culture, and sustainability. This chapter explores stories of leading in international development rooted in the unique perspective of student learning. These lessons are gleaned from years of coming alongside a community, but not as a traditional international development leader. While balancing the academic needs of Gonzaga University students, with their own power and privilege, we have found intentional ways to assist a community in their own development. The projects we have supported have been initiated by our Zambian partners and include sustainable chicken coops, bee keeping, and significant building projects such as a library, community building, and housing. These stories, illuminated by the lens of gender, context, culture, and sustainability, provide insight into the principles and values required for transformative change. While not always "successful," I believe that accompaniment and leadership are intrinsically tied together for those who want to serve and work in developing nations. These guiding sets of principles and values assist the accompanying leader in being an intentional driver in the positive process of transformation for communities (Burns, 1978).

LEADERSHIP AND ACCOMPANIMENT

We often gain credibility and leadership by demonstrating our capacity to take other people's problems off their shoulders and give them back solutions. While this can be an important skill, the leader who practices accompaniment mobilizes the work of others, rather than simply pointing the way. The leader reflects on ways to take the work off her shoulders and place it into the various factions within the organization to work on the problem together. While I intellectually believe this, it is hard for me to practice. In my role as a faculty member at Gonzaga University, I am rewarded for my individual contributions and for my ability to produce excellent teaching and learning and to manage programs and events.

When I strive to be a leader in international development, I must practice humility and vulnerability. I believe that we can disempower the communities that we seek to partner with by appearing to have all the answers. Ausland (2005) encourages international development leaders to "be honest about your own needs and vulnerabilities, to generate opportunities to receive in the places where you serve" (p. 6). This model of leadership, grounded in accompaniment, is fundamentally about relationship, and as such it invites us to redefine development. The role of the accompanying leader seeks to inspire hope and be part of a positive process of transformation. Accompaniment is only possible if leaders are willing to listen and share stories. Personal narrative gives us a unique window into experiences, needs, and potential ways forward. Chupp (2000) believes that "accompaniment involves observing, listening, and reflecting" (p. 114). Advocacy in the context of accompaniment enables those served to speak for themselves, often in ways that give rise to unexpected insights and creative solutions.

A project that developed from our engineering student work was a partnership with a local Zambian NGO building bio-sand water filters. One afternoon, I was installing these filters in the homes of community members in the village of Mize. We had 12 filters to place in various homes and, as the hours stretched on, I was feeling the weight of the work. After installing one bio-sand filter, I grabbed a bucket from the thatched roof home and walked quickly to the local watering hole to fetch some water to initiate the filter orientation. With a bucket full of water and an agenda to complete, I walked swiftly by a village elder sitting in the shade of an enormous tree. This man called out to me, and I remember feeling bothered by his intrusion to my work. After pulling up a chair for me, he proceeded to ask about our project. After satisfying his curiosities, I found myself pausing and *finally* entering into this moment of true dialogue. We shared stories of families and communities. I heard about his work, his history working for Zambia's independence, and the dynamics of leadership in Mize. I surprisingly found myself sharing about my own feelings of inadequacy in leading this community project, particularly after a lifetime of abundant water supply. After some time together, I invited him to join our classes and continue the relationship.

The most successful international development leaders are those who have become skilled empathetic listeners. Empathy at its most powerful is not merely good will and understanding from a comfortable and secure distance but friendship within a community of interdependent equals – it is not serving the other, but being one with the other. One way in which a leader can foster a mutually respectful relationship with the communities that they serve is through storytelling. Our leadership and capacity building seminars utilize storytelling and provide opportunities for our Zambian partners to share the important marker events of their life that influence how they lead. Our Gonzaga students are privileged to hear and share stories of great sorrow and joy that bind them and remind them of their shared experiences. As Buechner (1982) writes, "the story of any one of us is in some measure the story of us all" (p. 6). I strive to practice leadership that develops the opportunity to listen to my partner's stories and share my own honest and vulnerable stories with them.

GENDER

I enjoy running. I try to always start my day with a run while working in Zambia. Given our remote rural location in northwestern Zambia, it is a cultural experience for Zambians as I jog by their village. "Are you exercising?" or "who are you running from?" is often called to me as I meander my way through the African countryside.

One morning, I had run down to the mighty Zambezi River, the longest east-flowing river in Africa. It was a beautiful morning, with mist floating over this blue river as the sun was rising into the sky. After a couple miles, I turned into the savannah bordering the river and ran through the tall grasses while deep into my own mind about the upcoming development projects of the day. Without knowing it, I had run into a swampy delta area and found myself stuck without being able to pass. I tried to work my way around the large dense pool of water and became frustrated as I thought about the additional time and energy it was going to take to get out of this situation. My plight was one of inconvenience, not peril, but I stood there weighing my options. Just as I was preparing for the long run back, I spotted an ox-cart — a simple two wheeled cart pulled by oxen used in this area to transport local goods and people. With the power of these animals, the ox-cart propelled through the delta toward the dry land. As it approached, I greeted the older man and boy in their local language, *chimene mwane* and we made eye contact as we exchanged good morning greetings. Then the most remarkable thing happened. Without a word, the Zambian man began turning the ox-cart around and motioned for me to get into the ox-cart. Without any more words exchanged, he drove me across the area and delivered me to dry land. He first *noticed* that I had a basic need that he could address and then asked me to accompany him. It was an act of hospitality that is not uncommon in this part of our globe, but so greatly appreciated. During a year when we achieved many successful projects in regards to our international development work, this simple act served as a profound lesson.

I resonate with the belief that leading, is in some part, an "art of noticing." We are immersed in systems that function around us — these systems and patterns influence our social groups and communication patterns, they influence our organizations and the voices that get heard, they impact the challenges we see and our ability to bring about meaningful change. For the leader, it begins with training ourselves to "see the moments." Of course, there are conscious (and subconscious) reasons we often don't see (or pretend not to see) emerging moments. To notice a system that we participate in, that needs the change of a leader is often to bring about conflict. I know that I can fear this conflict because I worry that I might become defensive, emotional, or reactionary. But calling ourselves to notice means seeing our world with fresh perspectives and then doing the difficult leadership work to move toward change. In my experience, acknowledging gender within international development begins with the art of noticing.

In my leadership within international development, I have found my gender to most often provide me with opportunities and privileges. Particularly in the rural communities which we work in Zambia, my gender gives me power and a voice. I can ask to speak to the leadership of a local village and be confident that I will be given a seat at the table, a table that mostly represents male voices. However, the gender equation in international development is often more complicated than it appears.

It is easy to spot a traditional Zambian woman: she is usually dressed in a long, colorful *chitenge* skirt, simultaneously cooking and cleaning, with an infant strapped to her back, often with other children running around;

balancing something on her head; she might be cooking *nshima*: an arduous process of grinding corn meal into a paste, a staple of the Zambian diet. These are just snapshots of the incredible strength of Zambian women. In the capacity building lessons provided by Gonzaga students, we are constantly reminded that women feel that they do not have a voice. Their husbands are often unfaithful and deny to be tested for HIV; putting many at risk. Arranged marriages of young girls are not uncommon in rural Zambia. While this gender inequality is the context of our international development, I have found in the past decade that Zambian women have become our strongest partners in our community work.

A recent success in our international development involved a sewing project with a collection of Zambian women. During our month-long program in Zambezi, some women faithfully gathered for a class to develop sustainable feminine hygiene solutions. Rather than simply handing out these kits to girls in the Zambezi region, our Gonzaga students wanted to assist local leaders in developing a sustainable solution. These women learned to sew reusable pads and developed business plans to market these menstrual kits to rural communities where many girls stay away from schools during their cycle. While this project saw tangible success, one outcome was the relationships formed within various female community leaders. The female Gonzaga students teaching the course were inspired by the strength of the Zambian women and articulated an empowerment for their own voice. One of our students, Jessica Wilmes writes:

> After talking through all of the logistics of the class, we were all ready to jump into the project. The next Wednesday we got two sewing machines for the class, and quickly got to work. The women were so eager to help out, and we all had a really great time chatting and working on something together. On our last Wednesday, we had completed our kits! The women did such a wonderful job and their kits looked beautiful. After we had finished we all went outside to take a picture together, and before we were able to take a picture the women grabbed me, made a circle around me, and started singing and dancing. I asked Mama Josephine what the song meant, and she said they were singing about how thankful they were for me. At first I could feel myself feeling uncomfortable with this, because I did not feel like I deserved the

praise, but then I remembered that we are supposed to let those that we are serving also serve us. It is a part of accompaniment and is what breaks the wall between them and us. It shows that you cannot do a project like this with just one person, you need to form together with the community and work at eye-level.

While I was inspired, I was limited in my understanding of this resilience given my gender. I was often found quietly observing the relationships and development work, while not wanting to get in the way of the process. I felt the limitations of my gender in truly being able to come alongside these strong female leaders. The strong cultural norms of the local tribes reinforce gender roles and norms of masculinity. As an international development leader, noticing the gender dynamics and social expectations, I chose to provide space for gender empowerment and work toward gender inequality. While this work can certainly be with female local leaders, some of the most productive work comes from engaging men as agents of change and assisting them in understanding the power dynamics in relationships – dynamics that are often invisible or unnoticed by men but can be critical in gender justice work.

CONTEXT

My leadership in international development is committed to beginning with values as a critical starting point. Many well-intentioned leaders enter into community service volunteer work or international community development work without developing a set of guiding principles and values. By utilizing characteristics from servant leadership and the practice of accompaniment, leaders can facilitate true change that builds partnerships (Ausland, 2005; Greenleaf, 1977). The ethic of accompaniment has been defined as "walking together in solidarity which is characterized by mutuality and interdependence" (Padilla, 2008, p. 87). Accompaniment is the act of *being with* and *doing with*, rather than doing for; walking together along the same path with a community who identifies objectives, creates a plan, and manages these activities in its own leadership or development process (Aaker, 1993; Ausland, 2005; Chupp, 2000; Pope, 2015). In this way, accompaniment is not about giving service to the people, as a traditional charity would, but about *serving alongside them* in a relationship of mutual reciprocity.

Another accompaniment lesson comes from *Zambia Gold Honey*, a non-profit organization run by students from Gonzaga's Comprehensive Leadership Program (CLP) that exports fair trade goods from the Northwest Province of Zambia. The Zambia Gold Honey project began unexpectedly in 2007, when students participating in our study abroad program were encouraged to build collaborative relationships with the people of the community in hopes of bringing more opportunity to the region. After tasting this pure African honey, students spent time with local bee farmers, exploring ways to provide a sustainable market for fair trade organic forest honey in the US.

Near the end our leadership and capacity building courses, one of our trusted friends named Sandu told me, "We believe knowledge is the weapon to success in life." This core value has allowed the Zambezi community to shape the dialogue on change toward a focus on education. After careful listening, the Gonzaga program has come alongside a primary rural school in the Zambezi district to build the first community library in this region of Zambia. During the past 10 years, sales from Zambia Gold Honey and other goods have raised over US$65,000 for this community library. While we are financial partners in this endeavor, we have not spent our time physically working on the construction of the library, believing the Zambian people to be experts in this regard. Rather we have dedicated our time listening and posing questions that seek to understand the values and goals that will integrate this library into the fabric of the community (Ellerman, 2006). Sustainable change that allows a community to "stand on its own two feet" must be rooted in the core values of the community.

One of my undergraduate students, Hannah Van Dinter, beautifully captures the moment when books arrived in the Zambezi library and the mutuality shared through this celebratory moment:

> The large semi-truck slowly backs up, and women shoo eager
> children away from the truck's path. Silence overcomes the area, as
> we all carefully listen to the sounds of the heavy metal doors
> opening to expose the seemingly endless boxes of books from the
> truck's container. All sizes and colors of hands clap in celebration
> or reach up to touch the first boxes of books that are unloaded.
> Swarms of children and youth fight for the chance to support just
> one corner of a box. It seems as if the eager people below are still

unaware of the sheer number of books that will soon fill the Chilena library's shelves. Twenty thousand books will be accessible to a population that is always seeking new knowledge and further understanding. In the most disorganized and least efficient way possible, all 20 pallets of books find their way into the library building. The chaos of unloading books pushes me into a state of sensory overload, with sweaty bodies pushing past others in a rush to drop off one box so that they could transport another and an occasional team of eight young children who resemble a team of ants attempting to carry a fallen potato chip five times their size. Although I crave efficiency in this process, I recognize that the chaos is evidence of each person's desire to have a hand in the culminating event. In fact, this overwhelming number of hands did play an important role in the realization of a dream- a dream so profound that many may have thought it to be an impossible one.

The Zambia Gold Honey project was initiated when Gonzaga University students dreamt of creating a sustainable partnership in which organic forest honey from Zambia could be directly purchased from local beekeepers to be sold in the United States. Gonzaga student interns sat with local leaders in Zambezi and asked them to identify needs in their community. Through countless hours of these Gonzaga students sharing stories of Zambian bee-keepers, thousands of pounds of honey sold to US communities, years of construction to form the library, and months of books journeying by ship to Zambia led to the culmination of this shared endeavor. "Together, we have done this."

CULTURE

After years of working in Zambia, I am still surprised by my ability to misinterpret cultural practices and see my partners through my own cultural lens. One lesson that I continue to return to, centers on how difficult it is to "do good in the world." Zambia is littered with those with good intentions who have created more harm than good. In our community work, we are often working against years of colonial relationships that solidified the power dynamic in our favor and didn't empower communities with an honest mutuality that sustainable change requires. We are often asked (by individuals, institutions, and community groups) to fund projects without the necessary relationships firmly in place. My time in Zambezi is laced with explanations of our role in this community and conversations about coming alongside Zambians as they stand on their own two feet.

This was the context for a recent visit to the local Zambezi cemetery with one of my undergraduate students. As we walked through the overgrown site, honoring the dead in a place that buries too many, often too young, we stumbled upon a group of six men digging a grave. We approached them and offered our condolences, sitting in the silence and weight of the moment. Then one of the men turned to me and asked, "Can you give us a couple shovels?" This question went straight to my Western ears, and I thought, are you kidding me? We stop by this gravesite and you are asking me to go buy you some shovels? I was taken back.

We had been talking in our nightly reflections about sitting in the discomfort of a moment, and I listened to his question again though my Zambian cultural lens, *can you give us a couple shovels?* I suddenly realized he was inviting us into his experience, offering us a chance to join him in the mournful work of burying his sister. So we jumped into the emerging grave and shoveled – diving into the work with the passion of a heavy heart. As earth was moved, we heard about the 25-year-old women who had passed, about the upcoming day of celebrating her life, about those she was leaving behind. For a moment, we belonged. We were invited to participate in a sacred moment.

The opportunity offered by our mourning friends was one of kinship; as Boyle (2010) says, "There is no us and them; there is only us." This visit to a Zambian cemetery will stick with me for a while. Not just for the reminder that I am continually learning to hear our Zambian friends through *their* cultural lens, but also the affirmation that many Zambians have graciously invited us into the joy and pains of their everyday life in ways that continue to be spellbinding for me.

This learning to lead within other cultures is also seen in our partnership with the Chilena Library. During the construction of this library, I would often make cultural miscues that I teach my students to avoid. In my working with community leadership, I would often strive for efficiency. I would enter meetings wanting to "get to business" without spending the necessary time to connect relationally. I didn't fully understand the *ubuntu* philosophy that "a person is a person through other people" and wanted to designate individuals to be directly responsible for the library. We recently signed a memorandum of understanding with the community and Zambia's Ministry of Education to clarify the roles between the university and these governing entities. We are still learning how to negotiate our expectations for success while providing the community the full responsibility for sustainable achievement of a Zambian library. This takes constant cultural awareness and humility to recognize that the workings of a rural African library can and should be facilitated by Africans.

SUSTAINABILITY

In 2015, the UN adopted new Sustainable Development Goals to end poverty, protect the planet, and ensure prosperity for all. Many of the values within an ethic of accompaniment call to these sustainable goals and provide guidance as we come alongside a community.

One of my favorite evenings in our work with communities in Zambia each year happens at the end of our time in country. We ask each student to identify a cultural guide, mentor, or meaningful friend to invite to an "accompaniment dinner" where we honor their friendship and work. As students are teaching classes, working with partners, or engaging with the community, they are seeking opportunities for relationships, and this evening is an opportunity to celebrate these important friendships. With a team of nearly 20 students and faculty, these accompaniment dinners balloon into a formal dinner for 50 people. It begins late afternoon as Zambian friends begin to arrive in the yard in front of our building. An energy builds as Gonzaga students call for each other when their guests arrive and casual greeting and photos are taken. Students and Zambezi partners dress up for this special dinner and it is a moment to be captured. Once a critical mass of guests arrive, we welcome them into our space by having each student pour water for their guest in a hand washing station. We have learned this pre-dinner ritual from our partners, but it takes on a sacred moment when serving others in this way.

Before dinner, some welcoming words and blessings are shared between Gonzaga students and this collection of friends. During the meal, each Gonzaga student introduces their guest, mentioning the impact that this person has had on their three-week experience in Zambezi. The dinner is concluded with a number of speeches from faculty and Zambezi partners, affirming the development work and more importantly the relational foundation of the shared initiatives. This accompaniment dinner serves as a living embodiment of the sustainable development desired and longingly constructed within Gonzaga's partnership in this Zambian community.

However, for a university faculty member, sustainability of a project of this nature means paying attention to student learning outcomes as well as international development goals. International faculty-led study abroad programs can clearly contribute to significant international developmental outcomes, as outlined in the previous stories. Yet, we are also concerned with the development of cognitive, behavioral, and affective intercultural competencies within our university students. The leaders of the future will have to lead with intercultural competence and with the ability to develop this competence in others. International study abroad programs such as this offer one example of how leadership studies faculty might have an impact on student growth through deliberate encounters with diverse cultures. Conversely, it is our belief that simply traveling with students to developing nations will not provide this type of intercultural development. In this final section on sustainability, I would like to offer observations and insights for faculty, researchers, and practitioners interested in the power and potential of international study abroad that *partners* student learning with international development.

First, transformation and learning begins with the power of deep intentional reflection with students. Students enroll in study abroad experiences for a variety of reasons, particularly unique study abroad programs hosted in developing nations. Students bring aspirations to help others, seek a transformational experience, or a curiosity about different cultures. The outcome of the experience, however, may not fulfill students' presuppositions. As faculty we need to be sensitive to the complex emotions and outcomes that international education activates. The student learning which occurs in study abroad is enhanced through a careful attempt to process cultural experiences. In the Gonzaga-in-Zambezi program, students and faculty meet every evening to reflect, to share perspectives that enriched the sense-making learning. Students are required to maintain and write in personal journals, which encourage written reflection and meaning making. The students contribute to a group journal each evening, which summarizes the day's events while reflecting upon particularly transformational moments. Students are asked to write a thoughtful reflection examining a poignant learning moment described in a blog posting which opens a cyber-dialogue with students in this experience and members within the university community. In this way, students have to synthesize their thinking within this intercultural encounter, and the nature of their making meaning.

Second, it is clear that sustained engagement with those from diverse cultures is important for student leadership development. Gonzaga students are supported in the cultural immersion experience to utilize their service-learning projects as a vehicle for establishing deep cultural relationships. In this way, students who embody this notion of mutually indebted service have tools to reconcile the inherent power differential between the more "privileged" students and the local Zambian people. The ethic of accompaniment is a fundamental principle and practice oriented into each student as a means to walk in solidity with Zambians as they move to greater levels of community, self-sufficiency, and personal empowerment. Students are encouraged to challenge themselves to be served where they are serving. This distinct relationship encourages the type of sustained engagement necessary for developing intercultural competencies in new emerging leaders.

Finally, through these poignant stories of student learning we are reminded that while study abroad experiences can provide insightful learning about world cultures, it can also provide significant opportunities for understanding oneself. As anthropologist Mead (1972) stated, "I have spent most of my life studying the lives of other peoples – faraway peoples – so that Americans might better understand themselves" (p. 1). It was these increased moments of self-knowledge, particularly related to intercultural competencies that formed the basis of new understanding in international development and leadership.

This chapter explored leadership moments from over a decade of working with a community in Zambia and brings to light some challenges facing international development leaders. The unique opportunity to bring western university students into the development process illuminates values and practices that hold deep lessons. In particular, for transformative and sustainable change to occur, accompaniment and leadership must be intrinsically tied together. Examining these values through leadership stories of gender, context, culture, and sustainability allows us to learn from the global challenges facing international development leaders and commit ourselves to operating at eye-level within a community, serving alongside them in a relationship of mutual reciprocity.

ACKNOWLEDGMENTS

I am indebted to the communities of Zambezi, Mize, Chilena, and Dipalata for their eye-level relationships and deep learning. I am proud of what we have accomplished together, but more than that, I am a better human being because of our time spent in relationship.

REFERENCES

Aaker, J. (1993). *Partners with the poor: An emerging approach to relief and development*. New York, NY: Friendship Press.

Ausland, A. (2005, Spring). Staying for tea. Five principles for the community service volunteer. *The Global Citizen*,2, 5–15.

Boyle, G. (2010). *Tattoos on the heart: The power of boundless compassion*. New York, NY: Free Press.

Buechner, F. (1982). *The sacred journey*. San Francisco, CA: Harper Collins.

Burns, J. M. (1978). *Leadership*. New York, NY: Harper & Row.

Chupp, M. (2000). Creating space for peace. In C. Sampson & J. P. Lederach (Eds.), *From the ground up: Mennonite contributions to international peacebuilding* (pp. 104–121). Oxford, England: Oxford University Press.

Ellerman, D. (2006). *Helping people help themselves: From the World Bank to an alternative philosophy of development assistance*. Ann Arbor, MI: University of Michigan Press.

Gonzaga University. (2016). Gonzaga-in-Zambezi Faculty-Led Study Abroad. Retrieved from http://studyabroad.gonzaga.edu/index.cfm?FuseAction=programs.ViewProgram&Program_ID=10065

Greenleaf, R. K. (1977). *Servant leadership: A journey into the nature of legitimate power and greatness*. New York, NY: Paulist Press.

Mead, M. (1972). *Blackberry winter: My earlier years*. New York, NY: Kodansha America, Inc.

Padilla, R. M. (2008). Accompaniment as an alternative model for the practice of mission. *Trinity Seminary Review, 29*(2), 87–98.

Pope, S. J. (2015). *A step along the way: Model of Christian service*. Maryknoll, NY: Orbis Books.

12

LEADING CROSS CULTURALLY IN A FAITH-BASED INTERNATIONAL NON-GOVERNMENT ORGANIZATION

Gordon A. Zook

My leadership journey in international development over the past 35 years has provided a diverse and eye-opening exposure to the real-life challenges faced by people living in difficult economic and social settings. I have had the privilege of working with many highly committed and qualified people from multiple countries. Working together in multicultural teams, we have utilized our different perspectives in pursuing common objectives.

Understanding my journey requires first clarifying the specific sector of international development I work in: economic development from a faith-based perspective. Both parts of this description are important to the way I lead. First, this affects what we identify as the ultimate long-term goal of our work. Our organizational vision is to see communities living in right relationships with God, one another, and creation. We work toward this vision by sharing God's love and compassion for all by responding to basic human needs and working for peace and justice. Thus, while we desire to see people's living standards improve, we want this to happen within the context of improved relationships; one of these without the other is insufficient.

Second, my understanding of the sector keeps my focus on the people involved. I am concerned about how their lives, their families' lives, and their communities are impacted. This impact involves more than just improving individual welfare, but overall wellbeing. I also want to know how we as an organization and as individuals are being changed as we interact with partners and project participants. This focus on people reminds me that the important changes are the long-term, qualitative changes and that I will not likely see the full impact of my work. My calling is to continue to be faithful in the work I have, whether or not I see the results.

I am, of course, a product of my own culture; this has a great impact on my leadership style and expectations. My culture is first grounded in an American context, but my Mennonite faith heritage brings a minority counter-culture perspective to the dominant culture. We believe we are to "be in the world but not of the world." Balancing the two parts of this call is very important to me and has a definite influence on the way I lead. My faith also introduces another key leadership principle. Jesus told his disciples that their leadership needed to be different than what was found in the world. Leaders in his kingdom are to be servants following the example he provided rather than lording it over their followers. His example and call to leaders remain relevant today in my work. As a leader my primary responsibility is to look out for the welfare of those I am leading rather than focusing on my own position, privileges, or level of respect.

My journey began early through exposure to the work of Mennonite Central Committee (MCC) in areas and situations of need around the world. This work is a response to Jesus' call to demonstrate our love for God and for others by assisting them in meeting their physical needs. In university, I studied agricultural economics and international development to develop technical knowledge. Dr. Carl Eicher of Michigan State University was an important mentor based on his extensive field work with African agriculture and thorough knowledge of food, poverty, and economic development issues. This was in the late 1970s when concerns over the world's ability to feed a rapidly increasing population were widespread, but also an era when the early successes of the Green Revolution were giving hope that this challenge could be successfully met.

After further studies at Cornell University, I accepted an assignment with MCC in Bangladesh as its Agriculture Program Administrator. I was responsible for a diversified agriculture and rural development program with a multicultural staff of 15–20 expatriate volunteers and 100 Bangladeshis. I applied my organizational skills to facilitate the work of others and discovered that I enjoyed supporting other people's work. I had sufficient technical agriculture knowledge to understand the issues involved and to help evaluate alternative approaches but not enough to do the direct implementation work. Colleagues seemed to respond well to my style of leadership because I respected their knowledge and their work while helping them to work more effectively.

Our work in several program sectors resulted in very visible impacts. An early focus of MCC's work in Bangladesh was the production of temperate-climate vegetables such as cauliflower, tomatoes, radishes, and carrots during the winter season when Bangladesh's climate is sunny, dry, and mild. We researched which crops grew best and the most appropriate production methods. Our extension staff worked directly with farmers to help them master these techniques and to develop local markets for their produce. This work resulted in widespread availability and consumption of nutritious vegetables so we could then withdraw our direct involvement by supporting local networks to ensure good seed supply and market options.

Other staff developed and refined a manual irrigation pump, the Rower Pump, which farmers with small plots of land could use to irrigate crops during the dry winter season. We worked with local businessmen to develop a network to produce, market, finance, and install these pumps. Through this work, small farmers throughout southeastern Bangladesh could grow winter vegetable crops to market for additional income and for family consumption.

MCC played an important role in introducing soybeans into Bangladesh. In the 1970s, our staff identified soybeans as a high-yielding pulse that could potentially compete economically with winter rice and increase protein availability in the Bangladeshi diet. Since this was a totally new crop for Bangladesh, this work involved a diverse set of activities including research into production techniques, extending this knowledge to farmers, developing an assured seed supply, and establishing markets. We worked in cooperation with a network of government and non-government research and extension organizations. Due to our persistence for more than 20 years, today soybeans are well established as a crop in Bangladesh.

These and other visible successes whetted my appetite for further work in development. An equally important factor, however, was the Bangladeshi staff I worked with. We employed Muslims, Hindus, Christians, and Buddhists creating a multifaith working environment united by our common commitment to helping Bangladeshi farm families improve their lives and their children's futures. We shared values of respect for each other and for the poor, a commitment to simplicity in our work and lives, integrity, non-violence, and justice. This is one of the strengths of MCC's Bangladesh program and an important demonstration of harmony in a multifaith work context. I have been privileged to work with many of these persons over much of my career. From them, I learned about Bangladesh agriculture and how to work effectively with small-scale farmers. I learned about Bangladesh culture and worked with them in planning, implementing, and monitoring our programs. They have been colleagues in the complete sense of that word as well as lifelong friends.

Although most of my career has been spent in South Asia, my wife and I worked in Haiti for five years, a much different cultural and geographic setting, but one with similarities in terms of extreme population pressure on the available cultivable land.

Our work in Haiti revolved around community empowerment, an important element for sustainable long-term development. We supported the formation of community groups through a process of conscientization and worked with them to implement improved agricultural production techniques on sloping, rocky, marginal farmland, and basic preventative health practices. While these interventions were important on their own, the more important work was to help people in these communities learn how to work together. Done properly, this not only helps them solve their current problems, but it gives them the tools to address other problems.

The conscientization approach used in Haiti grew out of Paulo Freire's work with adult education in Latin America. In this approach, small groups are formed within each community. With the assistance of a trained group facilitator, group members discuss common problems in their communities, analyze their root causes, and develop a plan of action to address them. Through an ongoing process of discussion, reflection, and action, community members are empowered to address their own development issues and to challenge inequities in the larger society (Carroll & Minkler, 2000).

My wife and I returned to Bangladesh in 1995 where we renewed our relationships with many Bangladeshi colleagues from the 1980s. In this assignment, we had overall responsibility for MCC's work in Bangladesh including personal support for our expatriate staff and their families. One important initiative in this era was to train staff of small Bangladeshi NGOs in agricultural techniques and in how to work with farmers and communities to promote them. This project built on the knowledge we had gained in

MCC's 20 years of work in Bangladesh and allowed us to expand our impact beyond the areas we could reach directly. By equipping these organizations with technical skills, we could help them increase their effectiveness and their relevance to rural communities.

We also expanded our work in employment creation by establishing small businesses to provide employment for rural women. An additional goal with these enterprises was to develop local women's managerial skills so they could participate in the operation of the business. Eventually these enterprises were spun off into a new local organization to establish long-term sustainability. This organization continues to thrive today as it provides technical and management support, product design assistance, and export marketing services to these enterprises which have enabled thousands of rural women to improve their families' economic wellbeing and to educate their children. This has also helped raise the status of women in their families and in society.

I returned to Bangladesh in 2011 where my work for the next two years focused on stabilizing the program after an unexpected leadership transition, developing a new strategic plan, and developing new longer-term leadership. I worked closely with staff, partners, and an outside review team to examine our program and to determine the best way forward. The resulting plan had buy-in from all staff. Since the new leadership had participated in its development, they were able to proceed with implementation fully committed to this plan.

My wife and I moved to Kolkata, India in 2014 where we are responsible for MCC's work in India. We have the privilege of working with a dedicated group of Indian colleagues. As the only long-term expatriate staff, an important part of our role is providing connections between MCC's constituents in the US and Canada and our Indian partners. Living in India, we are better positioned to understand the Indian context and to work closely with Indian partners.

One current project I am very proud of is one we are supporting in Orissa to bring water to remote villages through gravity-based irrigation systems. The three-way partnership between MCC, our local partner NGO, and the local communities is an outstanding example of how community development work should happen. We supply a small amount of funds to purchase the pipe and cement needed to construct these systems. Our local partner provides technical expertise and relationships with these communities that they have developed over the past decade. Community members dig three to five kilometers of channel in which to bury the pipe and construct collection chambers. They also clear and level their fields on hillsides. We are a catalyst to get the development process started, but the critical resources and the ownership of the project and its impact belong to the villagers. The dramatic changes visible in these communities are a testament to what we can accomplish when we all contribute what we have available toward a larger, long-term objective.

I am particularly proud of the number of expatriate and national leaders that I have helped develop. While developing other leaders is complex and many other factors and people have significant roles in this process, I believe my approach as a servant leader and the example I set have inspired and helped others develop their leadership skills. I am most satisfied when I help others get opportunities to develop their technical and/or leadership skills. This has included facilitating short-term assignments in China, Myanmar, India, and Ethiopia which drew on specific skills of our staff and gave them unique opportunities to apply them in new settings. I have also sponsored staff for advanced study courses to develop new skills and knowledge that benefit them personally as well as help MCC meet its needs for skilled staff.

In developing other leaders, I need to be sensitive to cultural understandings of fairness. I continue to be surprised by the lasting power and influence of what different cultures view as appropriate behavior. One example involved choosing an employee to fill a senior management role. The response from the incumbent was not very enthusiastic. His objections were not based on competence which would be understandable within my cultural framework, but that this person was always looking for the next opportunity. The implication was that he was not willing to wait his turn but rather was too ambitious. In my culture this is usually seen as a positive expression of a desire to continually improve and to seek new challenges, but in that cultural context, it was often viewed negatively. When we look to restructure our organization, we must understand this aspect of the culture to preserve our staff's ability to work together effectively.

From 2010 to 2015, I was enrolled in Eastern University's PhD program in Organizational Leadership. This gave me the opportunity to critically analyze and reflect on my leadership experiences. I used real-life situations as the basis for research papers and class projects which, given my desire to apply my learning practically, grounded the academic approach of articles and texts. My studies exposed me to a wide variety of new information on leadership, non-profit organizations, strategy, and teamwork. This provided intellectual stimulation at a point when I needed a fresh sense of direction and new challenges. My dissertation explored how leaders of two faith-based international non-governmental organizations (INGOs) understand and assess organizational effectiveness within the context of their organizations. This research builds on my desire to examine and improve MCC's effectiveness. I am still working to develop a practical way of doing this that considers the difficulties of assessing the most important work we do, that of changing lives and empowering communities to take charge of their own development.

In my leadership journey, I have learned several important things about myself. First, I often see situations and issues differently than others. While this does not mean that I am either right or wrong, it does mean that if I do not actively participate in discussions, these ideas and views may never be part of the conversation to the detriment of the group's decision-making process. Consequently, I have needed to learn how to work with others to arrive at a group consensus that builds on everyone's perspective.

Second, I need a leadership style that works with my basic personality – introverted, thorough, and cautious. My preferred style is to be in the background working in a supportive role. I get stretched when I need to be more directive, either in responding to an emergency or a situation where the group is unable to arrive at an appropriate decision by consensus. My response, when possible, is to try to anticipate these situations so that I can prepare in advance. This gives me confidence that I have clearly thought through the issues and alternative solutions. Similarly, in developing strategy and tactics, I become as intimately acquainted with the situation as possible so that I am prepared to work with the group to develop an appropriate strategy and to identify the tactics required for successful implementation. In this I work closely with colleagues and trust their knowledge and capabilities. I also recognize that both strategy and tactics need to be flexible enough to change as the situation requires. Consequently, I work with my colleagues to assess how well the strategy is working and to identify changes that would make it more effective.

Third, I have learned that I thrive in situations where an organization needs to be stabilized to build further on its past accomplishments. My last four assignments have all involved situations of unplanned leadership change. An important part of my style is developing a sense of mutual trust with other people that then provides the foundation for working together even if we disagree on specific action steps to take.

To lead effectively, a leader needs to establish credibility and legitimacy. While organizations can and do convey positional authority, effective leadership requires more than this. I develop my legitimacy as a leader through two primary means: knowledge and listening. When starting a new role, I endeavor to learn as much as possible about the setting. This includes the area's history, the organization in general as well as the specific program, and a basic understanding of the current context. I want to understand what has happened prior to my involvement and why. I believe that others likely had good reasons for their decisions and try to take them into account before making changes. This initial understanding gives me a foundation to begin my work and then to learn more intimately how the program operates.

I listen to and learn from those who are currently working in the program or who have in the past. I recognized very early that I did not have all the answers to what we should be doing nor did I need to in order to lead effectively. A key in my leadership experience is to hire and develop good people, those who are passionate, committed, and skilled. As a leader, I work to provide them with the resources they need for their work. I trust their ideas and insights and spend sufficient time with them to understand what they want to do. I also support them by running interference as necessary with the larger organization to give them the freedom to work.

Leaders need to develop trust with colleagues and partners. This trust involves a sense that the leader is truly concerned about others' welfare and that he or she can be counted on. For me developing trust begins with establishing a personal relationship so that I better understand who people are, their dreams and aspirations, and their lives outside work. This not only enables me to better support them personally, but it also develops social capital which can be used when I need to deal with difficult situations or to hold difficult conversations.

A lack of trust was at the foundation of my greatest failure as a leader which involved managing the relationship with an expatriate volunteer who was creating a toxic organizational environment, both with other expatriates and our local colleagues. I had been unable to develop enough of a trusting relationship with this individual that would have enabled me to better address the problems he was creating. Eventually, this relationship broke down completely and the result was a need to terminate his assignment early, resulting in significant pain for everyone.

I learned several important lessons from this experience. First, not all situations can be resolved successfully and, as a leader, it is important to be able to make difficult decisions that are not the result of consensus. Second, I learned firsthand the negative implications of not having the necessary social capital. This is particularly critical in settings where the organizational structure involves not only work, but also personal and family relationships. I also learned that it is critical not to let emotions and personal feelings cloud judgment. Particularly when confronted with the need to make difficult decisions, the personal impact on the leader must be separated from the decision.

These lessons also extend to partnership evaluations and accountability. Issues related to this must be separated from likeability, friendliness, and the warmth of relationships. While these are important to establish and maintain, they do not obviate the need for accountability to ensure smoothly operating partnerships and projects.

Since most of our international development assignments have been joint leadership assignments, my wife and I have developed a pattern of shared leadership that works for us. Within these assignments we are each able to use our specific skills and interests to carry out individual parts of the assignment without feeling that one set of responsibilities is more important than the other. We have been responsible for the overall welfare of numerous expatriate staff in addition to the specific program work. By working together, we can ensure that the program work is effectively implemented and that our staff and their families are well adjusted and feel supported personally. Our ability to draw on our individual strengths in support of common program objectives has grown over time although we are still learning how to do this most effectively while preserving our personal relationship.

One challenge has been to demonstrate that we are both leaders of the program. MCC uses a co-leadership model in its international locations where spouses share the leadership responsibility. Since we bring different styles and approaches to our work, we divide the responsibilities to best fit our skills. In cultures where men are assumed to be the leaders, it has been important that we clearly identify areas where she leads and those where I lead.

Since my role usually focuses more on the visible parts of program leadership, at times it has been harder for others in the organization to value her contribution. While this lack of recognition is partly gender-related, it is also because she focuses more on the caring side of leadership as opposed to the doing side. We have needed to remind the larger organization and our local colleagues of the value of this work, particularly in MCC's style of working which includes all aspects of life, not just work.

Two leadership philosophies have been crucial foundations for my work. The first is Management by Walking Around. I spend significant blocks of time outside my office seeing what people are doing and the context(s) in which they are working. Through this direct engagement with staff I have time to engage in in-depth conversation and can better understand their thinking as well as challenging them to consider alternative ideas. I find it much easier to understand our work by seeing it firsthand rather than just reading reports; it is also much more personally rewarding. This also gives staff the assurance that their work is important to the organization's success.

The second philosophy is that of servant leadership which views the leader's role as developing other people through serving them. The leader functions from a desire to be a servant, which then leads to leadership as a way of serving others and the larger group or society. The servant leader desires to see others develop their ability to be leaders and draws true satisfaction from seeing this happen (van Dierendonck, 2010).

Two examples demonstrate how I have implemented these philosophies. My first work assignment was to lead a multifaceted agricultural development project in Bangladesh. I was young and inexperienced yet found myself in charge of a diversified development project where most of the staff were older and more experienced. My Bangladeshi colleagues understood the culture, context, and program history much better than I ever could. By spending time in the field, I developed an appreciation of the staff's work as well as an understanding of how I could be most supportive of their work. My ability to understand what they were doing and what they wanted to do coupled with my work to meet the administrative requirements helped me develop the necessary credibility to lead despite my youth and inexperience.

When my wife and I moved to Haiti, we began our work in the immediate aftermath of a failed leadership situation. We needed to establish trust with the field staff, both expatriates and Haitians, while also learning about a new country, context, and a new language. We did this by spending time getting to know staff personally, seeing their work and learning about it from their perspective. By spending time in their context, combined with our desire to be servant leaders, we were able to restore healthy relationships among team members freeing everyone to once again focus on their work without the distraction of struggles over the control of their work.

One of the most important contributions I can make now is to mentor new leaders. This has been an ongoing focus in my leadership journey; at least 20 persons I have worked closely with have gone on to serve in senior leadership roles within our organization and other organizations. Developing leaders in this fashion magnifies my impact beyond what I am personally able to accomplish.

There are several things I would like the next generation of leaders to know, all of which revolve around the need to truly understand the reality of the places where this work happens. First, it is critical that leaders have an intimate understanding of field-based contexts gained from extended hands-on experience to go along with solid academic study. This experience helps us evaluate and modify theory in line with reality. It enables us to better appreciate the complexity of the contexts within which we work and to be more aware of the constraints people face in adopting new practices or technologies. It also helps us understand that change rarely works in a straightforward, logical fashion, and that projects cannot always be thoroughly planned out in advance. Without understanding this complexity, our proposed solutions will far too often fail to lead to the type of change we want to see, especially sustainable change.

Second, I want leaders to understand the historical contexts within which we work. It is of course important to understand the cultural factors that affect how we can work, but the historical factors are also important as they constrain the choices people perceive they have. Leaders must understand the interplay between cultural, historical, religious, and other factors.

Third, I want these leaders to keep the focus of our work on people, not projects, plans, reports, or technologies. I believe our most important work is helping people learn how to solve their own problems. By focusing our attention on this rather than on just solving the problems themselves, we can find more relevant and sustainable solutions to their current problems as well as equip people with the skills to analyze their situation, problems, and steps they can take to address them. Leaders also must understand this work does not happen within the space of a three-year project but must be carried out with a long-term mindset.

Finally, I think it is important that leaders have an intimate understanding of the challenges of dealing with economic disparities. These disparities occur at many different levels, from the communities we work with to the staff of our local partners and within our own organizational staff. While we attempt to live simply and in line with lower middle class living standards in the country where we work, as expatriates we still have many more economic resources than do our local staff. In turn, they have more resources than most of our partner staff who in turn have more resources than the community members we are trying to assist. Working together effectively across these boundaries can be challenging, but finding ways to do it is critical for our overall effectiveness, both personally and organizationally.

One incident that brought this issue clearly to our attention occurred shortly after we arrived in Bangladesh. Our first son was born in Bangladesh a couple of months before a close Bangladeshi colleague and his wife also had a son. Within a few months, our son became very sick with something that could not be diagnosed in Bangladesh so we were sent back to the United States where he was diagnosed with zinc deficiency and restored to full health. In the meantime, our colleague's son was found to have a hole in his heart. Even though he was treated at one of the best hospitals in Bangladesh, he died. As we have continued to interact with this colleague, we have a constant reminder of the ramifications of these kinds of economic disparities. While I do not have answers on how to solve these disparities, I believe it is important to keep this issue in the forefront of our thoughts on how we organize and implement our work and work to reduce them as much as possible.

Sustainable development has always been an important concern in my work, both in terms of what we do and how we do it. I am not concerned as much with what we can accomplish during a project's duration, but rather about what changes local people can sustain after a project ends to create better lives for themselves, their families, and their communities. This desire also affects the pace of change we attempt. We desire to truly incorporate local knowledge and understanding into our work. This requires finding an appropriate balance between bringing new ideas and inputs from the outside and valuing local knowledge. Due to these considerations, our work often focuses on smaller and slower interventions, but ones we hope will be sustainable by the communities themselves.

REFERENCES

Carroll, J., & Minkler, M. (2000). Freire's message for social workers: Looking back, looking ahead. *Journal of Community Practice*, *8*(1), 21−36.

van Dierendonck, D. (2010). Servant leadership: A review and synthesis. *Journal of Management*, *20*(10), 1−34.

PART 4: LEADING MAJOR DONOR PROJECTS

The four authors in Part 4 have led projects or programs funded by major donors, either as donor staff or as a contracted implementer. Such projects and programs are generally of a different magnitude than most of the projects mentioned by other authors. They require meeting both the expectations of the donor and the expectations of the local stakeholders, which adds a significant "both/and" paradox to the leaders.

Nicole Rouvinez-Bouali, the author of Chapter 13, is a neonatologist who has led projects to reduce neonatal mortality in Benin and other countries. She writes that as a leader she initially creates a safe-space for the local healthcare leaders she is working with by acknowledging that neonatal mortality is the result of a multisystem problem and not only their fault. Using the "humble inquiry" approach, she focuses on building a close working relationship based on mutual trust, recognizing that the local leaders own the problem and the solution. Dr. Rouvinez-Bouali admits that her biggest challenge as an expert with knowledge of international best practice has been initially believe that her Western solution to improve newborn survival was the best solution for the local low-resource environment. As she writes "we tend to ask local teams to 'change' their procedures based on innovation and proof of concept issued from international evidence, which may or may not yield the same results in local conditions. Instead, it may be more appropriate to stimulate local solutions to generate culturally appropriate and affordable solutions that can be sustained by the local teams and health system" through the process of "Co-Production" that derives from partnerships based on shared values.

Dr Rouvinez-Bouali calls herself an "innovation manager" as she develops a program to introduce small innovations to improve patient care through an education program which she helps to sustain through employing a train-the-trainer approach reinforced by her regular follow-up visits. Knowledge is then disseminated by relying on "collective intelligence" as one health unit shares their knowledge and success with another unit and enquires about what they can do better via what she calls a "neonatal–perinatal network."

Maria Beebe, the author of Chapter 14, presents the notion of "leadership repertoire" as a sort of tool-kit to guide her leadership in various situations. Her notion of leadership involves a value-laden perspective that includes "why" and "how." As she writes "(a) the *why* of leadership involving a combination of having purpose and meaning, achieving impact, and giving back; and (b) the *how* of leadership focusing on relationships, values, and self-awareness, self-transformation, and self-transcendence." As a Filipina, the Philippine cultural norm, *kapwa* [shared humanity] is a key value in her leadership repertoire.

Beebe stresses the importance of understanding the local culture and context and of stakeholder consultation. She compares USAID's social soundness analysis with cultural practices of consultation, such as the Liberian *palaver* referring to a public meeting to bring issues forward; the Afghan practice *shura*, which is a consultation with those affected by a decision; the Setswana *kgotla*, public meeting, community council, or traditional law court. Consultation, local ownership, and leadership, along with clarity on assistance to be delivered, lead to effective development assistance.

Beebe concludes that learning to lead in different cultures requires recognizing and differentiating the *emic*, the insider's perspectives from the *etic*, the outsider's perspective, and trying to bridge the perspectives so various stakeholders can see the whole picture. Generally, we as outsiders need "to rely on that part of a culture that is visible" and only "make assumptions about underlying values which are mostly invisible." Based on these assumptions, we need "to adjust to cultural norms that do not call into question my integrity and my authenticity" in the countries in which we work.

The author of Chapter 15, Patricia McLaughlin's zigzag leadership journey in education included providing expert technical assistance on several educational initiatives in Egypt as well as leadership expertise in running international schools in several countries. McLaughlin's deep connection to the Egyptian culture provided her a lens through which to interpret her colleagues' behavior during the Uprising since she "understood what led Egyptians into the streets and having sheltered-in-place during the Uprising [she] developed a nuanced perspective that other expatriates often did not have …" She was able to empathize with them rather than simply sympathizing and felt honored that "they felt comfortable sharing their grief …" The Uprising gave Egyptians more courage to speak out and one of the Egyptian colleagues on her team used this opportunity to convince senior management that he should replace McLaughlin, an outcome that shocked her, although to some extent seemed to follow naturally from a sudden fear-lessness to confront the typical undercurrent of resentment of the "outside expert" which exists in virtually all development projects.

McLaughlin notes that her legitimacy as a leader derives from her trustwor-thiness. Trust, she learned, includes competence and character. Silence, she learned, is a rarely mentioned leadership competence. McLaughlin learned when to remain quiet when others were expressing themselves and when they were attempting to make her react defensively. She also learned how to handle betrayal, which is another all-to-common experience for leaders in international development. Her initial reaction, after her failed attempt to persuade her super-visor to change a decision he made that contradicted what he had promised her, was to feel betrayed, to resign, and to leave the country. Feeling disappointed in herself, she confronted her inner demons traceable to her childhood and was able to face "this invisible prison" and move beyond it. McLaughlin concludes that "among the most valuable leadership lessons I have learned is the impor-tance of self-awareness and self-reflection. Awareness of how I am perceived by others helps me relate effectively and knowing what gives purpose to my work helps me find joy in it. Reflection helps me find answers buried within me."

Randal Joy Thompson, author of Chapter 16, discusses leading the transfor-mation of the child welfare system and reproductive health systems in post-Ceausescu Romania. She describes the change process as being a highly collabo-rative and inclusive one in which her team facilitated the development of the new system through identifying Romanian change agents in key positions where they could use their power and influence to lead the change. Thompson describes her leadership as "intuitive leadership," because she sifted information that she gathered analytically through her intuition. She took steps and made decisions guided by her heart and from the perspective of the entire group that had formed a sort of collective intelligence and conscience. She suggests that the success of these system transformations was due to high-level governmental support, key change agents within the system who conceived of a vision them-selves, training that provided necessary knowledge, adequate funding to support the new approaches, a highly committed collaborative team, unified donors, and the conditionality provided by the European Union.

13

IN THE SKIN OF A "WORLDLY" FEMALE DOCTOR MANAGER

Nicole Rouvinez-Bouali

INTRODUCTION

Being worldly means to get into the worlds of other people — other cultures, other organizations ... managers should be exploring ceaselessly in order to return to where they started and know the place for the first time. This is the worldly mindset. (Mintzberg, 2013, p. 155)

Following efforts to reduce the burden of child death worldwide during the Millennium Development Goals, under-five-year-old deaths have fallen from 12.6 million in 1990 to 5.9 million in 2015 (UNICEF, 2015). Despite progress, disparities remain high, and above 90% of under-five-year-old deaths happen in low- and middle-income countries, especially in Sub-Saharan Africa. Strategies to reduce child mortality have mostly targeted the postneonatal period, so that the proportion of under-five deaths happening in the first 28 days of age — the "neonatal period" — is increasing, and represents now 45% of these deaths worldwide. Prematurity, complications from childbirth, and infections are responsible for close to 90% of all neonatal deaths in low-resource countries, yet most of these deaths are avoidable. Currently, 98% of all newborns die in places having less than 2% of worldwide resources. As pointed out by numerous organizations, the leading cause of death in children is not so much the disease itself, but the underlying socio-economic conditions, namely the "social determinants of health," so that half of the "Sustainable Development Goals" (SDGs) target the determinants of health.

This chapter, based on my own narrative, describes why I chose to advocate for underserved populations, my own experience in navigating the global health arena, and how tools learned during the "International Masters for Health Leadership" have contributed to increase my capacity to understand challenges and opportunities of healthcare systems in low resource countries and make an impact for underserved newborns.

SETTING UP MY SCENE

I am a Swiss neonatologist, working in an academic setting in Canada, passionate about health in developing countries. Initially a hobby, my global health involvement took a professional turn after a vacation in Benin, one of the poorest countries of Sub-Saharan Africa and of the world. During my first trip there, I had the opportunity to observe the living conditions of the population, including the critical lack of access to basic needs like electricity and water. I also had the opportunity to explore the medical infrastructure of the country, and to connect with local pediatricians, including Professor B, who has since been a key collaborator, playing a catalytic role in our projects. Major achievements resulted from this trustful collaboration, including the initiation of the first noninvasive ventilation program in the main neonatal unit of the country, and the creation of an International, Inter-University Diploma in Perinatology, providing perinatal training to gynecologists and pediatricians from various countries in Sub-Saharan Africa. Those successes encouraged me to be a co-applicant in a Global Development Alliance (GDA) Project, co-funded by a major International Development Agency, to reduce neonatal mortality in Benin. I became the Clinical Director of this project.

CHOOSING MY PATH

At the age of 12 years, I became strongly determined to become a pediatrician. I didn't even know any pediatrician or what they did, but I wanted to protect and heal children, and prevent them from suffering. I never changed my mind. I had to fight with my father to be able to go to a scientific college, as I knew this was going to help me enter and succeed in medicine. The scientific section was the only one having mixed boys and girls classes, and my father was afraid that this would divert me from my studies. Also, having learned medicine himself, in another epoch, he strongly believed that it was much more important to study Latin and Greek to study medicine. Thinking of it, this was my first leadership act, as my father was very imposing and not so flexible, so that I had to enter a true negotiation with him, and show that students with a scientific background were actually performing better during medical studies. Obeying my father's order might have prevented me from succeeding in medicine, and from pursuing my dream.

Clinical rotations confirmed that my path was indeed in pediatrics. More than in any other specialty, I felt in my element in pediatrics, easily finding ways and words to comfort children and their families, being stimulated by the diversity of diseases affecting children, and being thrilled by seeing a smile back on their face as soon as their health improved, as if all the pain was gone. Children are a great example of resilience! I also felt the need to learn how to support those with noncurable conditions and how to turn their fears and pains into an acceptable and even rewarding experience, for them and their family. Pediatrics above all was the area where I felt I could have a longstanding impact on the life of those critically ill neonates, children, and families.

FASCINATED BY GLOBAL NEONATOLOGY

As far as I can remember, I have always rejected injustice, especially injustice toward innocent children. "All human beings are born free and equal in dignity and rights ... " (United Nations, 1948). Yet, it is very difficult to imagine that a newborn in Africa has the same rights as a newborn in a high resource country. I have seen too many children die from a mild disease, because their parents could not access quality care, or could not afford to pay for it. Coming from two privileged countries (Switzerland and Canada), I feel the need to give back and help those who did not get the same chance. I am driven by the desire to heal newborns, as interventions provided in the first days of life can dramatically affect the rest of their life, and that of their

family. Trying to decrease neonatal death strongly fits my core motivational
values and expertise as a neonatology specialist.

FINDING BALANCE AT HOME AND IN THE WORKPLACE

What does it represent for a Swiss female physician, working in North-
America, to lead an international education program in a far-away country
such as Benin? What are the challenges associated with the realization of my
dreams, being a full time academic physician, and a mother with family
charges? This resembles the story of my life – somebody standing on the
edge, acting by passion and stimulated by challenges, often opting for the
tortuous path, with a succession of obstacles to overcome, with joy and tears
along the way, just because that is where I feel I have to go, where I feel the
most useful, and where I find most personal reward in the end! "We need to
take our best ideas, our strongest intuitions, and to test them [...] to be willing to fail, to be wrong, to start over again from lessons learnt"
(Duckworth, 2013a, n.p).

Being a full time academic physician, it has been challenging to convince
my colleagues that my global health work was serious and academic, and
most of my humanitarian missions' had to be taken out of vacation time at
the beginning, up to the time a famous grant gave serious support to my
work and credibility. Being active on multiple fronts has generated tensions
at home and in the workplace, and my family and colleagues have had to be
flexible so that I could take prolonged periods outside the country. They are
to be thanked for their indulgence and the successes they have facilitated.

My work has also generated tensions for me, trying to go beyond my limits to do my yearly full-time academic job within nine months, being away
on global health trips three months per year, on top of following a Master's
program, still dealing with family, household, and other issues. Dealing with
such a situation is when you challenge yourself on why you do all this, and
where you find out what is really important in your life, what you believe is
the right thing to do. In my case, I can say that global health, my patients,
and my daughter have had, and will always have the priority. They are the
ones keeping me going, and comforting me by the satisfaction they give me
on a daily basis. I would not engage myself so deeply, to the point of

rupture, if I were not truly passionate about my worldly activities! As Duckworth (2013b) contended:

> *You choose to do a particular thing in life and choose to give up a lot of other things in order to do it. And you stick with those interests and goals over the long term ... 'GRIT' is not just having resilience in the face of failure, but also having deep commitments that you remain loyal to over many years ... GRIT is the quality that enables individuals to work hard and stick to their long-term passions and goals. (p. 14)*

BEING A FEMALE MANAGER

Considering the gender inequity prevalent in most African countries, being a foreign female doctor may be considered a handicap. Being a white female certainly has the potential to add complexity to the task. As such, it sometimes makes it challenging to be taken seriously in my endeavor to provide education to doctors and nurses in Benin, and to interact with stakeholders. On the other hand, being a "Mom" has promoted interactions with mothers, nurses, midwives, and female physicians, allowing me to hear their voice and represent them as a silent majority. Also, my gray hair, considered as a sign of wisdom in local culture, may have incited my local colleagues to respect.

GAINING CREDIBILITY IN A CROSS-CULTURAL CONTEXT

Many projects to improve health care have failed to make a difference in the past, because of the magnitude of the problem, because of the limited scale of the projects, and because of resistance to change. What did I do to get respected and followed in a country I had no idea about before 2011? There are multiple plausible reasons to explain what:

- I do acknowledge that neonatal mortality is the result of a multisystem problem, and that healthcare providers' ignorance is not only their fault. This allows me to share my observations in a nonjudgmental way, and give them credit for their own efforts to change the system, despite multiple system barriers. I create a safe place for people to learn, fail, and strive for success.

- I was lucky to meet with a deeply influential and respected local pediatrician, Professor B, Head of the Pediatric Department of the main Faculty of Medicine at that time, who was the first to promote neonatal care and open neonatal units in Benin. Strengthened by his trust and influence, I was privileged to be accepted as a visiting Professor in many neonatal units of the country, being able to observe and interact closely with patients and healthcare professionals. Doing so, I gained precious information on what is really happening in those units and hospitals, what is working well, and what could/ought to be modified, and I gained respect from frontline healthcare workers. This is often not the case with international help, strategic decisions being made in head offices, with limited knowledge of the local context and the challenges frontline healthcare workers have to overcome in their daily work (Mintzberg, 2013).

- I am a "key listener," happy to support local initiatives, if deemed feasible, instead of imposing mine. The noninvasive neonatal ventilation program and the Diploma in Perinatology were both created following local requests that I supported as well as I could. In this "Co-Production model," the

> the 'learned' expertise of the professional [is combined with] the 'lived' experience of the user
>
> It is the user who ultimately determines the outcome, not the expert and their planned outcome (Alakeson, 2013, p. 210).

- My goals and interventions are realistic – keeping interventions simple and promoting those interventions with low cost but high impact.

- I am very patient and do not expect to see immediate results following interventions. This allows me to repeat my "take home messages" as often as needed to make my point. It promotes a "growth mindset": a learner may not be ready yet, but it is not a fail. Thanks to the "power of the yet," learners can "engage deeply [...], process the error [...], learn from it [...], correct it." You can reward for efforts, strategy, and perseverance, instead of requiring the result "now" (Dweck, 2014, p. 1).

- Going back multiple times to Benin and supporting local ideas has given a strong positive message to my local partners. As stated by Professor B, "the fact that Dr. Rouvinez Bouali came back multiple times made us believe we could do something to change our situation." This has allowed them to embrace and champion changes and stop thinking that newborn deaths are a fatality.

- Further buy-in and trust from local teams came once I started using the "humble inquiry" method (Schein, 2013) — "asking instead of telling" — using naïve questions to help them explore their own practice and how they could best promote change. "The client is the one who owns the problem and the solution" and the consultant role is to build a relationship with them to help them resolve their problem (Schein, 1998, n.p.).

THE CIRCLE OF INFLUENCE AND LEADERSHIP

Which are the key elements that promoted my personal leadership in global health?

- Finding a niche that people have not explored deeply before: caring for sick newborns is a huge challenge that low-resource countries can barely afford to provide as the required expert human resources and technical infrastructure are usually lacking. Hence, international help to support sick newborns has often been limited to interventions in large reference hospitals, especially when it comes to Sub-Saharan Africa. Stakeholders have perceived our multifaceted, multicenter program reaching out to community as a promising innovation, worth of support, be it financial, through official authorizations to participate to the program educative sessions, or informal.

- Having people believe in my capacity to promote local health: being the clinical director of our GDA project, I can act as a leader, but my leadership is only effective once key followers believe in what I believe, and that we can do it together. As such, being recognized by the most senior and respected pediatrician in the country has enabled me to act as a real leader. Professor B has been the determinant "First Follower" (Sivers, 2010) promoting our success. My local partners have seen my compassion and my vulnerability and trust that I understand and respect their reality well enough to follow me without feeling the blame. The trustful partnership established with them has also been crucial in promoting my own willingness to take a leadership role.

- Belonging to a renowned institution: "Me" as part of the University of Ottawa carries far more influence than "Me" alone for the newcomer. Yet, I have been the only entity involved in the education curriculum lead in Benin. Those achievements may not have realized if I was not officially under the cover of the University of Ottawa. If you are not famous, promote yourself under the umbrella of an official institution that people can trust, even though they may not know the institution itself. This will allow you to take time to build trust and credibility when working in cross-cultural teams.

- Similarly, association with respected organizations and agencies with established expertise in the field is a catalyst of success. This visibility did play a major role in obtaining our GDA grant. This grant has been a key determinant of success for the project and for my own leadership: it gave me the power to make changes based on academic recognition from my own center. Being the living interface between the GDA and local partners had a tremendous influence on local engagement into the project and local recognition of my leadership.

LEARNING FROM MY GLOBAL HEALTH EXPERIENCES

My biggest mistake has been to believe I knew what ought to be done to improve newborn survival in in low-resource countries. I may be a fully trained neonatologist knowledgeable of Western/Northern medical evidence, but I still had a lot to learn on local evidence and cultural beliefs, and their influence on the health system. We tend to ask local teams to "change" their procedures based on innovation and proof of concept issued from international evidence, which may or may not yield the same results in local conditions. Instead, it may be more appropriate to stimulate local solutions to address local problems, with international support using a "humble consulting" process (Schein, 2013), to generate culturally appropriate and affordable solutions that can be sustained by the local teams and health system. "Co-Production" (Alakeson, 2013) allows local people and healthcare workers to engage in their own project, to be more receptive to your observations, and to move from the "tell how" to the "ask how" (Schein, 2013).

Personal experiences in China and Vietnam also taught me that barriers are added when communication cannot be done directly between the international and local partners. Health professionals in those countries may not have access to the international medical literature, but instead refer to the limited amount of information written in their own language. Cultural aspects take another dimension when local leadership positions are attributed following "political" suitability instead of healthcare management expertise or medical expertise. Significant improvement had been made following years of intervention in the neonatal intensive care unit (NICU) in a referral hospital in South Vietnam where I have been involved for four years as a neonatal consultant. Unfortunately, we remained helpless to stop major backsliding when a new NICU Director was promoted, based on her position within the communist party, instead of medical expertise, as she blindly followed the outdated neonatal guidelines validated a long time ago by the party.

Partnerships need to be based on values, instead of technical support alone. There is no financial incentive for partnership based on values, so that actions based on values are more likely rewarded as they engage local partners in a true partnership. Finding common values is key to improving the capacity to develop projects with low-resource country partners, who sometimes denigrate international help, based on the perception that international help mostly serves foreign interests, instead of those of the low-resource partners themselves.

Learning from my previous experiences has guided my interventions in Benin, allowed me to establish a trustful network of international collaborators and to implement sustainable interventions with them.

CAPACITY BUILDING FOR HEALTHCARE WORKERS

Capacity building for first line healthcare workers is challenging in low-resource countries, as their initial professional training is often limited to some technical aspects of patient care and nursing or midwifery school is often the last education received. We cannot palliate to the inappropriate educational curricula in the country, but we can provide focused experiential learning to cover major gaps. These health care workers need to assimilate change piece by piece, adding complexity at each step. Regular follow-up visits to provide further education allows positive reinforcement messages about progress made, feedback regarding what has not been assimilated, and the opportunity to address resistance to change. Such follow-up visits are crucial, and contribute to increase the credibility of the international collaborator/educator.

EMPOWERING LOCAL LEADERSHIP THROUGH EDUCATION

The high neonatal mortality in Benin and other Sub-Saharan countries is the result of multiple dysfunctions at various levels of the healthcare system, including lack of knowledge, lack of human resources, lack of/or inappropriate equipment, lack of engagement from the community members themselves, as well as community, financial, and government leaders. One single intervention cannot fix all these dysfunctions, and change must be introduced gradually to allow progressive adaptation to change in order to support sustainable results.

Our program promotes a set of basic, cost-efficient interventions that complete each other in targeting the main causes of neonatal mortality altogether, along the continuum of care from the community to reference hospitals. As such, it may be more likely to make a difference on newborn survival than targeting one cause alone (e.g., preterm infants surviving the initial respiratory distress phase thanks to noninvasive ventilation often die of malnutrition or infection in the following weeks). I have put significant efforts in developing an innovative education curriculum to improve neonatal care, adapted to the different needs of doctors, nurses, and midwives, so that they would obtain the required knowledge of diseases and needs of preterm and sick newborns. I have involved my local partners in the development of six distinctive education modules and in a train-the-trainer model, so that they would contribute their knowledge of their system and culture, and so that they are now able to supervise the application of the program in a sustainable way. Interactive and hands-on simulation sessions allowed participants to practice new techniques, and to demonstrate their habits. Experiential learning allowed me to observe directly some unsafe practices, to promote good ones, and to identify champions for some of the interventions. Having doctors, nurses, and midwives participating together in the training sessions also allowed them to understand how they could work bet-ter together as a team instead of in silos.

I have maintained close contact with each unit involved in the project, and completed regular follow-up through team meetings and bedside visits. These follow-ups have allowed me and local teams to provide suggestions on how to optimize patient care on a continuous basis. They have proven to be fruitful and to empower local teams, who best know what can be done in their own unit. My role has then been mostly supportive of their own ideas, with individualized mentorship, helping them to progress at their own pace, and favoring the interventions that fit best their population.

MANAGING INNOVATION AND CHANGE

In their book *Beyond the Idea: How to Execute Innovation in Any Organization*, Govindarajan and Trimble (2013) describe three possible models of innovation:

> *Model S, for* Small *initiatives, attempts to squeeze innovation into small slivers of slack time ... Model R, for* Repeatable *initiatives, attempts to make innovation as repeatable and predictable as possible ... Model C, for* Custom *initiatives, is for all other and more complex initiatives. (Kindle loc 1427 of 1793)*

Change and innovation also come from "reframing" global health programs, as changing perspective often allows seeing new solutions or opportunities (Hurst, 2012).

Considering our GDA organization and my position of Clinical Director of the project, I can imagine myself as a "Middle Manager" (Mintzberg, 2013), with the privilege of having contacts with our local partners at any level — the organization "base" that we serve, as well as with the "top man-agement" represented by funding agencies and governmental institutions. My role may then be that of an *innovation manager* introducing small inno-vations, step-by-step, through a specific education program to improve patient care. Those small innovations are led by highly committed local part-ners, in their spare time, due to the extremely limited human resources avail-able in public hospitals in Benin. Hence reaching the full scope of our multifaceted project will require multiple small innovation initiatives.

I cannot agree more with the fact that "key to success of the Small Model is MOTIVATION: Model S is heavily reliant on front-line employees going the extra mile, squeezing in the innovation on employees free time" … and that "strategies to keep employees motivated include, among others, individual and/or collective pride in small improvements, and making visible the connection between innovation and the health of the collectivity" (Govindarajan & Trimble, 2013, Kindle loc 333 to 345 of 1793). Due to the extreme manpower restriction in healthcare workers in low-resource countries, the scale of innovations that can be driven exclusively by local teams is essentially limited to "small" initiatives. "Custom projects" are more complex and require substantial manpower support and extensive funding. Trying to apply a "custom model" of innovation to low-resource countries would also have the disadvantage of preventing local empowerment and sustainability.

THE POWER OF "COLLECTIVE INTELLIGENCE"

Through our educative approach, I have fostered the creation of a "neonatal-perinatal network," where healthcare workers from one unit share their success with others and enquire about what they can do better. Networking has been key in facilitating the dissemination of helpful interventions in Benin. In particular, sharing information between gynecologists and pediatricians around the time of problematic deliveries has fostered better joint management of high-risk newborns. I do believe that significant change will come from this improved collaboration in the coming years.

There is a huge need to improve communication between health institutions and patients at all levels, but even more so in the community. Poverty and poor clinical outcomes affect families and healthcare workers. There is a degree of fatality around neonatal death, and numbers of these babies die in the community before any attempt to transport a baby to a healthcare facility. There is a fear of going to the hospital as hospitals are often perceived as the place where people go and die. This fear contributes to the lack of trust toward hospitals and trained healthcare agents, and causes people to turn to traditional health practitioners and local divinities and voodoo, which may end up in life-threatening delays to receive quality care. Community's opinion has to be considered and work done with them to allow early recognition and optimal management of sick newborns to reduce perinatal deaths.

AIMING FOR LONG-TERM IMPACT AND SUSTAINABILITY

Many global health projects start with a personal story, with help provided to somebody in someone's sphere of influence. Those projects are very valuable and really do provide help to some people. But few become an "institution" with large scale influence and sustainability. High stakes connections are needed to have this large impact, from healthcare specialists to NGOs, to political and financial stakeholders. Our GDA grant is now over, but I keep making follow-up visits and I am delighted to see that the hospitals where the intervention was introduced are all keeping the project going, and building strategies to improve it, despite having no guarantee of any further financial support. The project has reached sustainability in that regard. Ownership of the intervention is now localized. Resistance to change is dissolving and there is space for suggestions and reflection. I can see the heathcare staff motivation to carry on the project. They are working with me to optimize what they do, to be held accountable for their actions.

I do believe that empowerment of our local partners, first line healthcare workers, families, and communities will bring a significant reduction in neonatal mortality in Benin in the coming years. Demonstration of this reduction will hopefully allow us to bring interventions to a policy level and engage key stakeholders − who need to take on the project and engage funds, allowing all babies to receive these low cost, life-saving interventions. Any intervention or program that can reach the policy level has a far greater chance of being supported by the countries themselves and to see funds put aside to support its implementation and sustainability. This fact, coupled with the international efforts put in place with the SDGs, other international initiatives to save the children and Paris Declaration may put enough knowledge and "ethical pressure" in the hands of developing countries governments to motivate them to put in place an infrastructure that allows hospitals to save newborns with promising futures, if they could receive the minimal treatments they need. I wish to see universal access to care for every newborn and mother. I also wish to see the end of the endemic corruption which prevents low-resource countries' citizens from accessing the essential health care they deserve!

TAKE HOME MESSAGES

Many initiatives to improve health care in low resource countries in the past have failed to make a difference, because of the magnitude of the problem, because of the limited scale of the projects, and because of resistance to change. Conditions and challenges found in Benin are also encountered in other low-resource countries, so that tools proposed are likely to apply to numbers of low resource facilities, patients, and healthcare workers.

Among others, I would like to emphasize some of the interventions susceptible to generate hope and success for future projects:

- The magnitude of the neonatal health problem is such that both local and international healthcare workers could easily get discouraged and abandon their efforts. At the same time, resources are very limited. "Reframing" (Hurst, 2012) the BIG problem into small pieces allows bringing solutions to the full puzzle one piece at a time, through "small innovations" (Govindarajan & Trimble, 2013) and stepwise changes. It may take time, but this time is also desirable to allow cultural adaptation, and to engage the community at large.

- Doing so, consider the "power of the yet" – don't expect immediate results – learn from mistakes done and reward efforts and perseverance to solve the problem. Having a "growth mind-set" is "a path to the future" (Dweck, 2014, p.1). Deliver positive messages and encouragements, reward success, and learn from failure.

- Believe in your dream and stick to your goal: "GRIT is passion and perseverance for very long term goals ..." (Duckworth, 2013a)

- Provide guidance according to the "humble inquiry" and "humble consulting" principles (Schein, 2013, 2015): local partners are the ones who know what are the real problems, and who own the solution to their problems – "Co-Production" allows local people and healthcare workers to engage in the project, to be more receptive to your observations, and to move from the "tell how" to the "ask how" (Schein, 2013). As Alakeson (2013) argued:

> *It is time for [local communities] to stop looking for someone to*
> *sort their problems ... to take on responsibility for what they are*
> *capable of doing ... to become active ... to take on responsibility for*
> *what they want to happen and how. (p. 211)*

It is also a good way to fight resistance to change as you are more likely to adopt ideas that you or your community have generated.

- Capacity building and networking are a way to benefit from the power of "collective intelligence" (Woolley, 2010).

Finally, I have to acknowledge that some of my personal qualities and flaws may not be generally replicable. That being said, advocacy and values are present in each of us — take the time to explore them, engage with those sharing your values and find your own path to help others. Find the right persons, the right context, listen to your heart, and seize opportunities as they rise. Let your passion guide you, even if it seems utopist — if you don't try you won't get it!

REFERENCES

Alakeson, V. (2013). Coproduction of health and wellbeing outcomes: The new paradigm for effective health and social care. *In The Art of Change Making*. Leadership center 2015, 210−212.

Duckworth, A. L. (2013a). *Angela Lee Duckworty Grit: The power of passion and perseverance*. TED Talk. Retrieved from: https://www.ted.com/talks/angela_lee_duckworth_grit_the_power_of_passion_and_perseverance

Duckworth, A. L. (2013b). Resilience and learning: The significance of grit (interview). *Educational Leadership*, September 2013, 71(1), 14−20.

Dweck, C. (2014). *The power of believing that you can improve*. TED Talk. Retrieved from http://www.ted.com/talks/ carol_dweck_the_power_of_believing_that_you_can_improve/transcript?language=en

Govindarajan, V., & Trimble, C. (2013). *Beyond the idea: How to execute innovation in any organization*. New York, NY: St Martin's Press, Kindle edition.

Hurst, D. K. (2012). *The new ecology of leadership: Business mastery in a chaotic Wworld.* New York, NY: Columbia Business School Publishing.

Mintzberg, H. (2013). *Simply managing: What managers do − and can do better.* Oakland, CA: Berrett-Koehler Publishers, Inc.

Schein, E. (1998). Process consultation revisited, building the helping relationship, Schein 1998: Ten principles as the essence of Process consultation: principle # 5.

Schein, E. (2013). *Humble inquiry: The gentle art of asking instead of telling.* Oakland, CA: Berrett-Koehler Publishers, Inc.

Schein, E. (2015). *Humble consulting: How to provide real help faster.* Accessed on Audiobook version, narrated by J Bronzi.

Sivers, D. (2010, February). *Derek Sivers: How to start a movement* [video file]. Retrieved from https://www.ted.com/talks/derek_sivers_how_to_start_a_movement

UNICEF. (2015). *Committing to child survival: A promise renewed progress report 2015.* Retrieved from http://www.childmortality.org

United Nations. (1948). *The Universal Declaration of Human Rights, Article, 1.*

Woolley, A. W. (2010, October). Evidence for a collective intelligence factor in the performance of human groups. *Science, 330,* 686−688.

14

PASSION, RISK, AND ADVENTURE IN DEVELOPING MY INTERNATIONAL DEVELOPMENT LEADERSHIP REPERTOIRE

Maria Beebe

"Why build university computer centers in Afghanistan when there is an ongoing war?" asked a student in a Leading with Impact class at the Asian Institute of Management in Manila where I had a month-long Fulbright specialist appointment.

This chapter examines the development of my international leadership repertoire after I turned 50, a "third chapter" filled with passion, risk, and adventure according to Sarah Lawrence-Lightfoot (2009). My "third chapter" included developing: (1) knowledge partnerships among South African and American universities, (2) networks related to telecommunications policy and regulation with African selected universities, and (3) alliances for the use of information and communication technologies (ICTs) for higher education in Afghanistan.

In 2010, I began efforts for giving back to the Filipino community by editing stories by Filipina women demonstrating leadership in the Philippines and elsewhere. A Fulbright specialist award in 2017 allowed reflection and exploration of leadership lessons.

THE CONCEPT OF LEADERSHIP REPERTOIRE

I posited that a leadership repertoire could be thought of as a toolkit, a set of resources, or skills that provides options for leadership tasks (Beebe, 2017). Repertoires afford Filipina leaders the flexibility to mix and match the *how* and *why* of leadership for dealing with different situations. In a discourse analysis of Filipina women leaders (Beebe, 2015), I suggested their understanding of leadership includes reference to (1) the *why* of leadership involving a combination of having purpose and meaning, achieving impact, and giving back and (2) the *how* of leadership focusing on relationships, values, and self-awareness, self-transformation, and self-transcendence. I indicated that the leadership challenge for Filipina women in the diaspora is twofold: (1) broadening and deepening of their leadership repertoires for success and (2) deciding on elements of the leadership repertoire that best fits a specific context. An important finding of both of my works (2015, 2017) is the role of the Philippine cultural norm, *kapwa* [shared humanity] in the leadership repertoire of Filipinas.

A leadership repertoire is consistent with George's (2016) view that authentic leaders "become skilled at tailoring their style to their audiences, imperatives of the situation, and readiness of their teammates to accept different approaches" (How leaders develop their authenticity, para 6). George explained that leaders need to inspire, coach, and build consensus; give tough feedback; and make difficult decisions that will not please everyone. Additionally, authentic leaders become more skillful in adapting their style, without compromising their character as they gain experience and develop greater self-awareness. Flexibility by leaders becomes the outward manifestation of their authenticity (George, 2016).

Another paradigm that helps with understanding leadership repertoire is Drath's (1998) concept of the "evolving construct of leadership." According to Drath, leadership has evolved from domination to influencing others and gaining committing to common goals. Leadership has shifted from commanding followers, to motivating followers and mutual meaning-making. Drath's construct suggested developing interpersonal skills, self-knowledge, and promoting interactions among group members. As part of a leadership repertoire, a leader's options could include mixing and matching of Drath's various elements.

This chapter expands on the concept of leadership repertoire introduced in "Developing an International Leadership Repertoire" (Beebe, 2016).

I frame my experiences by the *how* and *why* of leadership (Beebe, 2017), the concept of authentic leadership (George, 2016), the evolving construct of leadership (Drath, 1998), and the Philippine cultural norm of *kapwa*.

READINESS FOR GLOBAL ENGAGEMENT

The Global Competencies Inventory (GCI) by the Kozai Group (Stevens, Bird, Mendenhall, & Oddou, 2014) that I completed in October 2016 identified me as a "globetrotter." I scored high in perception management, relationship management, and self-management. These competencies, along with consideration of the socio-political-economic context, culture, gender equality, and sustainable development comprise my leadership repertoire. My repertoire developed as a result of my international development experience with diverse cultures and environments. In this section, I reflect on elements of my life that I believe have contributed to my readiness for global engagement.

I have repeatedly been told by my family that when I was born, the midwife exclaimed, "She will travel the world." I did travel the world after I married a US Peace Corps Volunteer, when I became a Peace Corps Volunteer myself, and during my husband's foreign service postings to the Sudan, Philippines, Liberia, and South Africa, with interludes in Corvallis, Oregon and Washington, DC. While accompanying my husband, I was also raising our two children and starting my career. At each posting, I applied for and was hired for positions that allowed me to work on meaningful activities that would make a difference.

My grandmother often reminded me that in addition to being "smart," I had the blood of a *katipunero*! The *katipuneros* were Filipino nationalists who fought for independence from Spain and my grandfather, as a young boy, was a runner for the *katipunan* during the late 1890s. To memorize the messages and run for his life to deliver the messages took courage. This could explain why courage to fight for social justice became a guiding force in my leadership.

Growing up in the Philippines immersed me in the Filipino social value of *kapwa* [shared humanity]. Thus, building and maintaining relationships was a competency I brought to my work in international development.

Like most Filipinas, I grew up multilingual, an often-overlooked advantage. Growing up multilingual appears to "facilitate the development of perspective-taking tools that are critical for effective communication" (Fan, Liberman, Keysar, & Kinzler, 2015, p. 1). After college, I taught high school where communicating was essential. I came to love Shakespeare while in the fifth grade. I took to heart the lines from *As You Like it*, "All the world's a stage ... And one man in his time plays many parts." These lines resonated with me as I recognized I was playing roles when I did not want to do yet another meeting with another governmental ministry official. I would tell myself, "Go to the meeting. Think about your purpose for being here." The ability to play a role while not feeling up to it can be authentic leadership when one maintains one's core values. As individuals we have numerous facets of our identity and we tend to assert different aspects of ourselves in different contexts by drawing from our leadership repertoire.

Marriage to an American was a cross-cultural experience. My first foray into cross-cultural international development was my Peace Corps assignment with the Bontoc Igorots, an ethnic group who were never colonized. They were as foreign to me as I was to them. Travel and graduate work in anthropology sharpened my appreciation of cultural differences.

SOCIO—POLITICAL—ECONOMIC CONTEXT CONSIDERATIONS

Culture, gender, and shared meaning shape international development assistance. Understanding these requires listening to local partners as they articulate their needs. Social soundness analysis is a tool for listening that had a significant impact on my leadership. As practiced by USAID, social soundness analysis includes understanding socio-economic feasibility, the benefits and burdens among groups, and the spread effect of the proposed initiative. Social soundness analysis involves stakeholder consultation. Consultation ensures ownership by those requiring the development assistance. Other cultures have a similar process. For example, the Liberians hold a *palaver* referring to a public meeting to bring issues forward. Afghans practice *shura*, consultation with those affected by a decision. In Botswana, the Setswana conduct a *kgotla*, public meeting, community council, or traditional law court. Consultation, local ownership, and leadership, along with clarity on assistance to be delivered, lead to effective development assistance.

Cultural Considerations

International development is about promoting social and economic change. These are not concepts that everyone understands in the same way. For example, family planning initiatives make assumptions about the desirable size of a family, mix of girls and boys, an ideal spacing of children, and who makes these decisions in the family. Gender equality programs are based on cultural assumptions about social relations. Development initiatives presume access to information; and, access is increasingly dependent on communication technologies and who controls the technology.

Learning to lead in different cultures requires recognizing and differentiating the emic, the insider's perspectives from the etic, the outsider's perspective, and trying to bridge the perspectives so various stakeholders can see the whole picture. For example, what constitutes sexual harassment in one culture might be considered teasing in another culture. Wearing "inappropriate" clothing could be read as a sexual invitation in some cultures.

The extent of cultural variability continues to surprise me. Despite this cultural variability, we, as outsiders in the international development process, rely on that part of a culture that is visible and make assumptions about underlying values which are mostly invisible. To the extent I understand the underlying cultural values, I adjust to the cultural norms that do not call into question my integrity and my authenticity. Here are some examples:

- As a woman, I dress appropriately, including wearing a head covering where expected. I do this to show respect for the culture, without necessarily embracing the religious beliefs that underlie the wearing of a head covering.

- Because of the centrality of family, allowing staff to take off from work for family reasons is acceptable to a certain extent.

- Disagreeing is better done in private rather than in public.

Gender Considerations

Gender identity, roles, and relations are often circumscribed by culture. My understanding of gender was influenced by my early experience in the Philippines where in my family girls and boys received equal treatment, including going to school. As a girl growing up in the Philippines, I was expected to behave to be responsible and to be respectful. My family called me "smart." I observed that the women around me had personal autonomy and influenced the decision-making processes at home. My belief about gender equality was tested, particularly by my work in Afghanistan in several ways.

- In 1996, when the Taliban took over, they imposed strict restrictions on girls and women. Girls, the term used for unmarried females, and women were not allowed to go to school or to work. Nine years later, in 2005, zero girls were enrolled at the university level but a year later in 2006, after the US occupation, about 25% of registered students were reported to be girls. Although girls were not allowed to go to school during the Taliban years, some attended literacy classes disguised as sewing circles. When I met the mother of a female staff member, I asked why she allowed her daughter to go to school. Her response was deeply personal: "When I was her age, my husband went for a scholarship abroad. When his letters arrived, I suffered the indignity of asking someone to read the letters to me and had to dictate my response. I told myself, this will not happen to my daughter."

- Girls and women were not allowed to go out in public unless chaperoned by a close male relative. I generally adhered to the restriction of not walking alone on a public street. As an outsider, I had fewer security restrictions than US Embassy and USAID personnel. With a male Afghan driver, I could go from my lodgings to Kabul University, Kabul Polytechnic University, Kabul Medical University, the government Ministries, other donor offices, the US Embassy and USAID, the airport, or shop or eat at restaurants. I kept a *burqa* in the car for added security. When I traveled outside Kabul, I took at least one male staff but always made sure I was accompanied by one female staff as well. Our female staff were allowed by their families to take public taxis when shared with other female passengers. When we started sending faculty members and masters students to the US and other countries, an initial request was for a male chaperone to accompany each female student. Since this solution would have been cost prohibitive, we agreed we would always have two or more females in a cohort.

The story of the boy who wanted to enroll in computer class but did not want to be taught by a girl is a vignette that I have shared (Njunguri et al. 2017, pp. 249–264). The boy came charging to my office and indignantly demanded: "Who is in charge here? My instructor is a girl. I do not want to be taught by a girl." To which I replied: "I'm Dr. Beebe. I'm in charge. She is the most qualified even if she is a girl. I hire only the best and the brightest, and in this case, the person happens to be a girl.

His retort: "Why should I listen to you? You're only a woman." The boy stomped out. The next day, two of his friends brought him back and apologized for his behavior. "If the girl teacher and Dr. Beebe would allow him back, we would make sure he will behave."

- An American male colleague passed an invitation to me from his Afghan colleague, the department chair, to join them at his house for *iftar*, the meal at sunset that breaks the fast during the month of Ramadan. He explained this would give his Afghan colleagues a chance to discuss how Afghan eQuality Alliances could benefit the faculty members of their department. Upon arrival, I was introduced to the other guests who were the all-male faculty members. When the meal was announced, my dilemma was whether to sit with the men so we could continue our conversations about the program or sit with the women (and their children) who were in another room and had not even been introduced. Although the men said, come sit with us, I decided to sit with the women first to honor that family's tradition of men and women and their children eating separately. This arrangement gave the women a chance to ask about my marital status, my children, and my work in Afghanistan. I showed pictures of my children and my husband. In turn, the women shared a little about their family life, introduced their children, talked about where they shop, and how they prepared the food we were eating. It gave the women a chance to teach me the names of food and the basic ingredients in Dari. It gave me a small window to the visible aspects of culture: holiday customs, what happens during Ramadan, and styles of modesty, including covering legs to the ankle, arms up to the wrists, and wearing a tunic top over loose pants. Dining etiquette was explained. Just before dessert, I joined the men. As an outsider, I was excused to sit with the men as the men wanted more information from me that was beneficial to them. I do not know if an American man or any outsider male could have sat with the women for a meal with this family. In subsequent invitations to other Afghan families, it became apparent that not all Afghan families observed the separation of sexes during meal time.

Commitment to the Sustainable Development Goals

Sustainable development presumes balancing economic, social, and environmental considerations. During our Peace Corps service in Bontoc, Mt Province, my husband also a Peace Corps Volunteer and I hiked two to five days to visit our community college students living in villages in the mountains, along the Chico River. These visits gave us a first-hand look at the rice terraces in the Cordilleras, estimated to be more than a 1,000 years old, and identified in 1993 as a UNESCO Heritage site. A community of small farmers created the rice terraces through the sustainable use of natural resources while honoring sacred traditions. Toward the end of our Peace Corps tour in 1973, tensions between economic and social considerations were exacerbated when World Bank consultants completed pre-feasibility plans to build a Hydroelectric dam on the Chico River. The proposed dam was deemed economically feasible despite the negative social impact on the residents. The traditional leaders attempted to dialogue with government leaders. The tensions made way for the communist-inspired New People's Army to make inroads among the indigenous people. Activists protested, and some died in clashes with government forces. In the end, the project was shelved. This experience, although peripheral to our work as Peace Corps Volunteers, influenced my thinking about the need to balance economic considerations with social and environmental concerns in any development assistance.

In 1983–1987, I was back in the Philippines as a USAID Private Voluntary Organization (PVO) consultant to help PVOs meet USAID requirements and to assess competing proposals for implementation by non-governmental organizations. Some of the projects were for micro-enterprises promising financial success. However, there were unintended consequences often involving the environment. For example, income generating projects based on gold-plating fruit, flowers, and other organic materials for sale as jewelry used acid copper and nickel solution that were dumped on the ground. Some projects based on collecting aquarium fish used sodium cyanide to stun the fish. There appeared to be a lack of understanding or even a disregard for the long-term impact of this practice on human health and the coral reef, the natural habitat of the fish. The World Resources Institute estimated that in 1996, as much as 20% of the live fish traded in the Philippine market was caught using cyanide (Bale, 2016).

Working with USAID in the Philippines strengthened my problem-solving skills, ability to make timely and effective decisions, and ability to negotiate the use of time, roles, and resources with diverse individuals and groups. I expanded my understanding of the importance of the environment. I began to understand what it takes for leadership in sustainability.

As a visiting faculty member at Oregon State University in 1990–1992, I learned of the Rio Declaration on Environment and Development (United Nations, 1992). In 1993, I worked as the principal advisor for the program activities of the USAID Central Office of Environment and Natural Resources in Washington, DC, with special responsibility for ensuring that projects were consistent with US legislation. Responsibilities included compliance with Initial Environment Assessments and Social Assessments. This experience was helpful in my awareness of the relationship among the various stakeholders and their perception of sustainable development.

BUILDING PARTNERSHIPS, NETWORKS, AND ALLIANCES

In the section that follows, I highlight the leadership actions in three projects that I helped design and implement during my "third chapter." These are (1) the Knowledge Exchanges and Learning Partnerships (KELP) in South Africa, (2) the Network for Capacity Building in Telecommunications Policy and Regulation (NetTel@Africa) in Africa, and (3) the Afghan eQuality Alliances in Afghanistan. Policies related to access and use of ICTs were the common elements in these projects.

In January 1994, our arrival in South Africa for James' assignment with USAID was quickly followed by the release from prison of Nelson Mandela in early February, all-race elections in April, and Mandela's inauguration on May 10. Mandela declared at his inauguration that "Never, never again will this beautiful land experience the oppression of one by another."

For KELP and Nettel@Africa, the opening of the World Wide Web in 1990 and the deployment of the web browser, Mosaic, in 1993 significantly increased access to ICTs in Africa. The use of ICTs made it possible to form partnerships that were not limited to face-to-face interaction. In 1996, USAID launched the Leland Initiative to improve Internet connectivity in Africa.

I will only highlight leadership actions related to social networks in these projects where the elements of Drath's (1998) evolving construct of leadership were evident. The objective of my leadership was to articulate common goals, meanings, and promote reciprocal relations with numerous partners. The focus of leadership development was to develop interpersonal skills and self-awareness to improve group interactions.

Knowledge Exchanges and Learning Partnerships

The objective of KELP was to achieve significant improvements in South African postsecondary education institutions. The purpose was to build learning partnerships based not only on face-to-face interaction, but also on the appropriate use of ICTs, including the Internet, video-conferencing, and CD-ROM. KELP envisioned engagement between South African and American centers of learning instead of transfers of expertise. The process included a commitment to sharing and reciprocity, with partnerships defined by mutual respect. Measures to improve integration of technology and education included improved use of technology use by instructors, increased African content, and policies concerning global and online education.

The KELP set of operating principles were:

- South African-led

- mutual benefits for South African and American faculty and students;

- reciprocal relationships shifted from one-way technical assistance to two-way knowledge exchanges; and

- shared objectives that included (1) integration of ICT into learning and teaching to complement face-to-face teaching, (2) joint knowledge generation and transfer, (3) attention to sustainable development issues, and (4) dialogue on cross-listing of courses, shared syllabi, joint certificates, and joint degrees.

Network for Capacity Building in Telecommunications Policy and Regulation (NetTel)

In 2001, I was tasked by the USAID Leland Initiative to work with the Telecommunications Regulators Association of Southern Africa (TRASA) to assist with the development of a coordinated training and capacity building program in telecommunications at the regional level. The regulators recognized that no one institution had all the expertise required by the association. I suggested a stakeholder consultation as the first step. I suggested that if the stakeholders came up with a viable plan, then financial resources would be made available. If financial resources could not be made available, there was no point in stakeholder consultation. Engaging the stakeholders early on ensured that ownership and leadership would be exercised by those who wanted the assistance. Ownership was identified as one of the principles for aid effectiveness by the Paris Declaration of 2004. The capacity building program, as articulated by TRASA stakeholders would: be interdisciplinary, go beyond basic to advance knowledge, allow for certification, and include peer-to-peer exchanges.

The policy makers and regulators outlined the basic and advanced skills required to be a successful telecommunications regulator. The academic stakeholders outlined a list of training programs that met the basic requirements identified by the policy makers and regulators. Stakeholders then considered which African University had the beginning expertise to be the lead institution to develop content and teach online and which non-African partner would provide external expertise. While I led the process, I acted as a facilitator. We scheduled a day to articulate the problem, a second day to brainstorm existing and additional training programs and courses, and a third day to start formulating syllabi for 10 key courses. The fourth day was community building time when we hiked part way up Mt. Kilimanjaro. The project was funded for an initial seven African universities, three US universities, and TRASA. The Internet made it possible for me to orchestrate from a distance, for participants to work together, and for students from many universities to have faculty members from within and outside Africa. Face time was important so once a quarter faculty, regulators, and policy makers met to discuss critical topics in policy and regulation after which the venue was rotated among the country regulators and the academic partners.

Afghan eQuality Alliances

My work with these USAID-funded activities in Africa was cut short by my unexpected involvement in Afghanistan. What I knew about Afghanistan I had learned from the news. Afghanistan was not on my radar until a

USAID colleague asked me to do a preliminary stakeholder consultation in Kabul in 2005. Thinking nobody would be excited about ICTs for higher education in the middle of a war, I agreed to visit Afghanistan. My first meeting was with the then President of Kabul University, Dr Ashraf Ghani. He had worked with the World Bank, and in 2014, he would be elected President of Afghanistan. During the first 5 minutes of our initial meeting, he said, "Distance learning. E-learning. Online education. That is what we need." And, with that, I was "called" to service in Afghanistan.

Lessons learned from organizing and leading the KELP in South Africa and Network for Capacity Building in the Telecommunications Sector in Africa (NetTel) were useful in designing and implementing the Afghan eQuality Alliances. The Afghan eQuality Alliances was a USAID-funded project implemented by Washington State University. The Afghan eQuality Alliances included leaders and stakeholders who shared a common goal of building capacity in higher education. By complementing each other's strengths, the institutions could achieve results beyond what any single organization could realize alone. Alliance partners came from within Afghanistan and included higher education institutions from the US, India, Japan, Europe, and Africa. The geographic distances and multiple time zones necessitated the use of electronic technologies for collaboration. Stakeholders recognized that institutions had varying capabilities and commitments but shared the goal of improving higher education in Afghanistan. The Paris Declaration encouraged finding better ways of working together. However, working together did not have the same meaning even within the same organization. I reported (Beebe, 2015) finding it useful to talk about ways of working together similar to those identified by Mandell (2003) emphasizing the need for different leadership styles and communication. These include networking, coordination, cooperation, and collaboration.

Networking for dialogue required exchanging information and creating a common understanding. These networks have loosely defined roles with low-key leadership, minimal decision-making, and informal communication. An Afghan example of networking was an informal donor group convened by the World Bank that met sporadically to share information about the use of ICTs.

Coordination required exchanging information, with partners implementing specific activities, facilitating leadership, and communicating formally. Coordination resulted in different levels of computer education to improve the use of ICTs and resulted in the Ministry of Higher Education chairing a working group, to facilitate the work of NATO to provide bandwidth for higher education institutions, and to review the activities and results of the training providers, including the Cisco Networking Academy, Technical University Berlin, and the Afghans Next Generation e-Learning Centers (ANGEL) of the Afghan eQuality Alliances.

Cooperation required sharing resources among partners. An engineering alliance composed of different universities from abroad worked with several Afghan universities on upgrading the engineering curriculum. This type of cooperation required shared leadership among the different teams involved in the activity.

Collaboration required the exchange of information, joint implementation of activities, sharing of resources, and capacity building of local organizations. To implement an executive master's degree program at the government-funded Kabul University, the curriculum and many of its instructors were initially provided by foreign partners but with increasing responsibility transferred to Afghans over the life of the project. Afghan faculty had to be trained and mentored in the use of the new curriculum.

Not all participants made a distinction between the different ways of working together to achieve the shared goal of improving higher education. One source of tension was when an alliance partner demanded approvals of actions when all that was sought was the sharing of information about actions. My leadership consisted of being low-key, facilitative, and collaborative. Sometimes my role was that of a translator and cultural informant for concepts that were often equally new for Afghans and non-Afghans or that of a referee in a game where the players and the rules seemed to be constantly in flux.

REFLECTIONS ON MY LEADERSHIP JOURNEY

Over time, I graduated from being affectionately called a sister, to auntie, to mother, to grandmother. Each term of endearment had gender roles and gender relations connotations. By the time I started working in Afghanistan, I had fallen into the grandmother category. In a country where female life expectancy was 46 years in 2006, I had passed the age of 50, and I was accorded respect. The intersection of gender and age, along with my

"Doctor" and "Professor" titles opened doors. And perhaps, because I looked like I might be from Afghanistan, I had a foot in the door but this also carried risks.

When I was growing up, I assumed there was gender equality. Gender practices around the world, particularly in Afghanistan, made me rethink the necessity of the sustainable development goals of the United Nations (2015). In DISRUPT 1 (2015) and DISRUPT 2.0 (2016), I edited stories by Filipina women who engaged in the struggle for gender equality. For the Filipina Women's Network (FWN) leadership summit in 2017, I organized a panel on sustainable development goals by exploring how Filipina leaders help to transform the world. Even after I stopped traveling to Afghanistan, I continued to work on website projects and other activities that used ICTs to empower Afghan women. Recently, I have promoted the use of ICTs in Central Asia and South Asia. In the US, my adopted home, the last elections shed light on the un-equal access to education, health care, decent work, and representation by immigrant women as well as by rural, working class, and poor women.

Upon reflection on my leadership journey, there was not one point when I recognized I was a leader. My leadership story is an accumulation of experience and growing realization of my ability to influence others. Being told I was smart and popular, being elected to student council, and being tapped for student plays were all positive influences. Receiving excellent performance reviews as a personal services contractor, project manager, program coordinator, consultant, and team director developed a sense of self-confidence. I developed competence in generic management and leadership tasks. Equally important was developing relational leadership competence such as coaching, collaborating, supervising, and managing conflict. Moreover, I strengthened my cross-cultural skills for networking. Yet, I was unable to name or own my leadership until I took a 1997 graduate course in leadership theory. The course helped me realize I was demonstrating and utilizing leadership skills without calling it leadership and without announcing "I am a leader." In retrospect, it might have helped if I had recognized early on that it was not enough to be good at what I was doing but I needed to be intentional about my role. I concluded I was a leader even as I continued to expand my leadership repertoire.

REFERENCES

Bale, R. (2016). The horrific way fish are caught for your aquarium—with cyanide. *National Geographic*, 10 March. Retrieved from https://news.nationalgeographic.com/2016/03/160310-aquarium-saltwater-tropical-fish-cyanide-coral-reefs/

Beebe, M. A. (2015). Harmonizing global teams in Afghanistan. In M. A. Beebe & M. O. Escudero (Eds.), *DISRUPT: Filipina women. Proud. Loud. Leading without a doubt* (pp. 279–297). Philippines: Filipina Women's Network.

Beebe, M. A. (2016). Developing an international leadership repertoire. In M. A. Beebe (Ed.), *DISRUPT 2.0. Filipina women: Daring to lead* (pp. 349–364). San Francisco, CA: Filipina Women's Network.

Beebe, M. A. (2017). The leadership repertoire of select Filipina women in the Diaspora and implications for theorizing leadership. In J. Storberg-Walker & P. Haber-Curran (Eds.), *Theorizing women and leadership: New insights and contributions from multiple perspectives* (pp. 163–182). Charlotte, NC: Information Age Publishing.

Drath, W. K. (1998). Approaching the future of leadership development. In C. D. McCauley, R. S. Moxley, & E. Van Velsor (Eds.), *The center for creative leadership: Handbook of leadership development* (pp. 403–432). San Francisco, CA: Jossey-Bass.

Fan, S., Liberman, Z., Keysar, B., & Kinzler, C. (2015). The exposure advantage: Early exposure to a multilingual environment promotes effective communication. *Psychological Science*, 26(7), 1090–1097. doi:10.1177/0956797615574699

George, B. (2016). The truth about authentic leaders. Working knowledge: Business research for business leaders. Harvard Business School. Retrieved from https://hbswk.hbs.edu/item/the-truth-about-authentic-leaders

Lawrence-Lightfoot, S. (2009). *The third chapter: Passion, risk, and adventure in the 25 years after 50*. New York, NY: Sarah Crichton Books.

Mandell, M. P. (2003). Types of collaborations and why the differences really matter. *The Public Manager*, 31(4), 36–40.

Njunguri, F., Almquist, J., Beebe, M., Elbert, C. D., Gardiner, R. A., & Shockness, M. (2017). Intersectional leadership praxis: Unpacking the experiences of Women leaders at the nexus of roles and identities. In J. Walker & P. Haber-Curran (Eds.), *Theorizing women and leadership: New insights and contributions from multiple perspectives. Women and leadership book series* (pp. 249–264). Charlotte, NC: Information Age Publishing, Inc.

Stevens, M. J., Bird, A., Mendenhall, M. E., & Oddou, G. (2014). Measuring global leader intercultural competency: Development and validation of the global competencies inventory (GCI). In J. Osland, M. Li, & Y. Wang (Eds.), *Advances in global leadership* (8th ed., pp. 99–138). Bingley: Emerald.

United Nations. (1992). Rio declaration on environment and development. (Annex 1). Report of the United Nations conference on environment and development. Retrieved from http://www.un.org/documents/ga/conf151/aconf15126-1annex1.htm

United Nations. (2015). Sustainable development goals. Retrieved from http://www.un.org/sustainabledevelopment/development-agenda/

15

AN EDUCATOR'S BACKWARD, FORWARD ZIGZAG LEADERSHIP JOURNEY

Patricia McLaughlin

INTRODUCTION

It was not a desire to lead, but rather a desire to serve that eventually led me into leadership. As a recent college graduate needing a job I accepted an offer to teach at a state school for the deaf, eventually transitioning into work with early childhood children with disabilities. While I related well to students with diagnosed disabilities, those with undiagnosed challenges had a special place in my heart, because I had struggled through childhood with an ambling gait that concerned my mother and caused me to increasingly struggle with sports and exercise activities in school. Observing these students with undiagnosed challenges I empathized as I remembered how it felt to do my best, but it never seemed sufficient, and I remembered how grateful I was to learn I had been doing my best. It was just that my best was within the limits of bilateral congenital hip dysplasia.

Knowing how important it had been for me to know what I was coping with, I made it my mission to be especially supportive of children with undiagnosed challenges. Ironically, where I encountered the most resistance was from school leaders and I became frustrated as the excuses they offered frequently implied prejudices I did not share. These experiences eventually led me out of the classroom. I wanted to influence policy and the practice of

carrying out policy. Most importantly, I came forward with a sense of purpose. I wanted to improve the human condition.

My career has remained centered in the education sector, initially in the
United States, and more recently in Africa. Although my leadership career, if
one subscribes to leadership "as a process whereby an individual influences
a group of individuals to achieve a common goal" (Northouse, 2016), has
been underway over three decades, this chapter focuses on recent leadership
roles I have had in international development and private K-12 international
education in Africa.

K-12 PUBLIC EDUCATION REFORM: EGYPT

One of the key opportunities to exercise my leadership was afforded in
Egypt with my participation as a consultant in the School Team Excellence
Awards Program (STEAP), implemented by the United States Agency for
International Development (USAID), to support the launch of a school
accreditation system for Egypt Ministry Of Education's (MOE) 16,000 primary and secondary public schools (Hunt et al., 2010). STEAP operated a
monetary incentive program to motivate school leaders and stakeholders to
embrace the newly developed National Education Standards (NES) as preparation for the new school accreditation system planned for MOE schools.
Prior to working on STEAP I had already led programs or initiatives in curriculum design, professional development, IT, special education, early childhood education, and elementary education, and I had worked as a leader
and/or teacher across all grade levels (K-12). Through these experiences
I gained knowledge of Middle States Association (MSA) and Council of
International Schools (CIS) school accreditation protocols. STEAP engaged
me in December 2006, as a consultant, because I brought technical expertise
they needed, as it was not present within the STEAP team.

My two primary deliverables were to create an accreditation protocol-
based on Egypt's NES that aligned with international school accreditation
standards and a protocol for conducting accreditation school site visits,
which served as the framework for STEAP's *Site Visit Guide to Evaluate
Egypt's Schools for Quality*. Developing the accreditation protocol deliverable was a multistep process, commencing with a comparative analysis of
NES with the MSA and CIS accreditation protocols, which informed

development of the accreditation standards, descriptive indicators for each standard, and evidence list for each descriptive indicator.

After my work with STEAP I reflected on how the varied experiences I had had prior to my work with STEAP had contributed to my success in developing the accreditation standards and protocols for STEAP. My leadership journey, which had often felt as if it was moving forward only to feel as if it was moving backward, as I transitioned from one specialization in education to another, now made sense. I could see it had equipped me with a uniquely broad, yet balanced, set of knowledge and skills that had not only enabled me to deconstruct and analyze Egypt's education standards and then reconstruct and organize them into a cohesive accreditation framework, but it had also equipped me for more senior level leadership roles than what I had previously thought. I had developed a broad field of vision that gave me the ability to view the whole of an organization, and because of my work in the various parts that made up the whole I understood how to organize and synchronize the parts.

K-12 PUBLIC EDUCATION REFORM: QATAR

Like many developing countries in the 1970s and 1980s, Qatar focused, primarily, on quantity of schools to ensure access to education, rather than on the quality of learning outcomes (Nasser, 2017). As the new century arrived Qatar leaders established progressive economic and social goals for Qatar but were not convinced their public education system could produce graduates capable of fulfilling those goals. To assess their existing public education system and offer education reform options Qatar leaders engaged RAND Corporation, an American nonprofit research and policy development institution, which recommended a standards-based system with curriculum standards designed to produce the desired learning outcomes; an assessment system to measure improvement of learning outcomes; and a professional development system for educators that would prepare them to produce the desired learning outcomes (Brewer et al., 2007). To implement the new standards-based system Qatar decided to convert Qatar's Ministry of Education (MOE) schools into independent schools, which emulated the American charter school model. To oversee the school conversion, Qatar created the Supreme Education Council (SEC), which opened in 2002.

The SEC contracted with foreign technical implementing organizations to staff and manage *School Support Organizations* (SSOs) to support each independent school's first year of operation. Each SSO, comprised of curriculum specialists for English, Math, and Science and a translator, was led by a school management advisor (SMA). In addition to leading the SSO team, SMAs core responsibilities were providing school board training, as well as mentoring the onsite school leadership team. The SSO team I led was assigned to a boys' primary school with a female staff led by a team of three Qatari women. I completed the last six months of a SSO contract another SMA had begun. By the time I arrived SSO team members were well underway completing their assigned deliverables and required minimal oversight, and as such I approached my team leader role collaboratively, supporting and guiding when required, but giving them space to get on with their work.

My engagement with the school in Qatar was similar in length to my engagement with STEAP, but my sense of accomplishment differed significantly. With STEAP I knew I had made a meaningful contribution, but with the school in Qatar I felt my one singular accomplishment was I had "ticked all the boxes." My approach to mentoring the school's leadership team, which I had applied successfully in previous competency-based leadership roles, was to come alongside team members to counsel and advise, but with this leadership team I experienced mixed results, which puzzled me at the time. Today I suspect one reason for this is that these three women had not come, yet, to own their leader identity. Oftentimes I felt as if I was back in the drama center of my early childhood classroom where children explored identities through role play. These women were wearing their "leadership costume" but had not yet embraced the role. As a result, I suspect they were not sure what to do with the help I offered. Another reason may have been my strong personality, which translates into a strong presence, which may have caused them to withdraw to within themselves. Perhaps, had I been aware then of my strong personality I could have been more effective.

K-12 PUBLIC EDUCATION REFORM: EGYPT

The USAID funded Girls Improved Learning Outcomes (GILO) was designed to be a three-year program serving underserved communities in four governorates to support elements of Egypt MOE's National Strategic

Plan for Pre-University Education Reform (Nielsen, 2013). In December 2008, GILO engaged me as a consultant to support the design of a professional development program aimed at strengthening school management. Working with the Egyptian technical advisor responsible for implementing the program, I advised on framework content while the technical advisor focused on practicalities of implementing it. As my consultancy was concluding I learned of a GILO initiative underway that would evolve into GILO's most recognized accomplishment and would lead me back to GILO two years later.

At the invitation of GILO, and with their support, Egypt MOE adapted the Early Grade Reading Assessment (EGRA) into Arabic and then conducted a pilot of EGRA in the spring of 2009. EGRA results, which embarrassed MOE leadership, led the MOE to ask GILO to help them develop an intervention program to address deficiencies exposed by the EGRA pilot. The intervention program, which became known as the Early Grade Reading Program (EGRP), consisted of teacher training modules and an array of instructional materials, such as EGRP teachers' manuals and flip charts (Nielsen, 2013). It was developed during the 2009/2010 school year, and piloted during the 2010/2011 school year, in the same primary schools where the EGRA 2009 had been administered.

EGRA was administered again in spring 2011 in the pilot schools where EGRA was administered in 2009, and in a set of control schools. EGRA 2011 results revealed that, even with Egypt's public schools closed for several weeks during the 2010/2011 school year because of the Arab Spring Uprising, students in pilot schools had made significant progress, compared to students in control schools. With EGRP's efficacy affirmed, MOE leadership decided to go to nationwide scale with EGRP, with GILO technical support. Within the span of one school year (2011–2012) all grade one teachers in Egypt received EGRP training and all primary schools received EGRP instructional materials.

As the MOE finalized scale-up plans, GILO engaged me to analyze results of a textbook analysis the MOE had conducted several months earlier. My analysis revealed reading textbooks were contributing to students' poor reading skills. For example, there were not enough repetitions of newly introduced words to facilitate student retention of new words, and there were too many multisyllabic words for beginning readers. The technical report I produced, published with the GILO/USAID imprint, remained posted on MOE website for the duration of the scale-up and referenced often in the scale-up discourse. A few weeks later I joined the GILO team as teacher professional development (TPD) director to support the scale-up, reporting to the Chief of Party. The TPD team consisted of five TPD advisors and four TPD specialists who had supported the EGRP pilot. The advisors were PhD qualified Egyptian educators, and the specialists were degree qualified Egyptian teachers. The TPD team members knew what needed to be done and how to get the work done, and as such my approach to leading the team was collaborative. I kept the team organized, focused, and synchronized so that TPD's role in supporting the scale-up happened how it should, when it should.

To keep TPD team members in sync I held monthly meetings in the GILO office, reviewing the previous month's work and planning the next month's work. While all of the TPD team members spoke English, to varying degrees, I engaged a translator to work alongside me in the team meetings, as my Arabic skills were not sufficient to conduct the meetings in Arabic. My approach to leading the meetings was to offer an observation or ask a question in English that was translated into Arabic, after which the team discussed, in Arabic, whatever issue I raised, with the translator simultaneously translating their conversation into English for me to follow the discussion. Initially I had tried to conduct meetings in English, but I observed that doing so was slowing down the process of arriving at solutions. With the translator our discussions became more productive.

When the Uprising erupted in January 2011, I had lived in Egypt more than six years and I understood what led Egyptians into the streets, and having sheltered-in-place during the Uprising, I had developed a nuanced perspective that other expatriates often did not have which continues, even today, to help me relate to Egyptians. The Uprising had brought about a roller coaster of emotions. First there was euphoria, then there was angst, and then there was anger. My experience riding this roller coaster helped me relate to the TPD team as unsettling events occurred. For example, just weeks after I began work at GILO Egyptian military tanks rolled over and killed more than two-dozen unarmed demonstrators in downtown Cairo. The next morning TPD team members came by my office, each in a state of shock. I was honored they felt comfortable sharing their grief, and their embarrassment about what Egypt's leadership had done. They knew I could empathize instead of simply sympathize with them. Like them I was frustrated and saddened, to see young people that had come out in the weeks after the Uprising sprucing up public parks, cleaning up public spaces, and painting curbs only to recede, out of fear of an unknown future, into the background. I had seen the change from jubilation to tribulation and I knew these uncertainties preyed on the minds of TPD team members.

My understanding of the political, social, and economic issues at play in Egypt helped me appreciate what team members were experiencing. Politically, there was considerable uncertainty. The Supreme Council of the Armed Forces (SCAF) was managing the country but, in the shadows of Mubarak's downfall, they were reluctant leaders, at least publicly. No one quite knew what would happen next. Socially, after diverse groups had joined together in Tahrir Square, they fragmented as the months went by. The Salafists, whose religious practices are derived from the Wahhabists of Saudi Arabia, had lived and worked in the shadows before the Uprising, but afterward they seemed to be everywhere. My husband and I watched this unfold in the months after the Uprising when a mosque across the street from our apartment building suddenly overflowed with Salafists. All of these things were unsettling to people, as these were outcomes that had not been anticipated, and many did not want. In conversations with TPD team members I could listen, and I could respond with more than passing "tourist" knowledge of the issues, which helped me relate with TPD team members and their concerns.

PRIVATE K-12 INTERNATIONAL EDUCATION

An outcome of my post-STEAP reflections was that I came to realize I am most satisfied when leading organizational change, whether revitalizing an existing organization or launching a new organization. In this section I will discuss my two most recent leadership roles, which have been head of school roles, leading change in both.

East Africa

Three weeks before my demobilization with GILO, a faith-based international school in East Africa reached out to me to explore my interest in joining their leadership team. While the position offered, deputy head of school, was not what I aspired for after GILO, I felt a sense of calling to accept. Someone capable of launching a learning support program for students with learning challenges was needed and that tugged at my heart, but perhaps the strongest tug was the frequently made comment from the head of school that, "I could learn so much from you." I had had a mentor that had groomed me for leadership and as I became increasingly aware of the impact that mentoring had had on my leadership development I became increasingly committed to being a mentor to those coming behind me. I had come to understand that when I can impact a leader's development I can impact the development of many others.

Unfortunately, this young leader was stuck in the "hero" phase of his leader development. He was not ready to collaboratively lead, nor learn. While disappointed, I went about launching the learning support program, and crafting the school's response to recommendations from the recent MSA accreditation team visit. With time I observed that, frequently, people had been assigned roles, and processes had been put in place, as a result of ad hoc decisions made in response to an immediate need, rather than strategically thought through. Perhaps most troubling was a blurring of lines of authority between the head of school and a specialist teacher. Wittingly, or unwittingly, the head of school had conveyed to this teacher significant informal power. By the time I arrived, this specialist teacher was the de factor deputy head of school.

Academically, the school was strongest at the elementary level, which the recent MSA accreditation team had noted, resulting in their recommendation the school strengthen its secondary program, in part by broadening the array of courses offered, which meant restructuring the school's schedule. As I continued my observations, I fell back on the broad, yet balanced, set of knowledge and skills that my backward, forward, zigzag leadership journey had equipped me with to develop a plan for reorganizing and revitalizing the school.

As the contours of the plan coalesced, the head of school announced he was leaving at the end of the school year. He had arrived four years earlier, two years after its founding, with the school on the brink of collapse in the aftermath of a walkout of the entire expatriate faculty, and in those four years he had brought it back from the brink and led it through the MSA accreditation process. But, his brusque leadership style, penchant for favoritism, and nonstrategic decision-making, had alienated stakeholders. While he was not forced out through contract nonrenewal, he was in effect forced out as he came to realize he had lost stakeholders' trust.

The board moved quickly to launch a head of school search. By the time I interviewed with them just before Christmas break I had a plan for bringing structure, processes, and systems to the school that addressed the school's most pressing needs. Soon after my second interview in early January I was appointed head of school for the following school year, but tasked, effective immediately, with sole responsibility for preparations for the following school year with the outgoing head of school responsible for day-to-day management of the current school year. While this type of leadership transition is not especially unusual when promoting from within, in this situation it created instant angst with the outgoing head of school, as he knew he could no longer protect favorites.

Immediately I began restructuring the school's schedule to accommodate more course options, which required reducing the number of periods per week the "special" specialist teacher taught. After three lengthy meetings with the teacher it was evident that, even though he knew renewal of his contract was at stake, he was unwilling to bend, having become accustomed to having his way. The day after he received notice his contract would not be renewed, he tearfully informed every class I had fired him.

A backlash quickly evolved in the parent community, to pressure the board to overturn my decision, but the board remained steadfast in their support. Repeatedly, for many weeks, at the required staff prayer and devotion gatherings, the head of school implied I had erred. These public exhortations were an attempt to provoke me to defend my decision, but I knew doing so would not be beneficial for me, my leadership, or the school and I remained silent. As a leader I had begun to grasp the importance, strategically, of choosing when to speak and when to remain silent. In this instance my silence spoke more powerfully than any argument I could offer.

Through this experience I realized my leader legitimacy is derived from my trustworthiness. Trustworthiness has always been important to me and as I grew into leadership I learned trust has two dimensions, competence and character. I came to understand the board trusted my competence, because they perceived my decision had been well thought out, based on fact and sound analysis. And, I came to understand the board trusted my character. They knew that because I had remained committed to my decision in the midst of the backlash, that their trust in me, manifested in their public backing of me, would not be betrayed, as it would have been had I succumbed to the backlash. This proved to be a defining moment in my leadership journey.

Looking toward my second year I knew building an effective leadership team was critical, and as I contemplated possibilities an experienced American teacher that had served in the country several years as a missionary alongside her husband, approached me about working at the school, as she was completing her master's degree in educational leadership and needed a position that would enable her to complete her required leadership practicum. She impressed me and I offered her the deputy director position. At first, she was taken aback that I saw that potential in her, but then she accepted the offer and worked hard to prove my judgment correct. I mentored her with the goal that she would be prepared to lead the school in my absence and, if the school board desired, to be able lead the school after I left. When I notified the board I would not return for a third year, they immediately approached the deputy director about succeeding me, as they could see she was prepared and capable.

While not by design, the leadership team I recruited was a multigenerational all-female team and it worked well together, which I believe was because of a shared sense of purpose, everyone wanted the school to reach its full potential. Collegiality came easy, because, with everyone at a different place in their leadership journey, there was no competition. Through weekly team meetings we addressed immediate needs related to school operations, and we remained focused on long-term issues that would position the school for growth.

With a capable leadership team handling day-to-day operations, I turned my attention to addressing expatriate staff retention and revising the school's business model. Working collaboratively with the leadership team a new remuneration plan was developed and subsequently approved by the school board, which resulted in the highest expatriate retention rate in the school's history.

As I began to fully embrace my executive leadership identity I began paying more attention to the nuances of leading than before. For example, at GILO I had revised my approach for leading team meetings, primarily to accommodate the unique needs of the language challenges that slowed the team's discussion. That approach proved beneficial, as I discovered discussions were richer than when I led discussions, as my comments as a leader had often cued staff members to my thinking, which, whether intentional or not, often skewed how staff would respond. Commencing with this school leadership team I began fine-tuning that approach. I tasked the deputy director with leading team meetings, which helped me focus on the issues, and as I did I noticed that by listening more, and by strategically choosing when to speak, my comments had maximum effect. I learned I got the best of the team this way, and even better, they were empowered and had ownership in the decisions and outcomes.

Two years after I left the school, it was rewarding to learn the school's finances had stabilized such that it was able to build a multiclassroom extension and that the academic program had strengthened such that enrollment had increased 50%.

NORTH AFRICA

When I accepted the offer to serve as the founding executive director of a new American curriculum international school in Egypt in early February 2015, it was seven months, almost to the day, until the school would open its doors for the first time. The school facility was still under construction; curriculum guides needed to be developed and written; school information management system selected, installed, and implemented; operational and academic policies written; school schedules created; student handbooks and staff handbooks written, and a full complement of administrative, support, and academic staff needed to be recruited and on-boarded in time for the opening of school on September 2. It was not supposed to be this way.

Several years earlier the owner family had engaged a school management organization headquartered in Dubai that, with their established protocols, provides client school owners turn-key school development and management services. This organization operated in multiple countries, with in-country consultants available to advise client school owners. In Egypt, the consultant held a degree in business administration from Cairo University. She had worked with the owner family for several years, from market research to site planning, until September 2014, when the organization decided to withdraw from Egypt's private school market. The organization offered the consultant a severance package with the stipulation she would forfeit it if she maintained contact with Egyptian clients and informed them of the withdrawal.

Suddenly, the owner family was without support, with the school's opening less than a year away. The family scrambled to find a way forward. More than two months later they found a consulting group to help them, who subsequently reached out to me, knowing I was living in Egypt. My initial meeting with the family was just before New Year's Day 2015.

From the moment, I met the owners I was impressed. Unlike so many private school owners, who view their school simply as a business, it was evident they were intent on doing good for their country and its people, while doing well for themselves. They owned other schools in Cairo, but this would be their first international school and they wanted it to become one of the leading international schools in Cairo, and they were willing to invest to ensure the resources were available. Said simply, they wanted a school of quality, knowing that quality would lead to quantity, of students and revenue, and from day one I sought to position the school in the marketplace accordingly. For example, while under considerable pressure to lower teacher qualifications standards, I remained firm that we must have expatriate teachers qualified to teach the American curriculum. Seven months after I became executive director the school opened with a qualified expatriate teacher in every classroom and every classroom at full capacity, save one seat in one classroom filled during the first week of school. When the school opened admissions for its second year, midway through its first year, its reputation was such that it was attracting students from the top American international schools. The school's parents recommended it to others, referring to it as one of the top five international schools.

My memories of this leadership experience are bittersweet. It was a daunting undertaking, but I thrive on challenges. I loved the school and its people and I had a vision for its future. Then, midway through the first year of operation a choice the board chairman made scrambled my feelings and dissolved my commitment. The owner family consisted of three family members, a father, whose father had opened one of the first five private schools in Egypt, a son, and a daughter. The young, 30-something-year-old son, with a recently earned MBA degree, was the board chairman. He was anxiety-prone, desperately wanting the school to be successful, and be viewed as such by his father. My first day on the job he asked me to speak with him as if he were my son.

Terms of my work agreement were that I had full authority for the school with all employees subordinate to my position. Throughout the fall months following the school's opening I searched for a business and operations deputy director, without productive results. In a meeting with the board chairman this frustrating search came up. He asked if I might want to consider the Egyptian consultant that had worked with them. After she received her severance package, she had contacted the board chairman, resulting in her working part time as we prepared for the school's opening. I found the idea intriguing and when asked if I would like him to approach her, I agreed. A few weeks later, I understood an agreement had been reached, but then, just prior to my departure for a short trip to the US I learned one last detail needed to be discussed. Upon my return, I learned that, in my absence and without consultation with me, he was persuaded to change the terms of my work agreement resulting in the deputy director, reporting directly to him, instead of to me. With time I came to see that this young, anxiety-prone, board chairman had been manipulated, but in that moment, all I could see was betrayal, and I felt diminished. I talked with him about the changes and asked they be reversed, but my efforts to persuade were not successful. His decision was not good for me nor for the school. I knew I needed to persist in my efforts to persuade him, but something within kept me constrained. Disheartened I gave notice I would leave when the school year ended.

Even after leaving the school I remained unsatisfied with myself. I had let myself down, and the school, by not persistently pursuing reversal of his decision and I kept reflecting on my life trying to figure out why. I had been in this situation once before as elementary school principal and I knew if I was going to continue my leadership ascent I needed to understand why I struggled to speak up when ill-treated. Finally, one day I understood. From my earliest memories my father made denigrating, caustic comments, and if someone dared respond, his retort was "I have never done anything I have needed to apologize for!" Feelings were left raw and unattended. With time I "learned" to remain silent when ill-treated. Intellectually, I knew I was entitled to assert myself but there had always been an internal unease acting as a restraint. It is difficult to express how powerfully this invisible prison affected me. It was just there, binding me, restricting me, and impairing my effectiveness.

CLOSING COMMENTS

Among the most valuable leadership lessons I have learned is the importance of self-awareness and self-reflection. Awareness of how I am perceived by others helps me relate effectively and knowing what gives purpose to my work helps me find joy in it. Reflection helps me find answers buried within me.

REFERENCES

Brewer, D. J., Augustine, C. H., Zellman, G. L., Ryan, G., Goldman, C. A., Stasz, C., & Constant, L. (2007). *Education for a new era: Design and implementation of K-12 education reform in Qatar* (pp. 1–13). Santa Monica, CA: RAND Corporation.

Hunt, B., Dye, R., Abreu-Combs, A., Said El, M., Nasrallah, A., & Fahmy, A. S. (2010). *USAID/Egypt education portfolio evaluation* (pp. 1–98). United States Agency for International Development, Egypt Mission.

Nasser, R. (2017). Qatar's educational reform past and future: Challenges in teacher development. *Open Review of Educational Research*, 4(1), 1–19. doi:10.1080/23265507.2016.1266693

Nielsen, H. D. (2013). *Going to scale: The early grade reading program in Egypt: 2008-2012* (pp. 1–44). Washington DC: United States Agency for International Development.

Northouse, P. G. (2016). *Leadership: Theory and practice* (7th ed.). Los Angeles, CA: SAGE.

16

LEADING RECOVERY FOR WOMEN AND CHILDREN IN POST-CEAUSESCU ROMANIA

Randal Joy Thompson

I never thought of myself as a leader in international development until I went to Romania and became the Director of the Health and Social Welfare Office of the United States Agency for International Development (USAID). Leadership was not a commonly used term in USAID. We were "managers." As managers, we implemented US government policy; we implemented development projects that had been meticulously designed, with or without the input of recipient country beneficiaries, according to pre-set plans, milestones, deliverables, and results; and we reported our successes to Congress. In USAID, we managed private sector implementers who had bid on and won our government contracts to implement projects we had designed and competed. I had stretched the boundaries of management as far as I could in Cameroon by organizing participatory evaluations with Cameroonian officials, at the time an innovative approach; and by insisting on stakeholder buy-in in the projects I helped design in Morocco. My major fieldwork had been working with the Moroccan military and flying with soldier-of-fortune pilots to fight the locust plague crossing the Atlas Mountains and threatening to destroy the food supply of the country.

In Romania in 1995, the situation was different. Recovering from the brutal reign of Ceausescu, Romania was in the limelight. The travesty of from

100,000 to 170,000 children in approximately 700 appalling institutions and the highest number of children infected by HIV/AIDs in all of Europe had created international outrage (Dickens & Groza, 2004; Greenwell, 2001; UNICEF, 2004; World Bank & UNICEF, 2014). Hundreds of groups had poured into Romania to cover the crisis and to either help or exploit the situation. Even the wives of the Beatles teamed with Elton John to create the Romanian Angel Fund and market an album *Nobody's Child* to help alleviate the suffering of the children (Hochman, 1990). Further, the horror story of women being denied contraception during Ceausescu's "reign," and the botched illegal abortions, imprisonments, and deaths had caused a public outcry. My leadership was mandated by this situation. I needed: to help create a vision for our program; to put together a cohesive, dynamic, and knowledgeable team who could design the program to achieve the vision; to inspire and empower change agents throughout the existing system to join us in a journey of major transformation; to form close relationships and alliances; and to maintain the perseverance and passion to address resistance and inertia and to influence individuals who could remove stumbling blocks along the way. Establishing my credibility, honoring the professionalism and excellence of our team and stakeholders, and engendering trust were essential to our success.

When I arrived in Bucharest in 1995, there were hundreds of organizations already working in Romania to improve conditions at the children's institutions. Moreover, international adoption agencies had already arrived in force and there reportedly already were about 10,000 children who had been adopted since 1990, representing one-third of all children adopted internationally (Rusi, Parris, Cross, Purvis, & Draghici, 2011). Working initially in "the period of the quick fix" and then "the period of unfocused and contradictory reform" (Rusi et al., 2011), organizations there to help were uncoordinated, driven by different intentions and different strategies, and focused on either removing children from their tragic conditions in this "terrible" country or easing their difficult lives in institutions.

As director of USAID's office in a country that wanted to join NATO and hence listened to the United States as well as having a significant budget to address a challenge that had received high-level interest in the US as well as in other countries, I had considerable positional leadership authority. I represented the USG's policy toward women and children. European donors, the United Nations Children's Fund (UNICEF) and the United

Nations Population Fund (UNFPA) were also deeply involved in these issues as was the European Union (EU) who made improvements in the conditions of institutionalized children a criteria for Romania joining the EU. Although I had positional leadership, I was not an expert in either women's health or child welfare. So, my first challenge was to build a team of experts in these areas. Fortunately, there was a US professor of social work on a Fulbright teaching fellowship working to establish the first social worker university degree program in Romania who joined our team after her fellowship ended. She was joined by another American professor of social work and a year later another social worker with many years of experience working in a US government agency. I practiced collaborative and inclusive leadership as they helped me develop policies and a program and educated me about the latest thinking vis-a-vis caring for abandoned children and children in need of protection. They coached me to become an "expert" quickly so that I could have the stature necessary to speak with authority to Romanian officials.

The American physician who held my position before me had established the foundations for a comprehensive women's health strategy. I expanded the strategy and also helped to develop a women's coalition comprised of influential Romanian leaders of NGOs and government agencies, and later helped to develop a health system transformation strategy. I eventually was able to hire another American health expert as well as a Romanian physician and Romanian social worker who had just graduated from the social work university degree program to help implement our program. Social work as a profession had been erased in the 1960s as part of Ceausescu's concept of the "Master State" that would manage all aspects of life. Our core USAID team worked closely with the child welfare and health organizations implementing USAID-funded projects, including International Nongovernmental Organizations (INGOs), US private sector development consulting companies, Romanian NGOs, UNICEF, and the US Department of Health and Human Services.[1] Because of the international attention Romania was receiving and because of the close scrutiny of the US Congress and particular Congresswomen on the child welfare issue, we were under exceptional oversight. Further, because of the international outcry and our own sense of responsibility to improve conditions, we were driven by a special "calling" that may not be typical in international development. Our calling infused our leadership with passion and determination that we were going to make a difference in the lives of Romanian women and children. Our passion helped us influence and inspire other stakeholders to join the "cause."

The USAID program prior to my arrival had funded innovative care models for the physical, psychological, and social rehabilitation services for children at risk and in institutions; teams of American volunteer orthopedic, plastic, ear-nose-throat, and ophthalmologic surgeons and nurses to help disabled children; support to the Romanian Adoption Committee so that children's rights could be protected; institutional staff training in new care protocols; and capacity building for Romanian NGOs. Our team quickly realized that although these services had been necessary to address the emergency situation facing Romania, we needed to facilitate a major child welfare system transformation. We offered technical assistance during this time to the National Committee for Child Protection and along with others influenced the emergence of new child welfare programs as well as helping both the governments of Romania and the US realize that "systemic child welfare reform was necessary" (Correll et al., 2006, p. ix).

The child protection system was centrally run by five different government institutions. Children aged from age zero to three years were placed in Infant Homes under the Ministry of Health and hence received medicalized treatment. Children aged from 3 to 18 years were moved to Children Homes managed by the Ministry of Education or to institutions for children with severe disabilities run by the Ministry of Health. Runaways or delinquents were placed in shelters or correctional facilities under the Ministry of International Affairs whereas offenders over the age of 14 years were sent to correctional facilities under the Ministry of Justice (Guth, 2014). The ministries did not coordinate care and children were often moved several times and could be placed anywhere in the country instead of in their own communities where their families could visit them. The large majority of the institutionalized children were social orphans, not actually orphans.

A system transformation would require legal reform, new policies, new organizations, a new system model, new knowledge and skills, changed attitudes, considerable public awareness and support, and an enormous amount of resources. The Romanian government began initiating major reform efforts in 1996, when they set up the Child Protection Department within the General Secretariat of the Government as the body responsible for coordination on child protection issues, an important step "to ensure a coherent strategy and implementation of reforms, particularly in response to the

resistance to change of the line ministries involved ... and associated opportunities to change of the labor unions (Guth, 2014, p. 4)." We developed a
close productive working relationship with the Romanian Head of the Child
Protection Department who was a young, brilliant, and ambitious man who
could make things happen in the realm of national policies and convince
Parliament to pass policies in support of new approaches for caring for children, which emphasized deinstitutionalization, family reconciliation,
community-based family-like living situations for children, and mainstreaming them into society.

In 1997, Emergency Ordinance 26 was passed in order to set up decentralized child protection services, called Specialized Public Services for Child
Protection (SPSCP) under County Councils (Correll et al., 2006; Guth,
2014). Further, responsibility for infant homes and children homes was
transferred from the Ministries of Health and Education respectively to the
SPSCP. Decentralization was necessary in order to provide the framework
for community-based services and to keep children in their own neighbor-
hoods and near their families. In order to help communities develop the policies and programs and motivation to take responsibility for their children,
we needed the support of community leaders.

We chose 10 counties to work in and proceeded to build relationships
with Secretaries of County Councils. We began in Cluj a county known to
be in the forefront of innovation and change. There, we met with the highly
influential Secretary of the County Council – a large woman who visually fit
the caricature of the stern and tough Communist bureaucrat – and
explained our task and invited her to participate as a leader. Far from fitting
the stereotype, she gushed with openness and willingness to collaborate and
quickly reached under her desk to offer us her homemade *tzuica*, a highly
potent distilled liquor made from plums, as an offering of a relationship
which would flourish and become true friendship throughout the five years
that I lived in Romania.

Each of the 10 county council Secretaries we worked with was a noteworthy and unique personality who deeply cared about children's welfare, who
wielded enormous influence and power in their counties, and who could
push through changes to completely transform the philosophy of and care of
abandoned children. Our team would meet with them on a regular basis in
each of the counties and explore the beauty of Romania as we closely
worked together to implement changes that they initiated. Our team acted as

facilitators, mentors, and trainers, forming a tight-knit group of leader-collaborators who jointly led our program.

Romanians had suffered terribly under Ceausescu. Lack of food, of heat, of hope, and terrible repression had worn them down and the sorry state of the children in institutions reflected the grimness that life had become. Leaders such as the Secretaries we were working with were saddened by the conditions in the institutions but these conditions were shared by the majority of the population. These leaders wanted to improve conditions and were anxious to learn how. They wanted to be change agents and system transformation needed such change agents. The first step was to help them construct a new vision of care and provide them the tools to carve out a new way forward. We designed a month-long study in the United States so that they could study and observe in practice the international best practices for child welfare and have the opportunity to work together to form a close knit team and to evolve their mindset from believing that institutionalization was the only option for abandoned children to one where they could envision the community as the caretaker. The Secretaries visited Washington, D.C., were shown models of child welfare and then settled in Santa Cruz, California for a formal customized course. By studying and living together, they formed a close bond and had the opportunity to discuss a new approach to child welfare in Romania and to create a workable strategy. By the time they returned to Romania, they were ready to lead major changes. We continued to send other groups of high-level civil servants to the US to study child welfare services. A total of 60 individuals were eventually sent to the US and "returned with a vision and began making changes without any additional funding" (Correll et al., 2006, p. x).

In 1998, the Government adopted the Child Welfare Reform Strategy that highlighted deinstitutionalization of children and their placement in alternative services, including, in the order of priority, reunification with their families, placement in foster care or in family like community services, or adopted nationally. At the same time, together with the Director of the Child Protection Department in Bucharest and with the Secretaries of the County Councils, we helped design a strategy for deinstitutionalization, helped to truly operationalize a foster care program and developed and implemented a training course for foster parents, helped to train the first major cohort of social workers in family reconciliation techniques and other concepts such as case management, and continued to fund community groups who were providing family-like care for children.

The notion that community-based groups could provide family-like care spread. USAID and other donors provided funding to community groups who set up living arrangements for children. We selected three counties to focus on initially, Cluj, Iasi, and Constanta, and funded a comprehensive suite of community-based services that other counties could learn from and that the government of Romania agreed to fund upon the completion of our support.[2] Our child welfare experts designed a series of trainings so that our Secretary change agents and others working in the system could continue to be trained. We took them on retreats at various locations in Romania to further their training and to allow them to work together to advance policies and influence major changes in Romania. Further, we funded the training of a group of nonprofessional staff called "social referents" who assisted mayors in rural areas with child protection issues. Mayors not initially involved in the program asked to be included and ultimately a network of rural social workers was built. By 2000, our programs in our three target counties included (Correll et al., 2006).

> *providing services for 3755 individual cases, reintegrating 693 children with their families, and counseling 1,599 families in medical units who were at risk of abandoning a child ... and trained 1,527 social assistants, 491 rural social workers, 91 supervisors, 956 case managers, 1086 professional maternal assistants, and 819 volunteers. (p. 13)*

Greenwell (2001) concluded that these three counties averaged 21% less institutionalization than other counties in the period 1997−2000.

We worked with other donors to establish a "gate keeping" system, a single-entry point into the child protection system and helped to develop Specialized Child Protection Services in the counties. These structures became County Directorates for Child Protection included in the Country Directorates for Social Assistance and Child Protection, and staffed by trained social workers. The Child Protection Commission functioned closely with these Directorates and made decisions regarding the placement of children outside their families. Only when parents disagreed, did the cases enter the court system. The Child Protection Department later was turned into the National Agency/Authority for Child (Rights) Protection. We worked with this Department to make the first attempt to develop quality standards of services as well as establish the basis for developing a Child Protection Information System.

The EU's original policy was to convince Romania to keep children in the institutions but to improve their care. We were able to influence them and convince them that instead their policy should support deinstitutionalization, family reconciliation, family-like community-based services, and foster care. Mainstreaming disabled children was a huge challenge that we made some inroads into and some community-based services were developed, but the social stigma against keeping disabled children in their own families remained relatively high. However, we were able to improve their care in institutions and also move them to their own communities so that their parents became more involved in their care and education.

We also worked closely with UNICEF in Romania who had developed the Convention on the Rights of the Child in 1990 and who was working closely with the Government of Romania to help them formulate their new policies toward abandoned and at-risk children, including street children. Street children lived in the sewers of Bucharest where steam kept them warm. Generally from institutions, dysfunctional families, or extreme poverty, the kids sniffed glue and resisted help because they were addicted and became used to their communal lifestyle. USAID funded several NGOs who were working to provide shelters and rehabilitation services for street children with limited success.

We did not work in the area of adoption nor promote any policy in this area. We funded two adoption agencies that were working to improve the care of HIV-infected children in one institution and to establish community-based services, but we did not support their adoption services. There were many scandals concerning adoption. Right after the fall of Ceausescu, adoption agencies poured into Romania and stories of child trafficking of abandoned children for body parts spread, as well as stories of institutions purposely putting their sickest children up for adoption. Corruption among government officials became rampant as adoption agencies bribed them to approve adoptions. One member of one county council told us that an adoption agency brought a brand new expensive vehicle to her home to approve an adoption. As a result, the Romanian government closed international adoption at one point. The government promoted domestic adoption but the stigma against adoption remained high. Since Romania has joined the EU international adoption has become legal again under certain restricted circumstances but is better controlled.

We developed a collaborative community of US organizations working on child protection in Romania and called everyone together to try to unify policies and approaches. The US Ambassador Jim Rosapepe and our team were very interested in unifying the approach so that we could collectively work toward a common goal of preventing institutionalization in the first place; returning abandoned children to their families whenever possible; and reducing the number of children in institutions by establishing community-based, family-like services. Because I had positional leadership within USAID and had the support of the US Ambassador, I was able to help organize an extensive network of NGOs and facilitate a common approach to child welfare. The Ambassador's wife, Sheila Kast, a well-known American journalist with her own radio program in the United States, participated in many of our events and hence helped legitimize our program in the eyes of the Romanian government who sought a close relationship with the United States. As they pointed out in their book *Dracula is Dead: Travels in Post-Communist Romania* (2014): "An American cannot spend more than a few days in Romania without hearing a native say, with a smile 'We've been waiting for you for 60 years'" (Rosapepe & Kast, 2014, Kindle loc. 485 of 5912).

In order to pursue our strategy of deinstitutionalization, we needed to address the causes. Doctors historically had encouraged poor women, especially Roma women, to abandon their children to institutions. Doctors especially advised women of all classes to abandon their disabled children since disability was a major social taboo and there were no community services for these children. Further, many children were abandoned by unwed mothers. Most of these children were unfortunately abandoned without identities, as their mothers, fearing social stigma, would abandon them without providing their names, hence preventing them from ever being reintegrated into their families, being adopted, or even having identity documents when they were released from institutions at the age of 18 years. Part of our program was to provide shelters for unmarried pregnant women and to try to convince them to at least give their babies an identity if they did not want or could not to keep them.

By 2000, institutions were renamed "placement centers" to indicate that they were not meant to be permanent care facilities. Institutionalization levels dropped by 27% during the period from 1997 to 2000 than previously with a reduction of time spent in these centers by 32% to 27.1 months (Rusi et al., 2011).

Together with the Government of Romania, other donors, and the NGOs that USAID funded, our team was able to transform the child welfare system from one where institutionalization was the first response to an abandoned child to one in which the community took responsibility for the welfare of their children and social services emerged to help families and children at risk preserve their families. The keys to success in this change effort included shared vision and inclusive leadership among different stakeholders in the Government of Romania, donors, NGOs, and the health and welfare professions; the international community spotlight on the issue of child welfare that brought resources to bear and established a "cause"; the EU conditionality to improve the conditions of abandoned children as a requirement to enter the EU that created significant pressure on the Government of Romania to take immediate and definitive action; and the changing mindset of the Romanian populace for communities to take charge of their social problems instead of relying on State intervention.

Correll et al. (2006) categorized the system transformation into five pillars: (1) political will, policy, and legislation; (2) child welfare services; (3) service delivery system; (4) coordinated programs and funding; and (5) community development and participation. Our approach contributed significantly to each of these pillars and helped to overcome resistance at several levels. Employees in the institutions feared unemployment and efforts had to be made to retrain them to work in community services or serve as foster parents. Leaders in the central ministries lost power and authority and had to be convinced that they would have more time for their other responsibilities and could still serve as advisors.

Unfortunately, a crisis hit in 1999 because decentralization had begun prior to the decentralization of the budget, exacerbated by a general economic crisis in the region. This was a universal issue in the entire transition process in Eastern Europe and the former Soviet Union. Decentralization was a major thrust of the democratization process and the delegation of responsibility often occurred before the decentralization of the budget, forcing the local level to assume roles that they could not afford, especially given the fact that they had little or no authority to collect local taxes. Fortunately, a legal framework was instituted to provide compulsory subsidizing of the decentralized child protection system by the Central Government and to directly fund National Interest Programs to keep the system working (Guth, 2014).

WOMEN'S REPRODUCTIVE HEALTH

Women's reproductive health was another significant issue that was attract-ing international interest and concern. Under Ceausescu, women were denied contraception and instead encouraged to have many children, receiving awards for having large families to fulfill Ceausescu's vision of the "new Romanian man." Abortion was illegal, while poverty was rampant. Illegal abortions were widespread with high rates of mortality and equally high rates of imprisonment. After the fall of Ceausescu, the government legalized contraception and abortion. Donors, including USAID, and NGOs began to provide contraception and set up women's reproductive health services. Some Romanian doctors, who made money off of abortions, worked against the effort to provide contraception by convincing women that abortions were better for their health than methods such as the pill. Abortion rates in Romania were the highest in Eastern Europe and had devastating impacts on women's health, causing serious infections, sterility, and even death. Hence, communication campaigns became necessary in order to provide correct information to women and contraception supply chains were developed to ensure that contraceptives were available.

Our team formed close collaborative relationships with the Ministry of Health and Ministry of USAID and funded US health organizations, which in turn provided funding to local NGOs.[3] Romanians took the lead on our program and we supported them, leading from behind. Romanian women were extremely anxious to obtain reproductive health information and they designed the initiatives that we funded. We funded women's health clinics and reproductive health education, funded the integration of women's repro-ductive health services in existing rural clinics, and funded a women's repro-ductive health NGO that was a leader in this area. Fortunately, we were able to contribute to the increased use of contraceptives and to the reduction of the abortion rate. According to national estimates, more than twice as many women in 1999, 30%, than in 1993, 14% had access to and were using fam-ily planning methods (Greenwell, 2001; USAID, 2013).

Our team also worked with a coalition of women's NGOs who were working for reproductive health rights as well as for women's equality and helped them develop advocacy campaigns. Democracy was a new concept and we worked with the coalition to develop their skills to influence government policy. We worked with them to lobby politicians to pass legislation to protect women and support their reproductive rights and helped them present reproductive health and women's empowerment platforms for candidates to employ in their elections.

We dealt with political pressures and resistance, as in our child welfare program. At one event for women's reproductive health rights that we organized in the town of Braila on the Danube River at which the Ambassador's wife was our keynote speaker, we were confronted by the Orthodox Church's refusal to allow contraception. The Orthodox priest who blessed the event spoke right before I did and decried the entire notion of contraception, applauding God's desire for large families. As the Ambassador's wife wrote in her book (Rosapepe & Kast, 2014):

> Mayor Lungu began speaking, then turned the microphone over to a sturdy, bearded Orthodox priest. Sheilah smiled and tried to look devout during his invocation, which lasted several minutes. Only later was it explained to her that his prayer went from beseeching God's blessings on us to denouncing birth control and asserting that women's highest calling was to bear as many children as possible. They all said "amen." Nothing altered Mayor Lungu's tranquil smile as he turned the microphone over to Randal Thompson, head of USAID's office of social strategies. She is a caring, adept champion of women's reproductive health; she delivered, in Romanian, a very different message. (Kindle loc. 4556 of 5912)

The mayor proceeded to call in a large group of women who were supposed to hear our message but instead were there to receive large plastic bags full of used clothing. The women had been selected because they had large families and eschewed the use of contraception. On another occasion when we visited a Roma community living in makeshift hovels in the dump outside Timisoara where they survived by recycling the trash, I met a very pregnant Roma woman who had several children living in institutions. I asked her what her plans were for her soon-to-be born infant and she told me that her doctor recommended placing the baby in the institution. I asked her why she did not use contraception and she told me that a missionary group had convinced her that contraception was a terrible sin. Our intent was not to force contraception on women, but only to offer them choices.

Products from the West that had been forbidden during the communist era were entering into Romania and companies often used slogans of democracy to market them, such as a huge billboard that exclaimed smoking American brand cigarettes was associated with democracy and freedom. Pornography could finally be marketed openly and a famous American men's magazine opened a branch in Bucharest. In their first issue, there appeared a pictorial spread titled "How to Beat your Wife without Leaving Marks" with tiny "how-to photos" showing step-by-step how to beat one's wife with a small rubber mallet. The Romanian editors included the article purportedly as humor, the sort of black-humor that Romanians relished.

Romanian women who we worked with in the coalition did not think the article was funny and loudly complained to me. I was expected to use my position as an American leader to do something about this affront to women. So, I emailed the magazine headquarters in the United States and explained our mission in reproductive health and women's empowerment and explained why Romanian women were so displeased with the article. The US-based editors were sympathetic and required the Romanian editor to come to my office with an official apology and to donate money to us so that we could fund a women's domestic abuse shelter. Up to that time, there were no such shelters and domestic violence was rampant, fueled by the transition period between communism and capitalism when state benefits declined, unemployment proliferated, and poverty greatly increased.

LEADING IN THE POST-COMMUNIST CONTEXT

The days in Eastern Europe after the fall of the Soviet Union were initially full of hope. Western donors moved swiftly into the post-communist world convinced that capitalism had won. Neoliberalism had become the dominant paradigm in what was touted "the end of history." The overarching policy in development was to implant capitalism and market-oriented economies and to "change the mindset" of individuals who had lived under communism. Recognizing that the people were well educated on the whole, the challenge was to shift them away from a mindset of dependency on the state to one of self-dependence and individualism and the motto of forging their own way. Entire 747s full of Eastern Europeans were flown to the United States for training and acculturation in the American capitalist way.

The International Monetary Fund and the World Bank along with certain US universities worked at the economic and country system level to dismantle the communist system by reducing social services and the social safety net, by reducing the number of workers at supposedly "nonefficient" state enterprises, by closing these enterprises or privatizing them and thus creating the famous oligarchs who have emerged to have enormous power in the region. Hope quickly died and poverty dramatically increased with the donor emphasis on privatization of state-owned enterprises, which displaced many workers and caused massive unemployment, coupled with reduced expenditures on social safety nets, so that the unemployed could not get benefits to survive.

As development professionals, we were told that we were supposed to change the mind-set of the populace who was "dependent" on the State to solve all their problems to that of the rugged individual dependent only on herself or himself. We were assumed to despise everything about the communist system and were to infuse this abhorrence in those we worked in. This was virtually impossible for me to do because, working on social systems, I saw the negative impact of unemployment, lack of social support, lack of services and resources for poor families who wanted to keep their children, and lack of the systems in place to replace the State. The assumption was that NGOs would provide services that the government could no longer afford, but NGOs depended upon donor or government grants. Further, employees of the child welfare institutions often felt patronized and minimized by all the good-doers and "volunteer tourists" who worked in the institutions often for only two weeks at a time. The experience raised the challenge of how to lead when not completely supporting the overarching development approach and having little influence on changing it.

Dickens and Groza (2004) claimed that they practiced an empowerment approach to child welfare in Romania and criticized others for not so doing. Empowerment, they argued, included six components: (1) a clear shared vision; (2) a focus on what Romania wants for its children; (3) a focus on strengths and resources rather than only problems and deficits; (4) the recognition of the universality of social conditions and not blame Romania for conditions which our country's share such as poverty, abandonment, abuse, and so on; (5) the inclusion of public policy reformation; and (6) the community context of change. We feel strongly that we practiced such an approach although we admit that other donors such as the EU did not practice empowerment largely because they employed a conditionality approach to achieving EU membership.

Eyben (2014) labeled Reflexive Practice as the ability to practice double-loop thinking and reflect on our own assumptions, worldview, and values. Reflexive Leadership, I argue is going a step further in an attempt to see oneself as others see us. One of my Romanian staff once asked me why I seem to want to make everyone in the world happy. I had no reply. We often get so wrapped up in our zeal and intentions to "do good" that we may lose sight of the fact that we may be imposing our view of reality on others, that they feel minimized by us, and that they fear expressing their own point of view. In Romania, we promoted a system that we thought was the best for their country and for their children. Yet, Romanians were in a vulnerable position after the fall of Ceausescu, during "transition," and even since joining the EU. I can only hope after all is said and done that we truly initiated a transformational process that was, is, and will be one that will establish a sustainable system to achieve the wellbeing of Romania's children and of Romanians writ large.

DISCLAIMER

The author's views expressed in this publication do not necessarily reflect the views of the USAID or the United States Government.

NOTES

1. As part of the child welfare reform, USAID funded the following INGOs with a total of $44.7 million: World Vision, World Learning, PACT, Operation Smile, Catholic Relief Services, Brothers Brother, Feed the Children, Project Concern International, Support Centers of America International, World Association for Children and Parents, Holt International Children's Services, and Bethany Christian Services. Romanian partner NGOs included *Salvati Copii,* Romanian Committee for Adoption, Romanian Association against AIDS, National Association of Social Workers, and several other local NGOs. USAID also funded UNICEF to elaborate an

operational framework for implementing a national Plan of Action for the Protection
of Children and provided an additional $14 million to the government for child pro-
tection (Correll, Correll, & Predescu, 2006).

2. These services included: (1) family support or prevention services such as parent
education, daycare, family counseling, and family planning; (2) family preservation
services, crisis counseling, intensive family interventions, parental assistance, and
emergency financial aid; (3) protective services, referring to assessment of abuse and
neglect and subsequent planning and interventions; (4) temporary substitute care,
including foster care, permanency planning, family reunification, and mothers' shelters; and (5) permanent substitute care, including adoption, foster care, and group
homes (Correll et al., 2006, pp. 11–12).

3. USAID funded Management Sciences for Health (MSH), John Snow International
(JSI) and also provided funding to Romanian NGOs, including the Society for
Education on Contraception and Sexuality (SECS), Population Services International
(PSI), the Romanian Association Against AIDs (ARAS), Youth for Youth Foundation
(TFY), and the East European Institute for Reproductive Health.

ACKNOWLEDGMENTS

I would like to acknowledge the dedication and hard work of our core team,
including Rebecca Davis, Bill Saur, Lucia Correll, Susan Monagan, Ecatrina
Vasile, and Dana Buzducea, and our extended team, including Daniela
Draghici, Luminitza Marcu, Anemona Munteanu, Borbola Koo, all the
women NGO leaders in our coalition, Secretaries of the County Councils,
Ministry of Health colleagues, and all the other stakeholders we worked
closely with. Also special thanks to Ambassador and Mrs Jim Rosapepe who
supported our work and ensured its credibility to high Romanian officials.

REFERENCES

Correll, L., Correll, T., & Predescu, M. (2006). *USAID and child welfare
reform in Romania: Challenges, successes, and legacy.* Aguirre Division, JBS
International, Inc. Retrieved from https://www.brandeis.edu/investigate/
adoption/docs/final_romania_legacy_report_090506.pdf

Dickens, J., & Groza, V. (2004). Empowerment in difficulty: A critical appraisal of international intervention in child welfare in Romania. *International Social Work, 47*(4), 469–487.

Eyben, R. (2014). *International aid and the making of a better world: Reflexive practice*. London, England: Routledge.

Greenwell, K. F. (2001). *Child welfare reform in Romania: Abandonment and deinstitutionalization 1987-2000*. Report produced for USAID. Retrieved from https://pdf.usaid.gov/pdf_docs/PNACN639.pdf

Guth, A. (2014, April 12). *Reform steps towards child protection Bulgaria – Romania: A comparative approach*. ChildPact. Retrieved from http://www.childpact.org/2014/04/10/reform-steps-towards-child-protection-in-bulgaria-and-romania-a-comparative-approach/

Hochman, S. (1990, July 24). Wives of Beatles Lead a Crusade to Save Orphans: Charity: An all-star album featuring George Harrison, Ringo Starr and a relief fund aims to ease plight of abandoned children in Romania. *Los Angeles Times*. Retrieved from http://articles.latimes.com/1990-07-24/entertainment/ca-721_1_george-harrison

Rosapepe, J., & Kast, S. (2014). *Dracula is dead: Travels in post-communist Romania* (Kindle ed., 2nd ed.). Kast and Rosapepe Publishers.

Rusi, A. V., Parris, S., Cross, D., Purvis, K., & Draghici, S. (2011). Reforming the Romanian child welfare system: 1990–2010. *Revista de cercetare [i interven]ie social, 34*, 56–72. Retrieved from https://www.rcis.ro/images/documente/rcis34_04.pdf

UNICEF. (2004). *Child care system reform in Romania*. Retrieved from https://www.unicef.org/romania/imas1.pdf

USAID. (2013). *Family planning in Eastern Europe and Eurasia: A Legacy of change*. Unpublished Report. Retrieved from https://www.usaid.gov/sites/default/files/documents/1864/EELegacy.pdf

World Bank & UNICEF. (2014). *Romania: Children in public care*. Retrieved from http://documents.worldbank.org/curated/en/148571505811999132/pdf/119791-WP-P147269-PUBLIC-RomaniaChildreninPublicCaresite.pdf

PART 5: LEADERSHIP LESSONS TO REFLECT ON

For the conclusion of this volume, the authors of Chapters 17 and 18 provide several key leadership lessons that encapsulate many of the leadership moments described throughout this volume. In Chapter 17, Dick Daniels recounts his key learnings derived from his career of following his "leadership itch." Leadership, he concludes, combines positive influence and effective action. Positive influence represents the soft skills of leadership with a focus on relationships. The effective action represents the hard skills of leadership with a focus on results .... The art and the science of leadership is determining where the emphasis on that continuum is needed by each team member, each organizational development season, and each obstacle that tries to get in the way of vision, mission, values, and strategy.

Daniels summarizes his leadership journey as following three steps. During his first step, "calling," Daniels noted his tendency to always be in leadership roles, a tendency that motivated him to build his "capacity" as a leader, his second step, by taking on more challenging assignments and honing his personal drive, and to continue a lifelong "development" process, his third step. Daniels learned that leadership legitimacy is rooted in competency, respect, outcomes, and humility. While working in international development, he also learned that "sustainable leadership is committed to the development of global competencies as well as the agility to adapt."

Daniels argues that the achievement of the United Nations Sustainable Development Goals requires collaborative partnership, a competency that "requires the interpersonal savvy and cultural sensitivity to work across typical borders and boundaries to serve a greater purpose together." This competency also requires humble leaders who are capable of breaking down "global silos that prevent a sustainable resolution to eradicating poverty in all its forms and dimensions."

Daniels argues that a "train-the-trainer" approach is essential in leading development projects in order to avoid dependency of both expatriate leaders and national leaders and stakeholders. As he writes, "with good intentions we lead projects that make us feel good ... Intense experiences of helping can create dependency in both directions. While the intentions are notable, the results often do more damage to those being served as well as to those serving. A train-the-trainer approach provides skills and resources for people within a specific culture."

Finally, Daniels reflects, as many leaders in development have, on the recognition that he has benefitted "more than whatever I offered to the team on the other side." As he concludes:

> *Leadership in international development is a journey of humility. Each time, I left a community of abundance to partner with a community of scarcity. I have been reminded in each initiative that joy and happiness are never tied to affluence but result from a quality of human connection and interaction. Relationships break down the polarization and isolation of individuals who lead and also those who follow. The leadership challenge is to carefully balance the attention to results alongside an investment in relationships with all stakeholders.*

Kathleen Curran, in Chapter 18, has identified the leadership state of being, which she calls "Global Resonance" that exemplifies the relationality that virtually all authors in this volume have identified as the most important competency of leaders of international development. Including and transcending competencies commonly identified in the global leadership literature, namely intercultural competence, cultural intelligence, and global mindset, Curran asserts that Global Resonance begins from inside the leader and moves outward. Global Resonance, that is, is initiated with a very conscious "intent to connect." The typical competencies of global leadership are cognitive and are based on knowing and doing, whereas Global Resonance is "being." Although they are important to develop, global leadership competencies do not equalize the "I–you" relationship, nor do they break down the hegemonic relationship between expert and client, as Curran contends. By intent to connect, the global resonant leader commits to entering an equal discovery relationship with the client or partner in development. This intent leads to a process of co-creation. Such an intent counteracts the typical, "outdated, yet well-intentioned, albeit unjust and unsustainable positions of rushing to solutions developed, owned, and delivered by experts."

Generated from the inside-out, Global Resonance completes a global leader's *being-knowing-doing cycle*, and, in Curran's own words from her chapter, proceeds through the following phases:

Intent: Conscious Receptivity

Global Resonance begins from a place of conscious receptivity, not only accepting difference but expecting and inviting the possibility to be changed by the interaction with another.

Expect Brilliance

This phase catalyzes an emergent process that is underpinned by honor and respect for the belief in the brilliance of the other, not as a hope, but as an expectation.

Cultivate Space for Discovery

Cultivating transformative space for discovery begins co-creation possibilities; unfolding and emergent meaning is allowed for and uninterrupted. This dialogic space is where the "I" is transformed to "We." In other words, the "we" begins to take on a collective and meaningful shape.

Co-Create

In the space of co-creation, an issue of concern is seen as an object facing global leaders and stakeholders; the focus therefore shifts to an individual's contributions to the partnership and shared vision, and away from potentially adversarial blame or responsibility. Acknowledging their co-created partnership and balancing power differentials opens a window to their diverse influences, enriches both the connection and the shared outcome, and promotes commitment to action.

Advocacy: Courageous Consciousness

Consciousness of what is and has been discovered increases awareness of influences, differences, and possibilities that can longer be ignored; courage to give voice to them is the global leader's responsibility. In spiralic fashion, advocacy, therefore, completes the cycle.

In summary, Global Resonance brings the inherent and somewhat neglected attention to the dynamic relational aspects of global and international development leadership.

17

LEADERSHIP MUSINGS

Dick Daniels

HOW IT ALL BEGAN

Leadership caught me by surprise during my junior year of college. It was spring, the season of student government elections. I decided to run for Student Body President at a small Midwestern college. Winning that election was the beginning of my leadership journey. The Dean of Students became a mentor who affirmed my leadership skill set. I discovered that leadership was a collaborative process with all members of the student government organization. I simply clarified the vision and strategy and invested in setting them up for success.

In that first leadership role, I felt the leadership itch. I discovered that I could work with teams of people toward shared outcomes. Over time, I learned that leadership combines positive influence and effective action. Positive influence represents the soft skills of leadership with a focus on relationships. Effective action represents the hard skills of leadership with a focus on results. One without the other misses the mark needed for sustainable leadership. The art and the science of leadership is determining where the emphasis on that continuum is needed by each team member, each organizational development season, and each obstacle that tries to get in the way of vision, mission, values, and strategy.

I eventually determined that my career has followed the path of an entrepreneurial leader. I love the startup phase. Once the organizational machine is well oiled, then I get bored with maintaining and managing. This was the beginning of understanding where my leadership skills could take me. It was an introduction to aligning a group of people around a shared goal. There was a sense of fulfillment that I had never experienced before as I learned to lead in that student government role. That experience led me to pursue graduate work in student development in higher education. Eventually, I was Dean of Students where I had the opportunity to work with student leaders developing their leadership competencies and leadership behaviors. The career roles that followed pushed me into the development of talent at all levels of an organization.

Gender realities were interesting in my early career. There were not as many women competing for senior leadership roles. The candidate pool was not only smaller, but that pool did not have the competitive quality that we see today. As a result, it was less competitive for men to get into senior leadership roles than it is today. Another result of that generational season is that the "good old boys' clubs" protected their turf from an emergence of women into the marketplace. The glass ceiling was a reality and still is when considering salaries and senior roles. Women can bring a perspective different from men. Yes, that is a generalization, but the point is that a gender-balanced leadership team adds a richness of perspective, criteria for strategic decisions, and most importantly, results. This becomes a very important factor for leadership in international development.

When leadership opportunities occur, the women and men who succeed are the ones who connect the relationship-oriented skills to the results-oriented skills of leading. In the end, they get the leadership assignment completed and earn the respect of their employees. If they stop long enough to reflect on how to do the same thing even more effectively and more efficiently the next time, they are well on their way to a career of effective leadership. I experienced three key steps in my leadership journey:

Calling. Some will quickly discover, as I did, that they have a tendency to be in a leading role as well as continue to develop their leadership skill set. Success in the simple leadership assignments becomes a calling for some to grow and develop competencies required by other more complicated challenges. Recognizing my calling in leadership motivated me to identify the next steps in my journey.

Capacity. Leadership capacity is one's ability to continue to lead at higher levels of organizational complexity. Capacity to lead increases in an emerging leader by enhancing one's potential through taking on more challenging job assignments. Consistently surpassing expected outcomes also increases one's capacity. Personal drive is the final capacity element. I discovered that my leadership capacity varied by the season of life I was in as well as the season of organizational development of the company where I was serving.

Development. My leadership development grew into a lifelong commitment to never stop learning about myself, about people, about leadership, and about organizational health. It was never to focus on my identity as a leader. It was about connecting the right competencies to the needs of the organization. A good leadership agenda emphasizes working with and through a team of people to consistently achieve strategic outcomes while sustaining the values that define the culture of each organization.

DEVELOPING LEADERSHIP COMPETENCIES

Legitimacy Multipliers. Leadership is rooted in the following legitimacy multipliers:

Competency. Does the leader possess the specific leadership competency mix from training and life experience to lead effectively and efficiently in the assigned role?

Respect. The respect of reports, peers, and senior leaders is earned by the consistency of leadership presence, leadership behaviors, and leadership skills. Respect is slow to be earned and yet can be lost in the moment of a premature decision or a word spoken out of turn.

Outcomes. Legitimacy is demonstrated in the timeliness of achieving expected outcomes as well as surpassing those expectations in whatever way possible.

Humility. Leaders learn the value of giving credit and taking blame. They recognize the contribution of every team member. They appropriately reward the individual in line with how they are wired and motivated.

Leaders celebrate the team achievements in a variety of ways by investing time and money in celebration events.

LEADERSHIP BASICS

Leadership is always tied to context. Leadership development is executed within the context of the organization to address growth-related challenges and build on opportunities. First, leaders determine the stage of development for an organization (see the Adizes model of organizational maturity at www.adizes.com). Then, leaders assess the current culture of the organization (see the Four Frame Model, Reframing Organizations by Bolman and Deal). The call of leadership is to determine the cultural frame needed to meet strategic outcomes. Finally, the leader adapts her/his style and competency mix to transition the organization to the best cultural frame suited to move the organization forward. The order of priority begins with vision, mission, and values to determine strategy. From strategy, the leader moves to structure, then systems, and finally staffing.

LESSONS LEARNED

Leadership is applied to international development. My greatest success has been the agility to adapt to the changes in organizational context and culture. This is essential to sustainable leadership. The development of courageous followers who are learning to expand their own capacity to lead at higher levels of organizational complexity is also essential. I have also learned the incredible value of distinguishing between culture and climate. Leaders must address both. Culture is how the organization is reflected through its values which inevitably influence how employees will work together toward strategic outcomes. Climate is the reality of how closely the daily life of the organization matches that ideal. The culture − climate gap reflects the pain point for leaders. Climate is determined in each department and in each team by the personality of the leader or any team member at any given moment in time. Personal baggage and toxic temperaments can render a leader ineffective. The wider the gap, the unhealthier the organization, and less engaged are the team members. My greatest lesson within a global perspective was discovering how to approach projects from a train-the-trainer perspective. This insight resulted from reading, listening to presentations, and discussions on books such as, *When Helping Hurts: How to Alleviate Poverty Without Hurting the Poor ... and Yourself*, by Brian Fikkert and Steve Corbett (Corbett & Fikkert, 2012). With good intentions we lead projects that make us feel good. We especially like global projects that require travel. Intense experiences of helping can create dependency in both directions. While the intentions are noble, the results often do more damage to those being served as well as to those serving. A train-the-trainer approach provides skills and resources for people within a specific culture. The trainer allows local leaders to use the resources in the way best suited to that culture. It is an approach that develops local leaders to train others, which in turn multiplies the impact in culturally relevant applications.

APPLYING LEADERSHIP COMPETENCIES TO INTERNATIONAL DEVELOPMENT

- *My Leadership Sector Set the Stage.* I have worked most recently in a healthcare context. My motivation was to experience leadership development in a large, complex, and organizational setting. The healthcare sector has influenced my leading, in part because of its complexity, but also in terms of the clarity of its mission which is to provide quality healthcare and wellness education to the demographic it serves. When considering Simon Sinek's concept of The Golden Circle (what, why, and how), healthcare has clarity on what and why it does what it does (Partridge, 2014). How quality patient care is delivered is always evolving with new research and best practices.

- *The Paris Declaration Provides a True North Perspective.* The OER (Open Educational Resources) aspect of the Paris Declaration calls on governments worldwide to openly license publicly funded educational materials for general use (What is the Paris OER Declaration?, n.d.). This challenge or invitation is at the core of the global leadership development in the train-the-trainer approach when providing resources otherwise not available. The development projects I have been part of have generally been in underdeveloped and/or under-resourced areas of the world. The work has focused on providing resources and training in a train-the-trainer approach. Providing educational resources in a way that can be applied by local leaders in culturally appropriate ways will far outlast our direct involvement.

- *Learning to Lead in Different Cultures.* In preparation for the first international development project, I sought out a leadership development specialist who worked in a global company. At the time I lived in Minneapolis, where 3M is headquartered, and found them to be a great resource with operations in more than 65 countries, including 29 international companies. The leadership development department at 3M addresses global leadership competencies and leadership behaviors for their global workforce. I explained my upcoming project and asked for insight in order to prepare appropriately. One of the resources recommended was the book by Richard D. Lewis, *When Cultures Collide: Leading Across Cultures* (Lewis, 2006). It provided insights and strategies for leaders to embrace differences and work successfully across increasingly diverse business cultures. Each chapter addresses a specific country with sections on culture, key concepts in that region, cultural factors in communication including communication patterns, listening, behavior at meetings, and negotiations, as well as manners and taboos. This resource became a continual reference for each international project that followed.

- *Surprises in Understanding Culture and Leadership.* I have been surprised by the insensitivity to cultural differences in both directions. Sometimes the clash is not intentional but comes with a lack of understanding. So the leadership challenge is one of educations and also learning how to execute leadership practices in a way best suited to a diverse cultural setting or a unique cultural subgroup within an organization, region, or country.

- *Leading Sustainable International Development.* I am a proponent of sustainable leadership in my writing and practice of leadership development. Effective leadership development is tied to sustainable leadership. If I am not learning to lead in a way that fosters sustainability within an organization, then I will fail to establish sustainable development within a cultural context globally. Sustainable leadership is committed to the development of global competencies as well as the agility to adapt. Leading for the long haul translates into sustainable development for the long haul.

AN UNDERSTANDING OF THE UNITED NATIONS SUSTAINABLE DEVELOPMENT GOALS

The United Nations 2030 agenda for sustainable development provides a plan of action for people, planet, prosperity, and universal peace. The 17 Sustainable Development Goals and 169 targets within those goals demonstrate the need for collaborative partnership (The Sustainable Development Agenda, n.d.). This leadership competency requires the interpersonal savvy and cultural sensitivity to work across typical borders and boundaries to serve a greater purpose together. The impact on leadership touches the need for humility in the leader and the necessity to break down global silos that prevent sustainable resolution to eradicating poverty in all its forms and dimensions. This is perhaps the most significant requirement for sustainable development. I am not close enough to the leadership on a national or global scale to see any indication yet of a mindset shift among leaders to impact international sustainable development. The resources and solutions are there, but it will require a different leadership mindset to think and act globally rather than regionally, nationally, or personally.

LEADERSHIP ALIGNMENT CRITICAL TO LEADERSHIP IN INTERNATIONAL DEVELOPMENT

Sustainable development implies aligned leadership and a shared commitment at all levels to the priorities identified in the 2030 Agenda for Sustainable Development. We should understand more of how this is being diffused locally as well as internationally. Alongside that observation is the simplicity of understanding of how relational leadership brings results. One without the other is never sustainable for long-term results. Effective leaders understand the interpersonal dynamics reflected in differing values and cultures. They are savvy in adapting to the context and showing respect for the values that rest beneath a particular culture. They also know how to work cross-functionally to get to tangible results. Sustainable development implies leadership agility from a global mindset.

LESSONS FOR THE NEXT GENERATION OF LEADERS IN INTERNATIONAL DEVELOPMENT

Failure. It's never final. Allow for it. Own it. Learn from it so you fail less in the future.

Conflict. It is the pathway to team innovation and creativity. Train teams to expect it and to keep it centered on ideas, never between individuals.

Settle for More. Never settle for less. Maximize what is working so it works more effectively and efficiently. Fix what isn't working.

Clarity. Know and own your vision, mission, and values so well that you can say "no" to the good in order to say "yes" to the best.

Divisiveness. The continual underperforming team member and the divisive team member are like cancer to the team. Most senior leaders admit that they invest too much time discussing the situation and delay in doing the right thing in the right way. Many say their delay resulted in costly damage to the team and to the bottom line. Some companies make a regular practice of cutting the lower 10% of underperformers as well as divisive personalities. This creates a culture of performance rather than acceptance.

A COLLABORATIVE CASE STUDY IN LEADERSHIP FOR INTERNATIONAL DEVELOPMENT

In the last 19 years, I have been involved in humanitarian service projects on a global basis as a way of investing in the development of leaders internationally. The countries include: Kuwait, Norway, Ecuador, South Africa, and Ghana. In 2015, I invited the leaders of five global organizations to join me in Orlando, Florida to discuss what each organization does in its global silo. All participants are doing significant humanitarian work around the world. My invitation was to consider a collaborative project somewhere in the world to maximize efficiencies and impact. It would serve as a pilot for how to break down global humanitarian silos.

Our collaborative work was influenced by the humanitarian philosophy of books such as: *When Helping Hurts: How to Alleviate Poverty Without Hurting the Poor...and Yourself* by Steve Corbett and Brian Fikkert

(Corbett & Fikkert, 2012) as well as *Toxic Charity* by Robert Lupton (2012). The perspective of these authors and others is focused on compassionate work that does not create dependency or co-dependency on those who serve or those who are served. This is wrapped in our train-the-trainer methodology. We wanted to provide resources that local men and women in leadership could continue in culturally relevant ways without our ongoing involvement.

THE PROJECT

The Leadership Development Group, providing leadership development training to leadership teams, agreed to partner with Francis and Pamella Bukachi who lead Hope Alive Initiatives (hopealiveinitiatives.org/). The Bukachis are Kenyan missionaries who started 30 Christian churches in Northern Ghana. Their mission is "To build the capacity of native churches and organizations in poor and vulnerable communities" (Hope Alive Initiatives, n.d.).

THE OTHER COLLABORATIVE PARTNERS

Indigenous Technology and Education Center (I-TEC) (www.itecusa.org) – a resource for training and tools including I-See (glasses), I-Dent (dental), I-Med (medical), I-Fix (repair training), and I-Film (video training).

Kids Around the World (www.KATW.net) – (1) Play – Building playgrounds for children in poverty-stricken communities, (2) Feed – Partnering with volunteers to package and deliver the nutritional requirements for undernourished children, and (3) Train – Equipping children's teachers to provide orality Training – a non-literary based approach to teaching Bible stories to children.

Renew World Outreach (www.renewoutreach.com) – Empowers others with solar-powered equipment and audio/visual media to reach the world's most remote people.

GoTandem (www.goTandem.com) – A resource app that provides churches and pastors with a "toolbox" of resources including this app which brings Bible content to smart phones for personal spiritual growth and development.

THE RESULTS

Teams from all five partners collaborated for eight days in August 2016 to train and equip local leaders with resources not otherwise available. This joint project modeled a breakdown of humanitarian and ministry silos which rarely happens. The impact on local leaders touched the following leadership in international development priorities:

Gender. The opportunity to train and equip women and men in local leadership roles appropriate to the cultural context.

Context. This collaborative initiative was executed with a culturally sensitive philosophy that equipped leaders with resources to create sustainability without co-dependency.

Culture. The project reflected world views, values, and approaches different from Western ideas. That is always the learning agenda for those of us coming from a Western mindset.

Sustainability. The train-the-trainer approach was a commitment in our approach for the goal of local sustainability. The initiative was focused on training local leaders who would train others at the local level.

The entire experience was extremely rewarding! Our collective take-away includes ongoing discussion of how to model this type of collaborative compassion work as well as seeking new opportunities for this collaborative group, or others, to do it all once again.

THE PERSONAL PRICE OF LEADING FOR INTERNATIONAL DEVELOPMENT

The gift of one's expertise is reputable. The contribution of one's experience is noteworthy. The offering of one's resources is impressive. But, the investment of one's time is sacrificial. In my experience, each international development opportunity has included expertise, experience, and resources. But the transformative moment of leadership is giving without an expectation of getting back. It avoids creating the debt and debtor transactional dynamic often present in a traditional humanitarian venture. I am far from having arrived as a transformational leader, but I have returned home each time with an understanding that I have benefited personally more than whatever I offered to the team on the other side. Leadership in international development is a journey of humility. Each time, I left a community of abundance to partner with a community of scarcity. I have been reminded in each initiative that joy and happiness are never tied to affluence but result from a quality of human connection and interaction. Relationships break down the polarization and isolation of individuals who lead and also those who follow. The leadership challenge is to carefully balance the attention to results alongside an investment in relationships with all stakeholders. Without positive influence between leader and team, one's effective action is inhibited and unsustainable for the long haul. The leadership itch includes a price to pay, but the return on investment is the ongoing legacy of the emerging leaders who follow.

ACKNOWLEDGMENTS

I would like to express appreciation to Heidi Sheard of Minneapolis, Minnesota, who provided professional editing of this chapter in preparation for final submission. In addition, I am grateful to each member of the Ghana Collaborative Project with whom I served. Team leaders include Jim Rosene and Gary Strudler from Kids Around the World, Steve Buer and Jaime Saint from Indigenous Technology and Education Center, Paul Veerman who represented Go Tandem, and Francis Bukachi from Hope Alive Initiatives. Each individual modeled servant leadership in international development. I was humbled by their commitment, attitudes, and global wisdom.

REFERENCES

Corbett, S., & Fikkert, B. (2012). *When helping hurts: How to alleviate poverty without hurting the poor and yourself* (2nd ed.). Chicago, IL: Moody Publishers.

Hope Alive Initiatives. (n.d.). *About us*. Retrieved from http://hopealiveinitiatives.org/about-us/

Lewis, R. D. (2006). *When cultures collide: Leading across cultures* (3rd ed.). Boston, MA: Nicholas Brealey Publishing.

Lupton, R. D. (2012). *Toxic charity: How churches and charities hurt those they help, and how to reverse it* (1st ed.). New York, NY: HarperOne.

Partridge, A. (2014, August 27). *Executive summary: The golden circle with Simon Sinek*. Retrieved from https://enviableworkplace.com/executive-summary-golden-circle-simon-sinek/

The Sustainable Development Agenda. (n.d.). Retrieved from https://www.un.org/sustainabledevelopment/development-agenda/

What Is the Paris OER Declaration?. (n.d.). Retrieved from http://www.unesco.org/new/en/communication-and-information/access-to-knowledge/open-educational-resources/what-is-the-paris-oer-declaration/

18

DEVELOPING GLOBAL RESONANCE FOR GLOBAL LEADERSHIP

Kathleen Curran

A request for cross-cultural training landed in my inbox from a new client who found me on the web. The CEO of the company had recently had his photo taken with a counterpart in Saudi Arabia. The executive had posed for the photo with his hand in his pocket, a sign of disrespect in the Saudi culture, and someone in the UK had shouted for cultural sensitivity training.

As an intercultural relations specialist with over 20 years' experience in global skills consulting, coaching, and training, I immediately went into my expert role as solution provider. I assumed from my years of academic studies and professional experience that I understood the issue, impact on the business partnerships, and what needed to change. So naturally, as an experienced consultant, I set up an appointment to meet with the sponsor of this potential client, ready to share my wisdom and propose a solution that would meet the intercultural sensitivity needs.

Early for my appointment, I sat in the lobby, thinking about what I wanted from this meeting. I went through the usual process anyone in the corporate, private, or NGO sectors would do when attempting to bring a solution to the client: What's my objective for this meeting? What do I need to do in this meeting to reach my objective? What more do I need to learn about the issues and why the company thinks they are a problem? What's being impacted and how can I help? What are the programs I want to present that will best match their needs? What questions can I ask that will gain for me the things I want to know?

Suddenly, I paused. A light bulb went on! How many times had I just used only *I, me,* and *my versus we, us,* and *our?* All of what I was targeting in my preparation was important, but very limited. My individually motive-oriented objective would put in motion a very linear process and potentially myopic focus, allowing for a restricted exchange and implicitly creating an unequal relationship based on my conception of our roles as expert and recipient of expertise. Exploration would undoubtedly be restricted by such narrow parameters I had unwittingly set.

I had, in fact, just fallen into the trap commonly experienced by many leaders in the present day global environment characterized by complexity, ambiguity, and continually changing terrain. Without questioning my assumptions, I believed the multiple embedded and taken-for-granted suppositions and judgments I was making about the *problem* – even calling it a problem. I was seeing the client as the unequal and less knowledgeable counterpart in this relationship, and myself as the expert who could solve the issue as I led our encounter with supposed wisdom gained from my years of international experience, and directed with questions about things *I* wanted to know.

All too common, as I have found in my global leadership coaching practice, leaders in many domains unwittingly encounter the same pitfall and create hegemonic relationships and processes for achieving goals that have been interpreted by an entity external to the context in which implementation would occur and do not take all party's priorities into account. Again, the assumption is that the leader and driving organization know best. Unfortunately, such initiatives launched by leaders in the international setting often prove to be unsustainable, as the internally relevant elements and expertise in the local context have been neglected.

It's not surprising. As I have found after many years as an interculturalist, cultural systems of beliefs, assumptions, and values are strong teachers of behavioral norms. As such, "most learning may be incidental; when we confront a problem, we seek to solve it and act to apply our solution" (Jarvis, 1999, p. 21). Peters (2012) argued that, historically, western philosophy has sought an all-embracing rational system of absolute truth and uses "universalizing and totalizing concepts that attempt to enclose the unity and totality of being" (p. 36). In other words, in the attempt to understand self, identity, and one's place in the world, the western approach has produced a polarized view of *us and them*, which can impact many leaders' perspectives on problems, solutions, and implementation.

Intercultural philosophy originating in western cultures has also often been critiqued as historically distorted due to unjustified and unquestioned claims of superiority, rationality, and universality. Philosophically and in practice, therefore, the tendency to employ the expert "helping model" in international development, global business, education, or other contexts may be explained but not excused. Many examples of leadership in practice show a tendency to default to the outdated, yet well-intentioned, albeit unjust and unsustainable positions of rushing to solutions developed, owned, and delivered by *experts*.

I may be able to explain rationally why I initially approached my client as I did, but I clearly needed to look at this interaction with new eyes. If I changed my glasses, so to speak, my attitude toward my client and choice of actions would also dramatically shift. Instead of asking *what's my objective*, I would consciously choose *what kind of person I want to be in this relationship? What's my intent?*

INTENT: WHAT IS THAT?

Intent is more than simply being friendly; that's very nice, but relatively surface level. It's more than being open and transparent; that's necessary but often inappropriate in many cultures if engaged in before enough trust has been built to make sharing comfortable. It's not even empathy, which can be cultivated by standing in another's shoes. Instead, intent is a will, a will to reach a different place of shared understanding, which declutters the space of preconceived notions, judgments, and personal agendas, and clears the way for exploration, innovation, and co-creation. The resonance produced by two in synchrony springs from *intent*, the personal will to connect.

When I declared myself an explorer and *conspirator*, in the purest etymological sense (L. *conspirāre* – *con*, together, *spirāre*, to breathe, Chambers's Twentieth Century Dictionary) everything changed. My previous objective that included persuading or convincing another of my solution had no place in my vision. Our relationship became a collective as opposed to a polarized client and consultant.

What had I actually done so differently to make such a deep and meaningful difference?

Intent to connect. My intent to connect shifted my view of our relationship. Importantly, in that shift, I approached our engagement as a catalyst, similar to that used in chemical reactions. I saw opportunities to leverage for connections, not for taking advantage. The genuine invitation my attitude extended greatly impacted the partnership that ensued.

Challenge expectations. My intent to connect directed my expectations, which I became conscious of. I suspended my judgments about what past experience or cultural knowledge made me expect. I fully believed that my client had wisdom, which I needed to learn. My attitude of trust created a fertile climate in which to engage.

Create space for exploration. Freedom from agenda linearity allowed our exploration to go where emergent meaning took us. We may well have reached the same place if following a more linear agenda, but the process would not have given us the time and space to cultivate creativity or potential for novel co-creation. This space also removed the need to offer solutions or answers in a directive, problem solver way; instead, the invitation to learn and understand another's point of view more deeply was implicitly offered.

Trusting in our winding path, deeper and more integrated meaning emerged. We were seeing broader contexts and systems, not just a point in isolation. With space for flexibility, I found the right questions and could say I don't know, triggering more valuable reactions to occur as we explored possibilities.

Co-create innovative outcome. My client and I had co-created *our* more sustainable solution together. Any sense of intellectual hierarchy was dispelled; all borders were crossed seamlessly. We felt awe at the power of the moment, intensity of our presence, the resonance we reached, and the outcome we had achieved, all of which were greater than we could have achieved alone in prescribed roles.

Due to my extensive academic background in intercultural communication, and global coaching and consulting experience, I had access to a personal cultural database for background context and explanations throughout our conversation. For example, I noted that my client appeared reluctant to challenge the recommendation of the colleague who had called for the delivery of intercultural sensitivity training across the organization. She also protected the hierarchies and networks that had organically produced an unquestioned way of working. I could detect that cultural influences, embodied in differing ethnic, organizational, and professional priorities, were clearly in play. However, due to my intent to connect, I could draw on my crucial cultural data to inform, but not distort our interaction. We were connecting as two individuals, not as representatives of our cultures.

CULTURE IS A VERB

Working in the global leadership development and practice field, primarily in Asia, has exposed me to countless instances where the requests from clients were often similar to that of my earlier scenario. How could leaders manage their multicultural team more effectively; how could they motivate their staff in China more appropriately; how could they create a high performing team in India? Embedded in their requests was frustration with ambiguity and unmet expectations as well as the hope that each leader could learn culture specific information, translate cultural data to adaptive behavior, and thus achieve their goals in spite of cultural differences. The desired changes in leaders were conceptualized as add-ons instead of transformations.

Many researchers and practitioners in the cross-cultural and intercultural competence field have attempted to answer these questions using an anthropological approach to culture and tried to describe systems of values, attitudes, behaviors, and norms of particular cultures around the world (Hofstede, 1991; Kluckhohn & Strodtbeck, 1961; Trompenaars, 1993). Comparative management studies and cultural relativity models emphasized knowledge and skills, patterns of understanding of cultural differences and implicit leadership models, and strategic behavioral adaptation applied to specific cultural contexts and functions (Ananthram & Nankervis, 2014; Bird, 2013; Hammericha & Lewis, 2013; House, Javidan, Hanges, & Dorfman, 2002; Jokinen, 2005; Levy, Beechler, Taylor, & Boyacigiller, 2007; Meyer, 2014).

Often grounded in the expatriate experience, other researchers explored inter-cultural, and cross-cultural competence (Hall, 1981), cultural intelligence (Early & Ang, 2003), and global mindset development (Javidan & Bowne, 2013). Their work provided insights to the (1) impact of cultural differences on business and transnational initiatives, (2) help for managers to communicate within multicultural contexts, (3) culturally influenced approaches to work-related tasks, and (4) explorations into why some individuals could adjust to new cultures while others could not (Rogers & Tan, 2008).

Culture as a complex, socially constructed process, however, cannot be reduced to predictable patterns as I have found in my lengthy international practice. While such cultural frameworks have provided valuable assistance to international executives, international development professionals, and sojourners of all ilks, the static and unrealistic simplification of the myriad of kaleidoscopic differences found among any cultural group often created more stereotypes and misinformation about a population that consisted of multiple generations, disparate socioeconomic conditions, dispersed geographic living circumstances, and varied levels of education than it helped. This distorted picture that was based on inaccurate perceptions of homogeneity often perpetuated an unconscious polarized perspective of peoples and practices that tended to place the other in an unequal relational position. If an international executive or international development professional wanted to motivate staff in China, the framework could suggest advice as though it applied to all 1.3 billion people in the country!

Globalization has brought increased contact among cultures, which concomitantly has increased cultural complexities and interdependencies. In this modern day context of hybridity and cultural blending, leadership must shift from *leading globally*, which simply applies traditional methods and models in new geographies, to *global* leadership, defined by "the processes and actions through which an individual influences a range of internal and external constituents from multiple national cultures and jurisdictions in a context characterized by significant levels of task and relationship complexity" (Reiche, Bird, Mendenhall, & Osland, 2016). Globalization is clearly recognized as an impetus of change, but "not often enough do we emphasize the globalization of responsibility" to challenge privilege and a taken-for granted social order (Rosenmann, Reese, & Cameron, 2016, p. 202).

It can be said that the aim of making knowledge as concrete and predictable as possible is incomplete, if not unrealistic. Boundaries among cultures have become increasingly permeable, calling for attention, not to the cultural core, which previous cross-cultural models attempted to define, but to contact zones where cultural diversity meets and challenges the status quo. In the volatile, uncertain, complex, and ambiguous (VUCA) environment, not being surprised by surprises and possessing the agility to pivot as needed are requisite capacities of global and international development leaders. As Hermans and Kempen (1998) declared:

> *Cultural dichotomies do not and cannot meet the challenges raised by the process of globalization ... which involves social processes that are complex and laden with tension .... We need an alternative approach that is sensitive to the process of cultural interchange, the complexities of social positions, and the dynamics of global interconnectedness. (p. 1112)*

More profoundly relevant for global leaders, therefore, is the capacity to simultaneously thrive in the dynamic culture contact zones, while accessing learning from experiences in the relatively more established and comfortable cultural core.

THE NEED FOR DYNAMISM IN GLOBAL LEADERSHIP DEVELOPMENT AND PRACTICE

Clearly, global and international development leadership is not an individual, independent activity. Such leadership is, notably, an interdependent and facilitative one, whether in business, education, or international aid. Mendenhall, Reiche, Bird, and Osland (2012) concurred, citing the contextual multiplier effects of elements such as interdependence, ambiguity, and flux, which increase the magnitude of importance of the dynamic process of connection. Global leadership also stands on the foundation firmly built by previous research and models of *intercultural competence, cultural intelligence,* and *global mindset* and expands to include the dynamism of *Global Resonance*, a concept I have discovered, as detailed below.

Intercultural competence, "the ability to think and act in interculturally appropriate ways" (Hammer, Bennett, & Wiseman, 2003, p. 422), receives attention as it pragmatically enables strategic task completion with targeted global stakeholders. Intercultural competence pertains to culture specific awareness, knowledge and skills, and assumes knowledge of target culture-specific norms in a task-focused, cultural contrast way. This competence is most often concerned with learning about specific cultures and contexts with an individual's motives and hoped-for outcomes in mind and adaptation as the measurement of success.

Cultural intelligence, as a construct (Early, 2002; Early & Ang, 2003), is defined as a "system of interacting abilities necessary for adaptation to, as well as selection and shaping of an environment that is characterized by cultural diversity and cross cultural interactions" (Thomas et al., 2008, p. 125). There is also an implied assumption that knowing the priorities and ways of accomplishing goals in one culture will translate into adaptive behaviors that will facilitate goal accomplishment in a second (Johnson, Lenartowicz, & Apud, 2006). However, as I have discovered over the years after coaching hundreds of leaders, simply knowing about culture-specific values and norms does not necessarily mean that appropriate behaviors will be deployed in cross-cultural situations.

An additional element in this construct, *cultural meta-cognition*, acts as a link between knowledge and application of knowledge. Meta-cognition facilitates access to and integration of new culture learning, and "allows the emergence of cultural intelligence from the interaction of its constituent elements" (Thomas et al., 2008, p. 132). Meta-cognition, also known as *mindfulness*, supports the cognitive comfort zone as it is described as "putting patterns into a coherent picture even if one doesn't know what this coherent picture might look like" (Early, 2002, p. 277). Cultural intelligence, however, is directed at individuals not relationships; hence, it appears to lack the dynamism that relationships can foster.

Global mindset, the lens through which the world is seen, made sense of, and experienced, is the third, equally significant construct (Gupta & Govindarajan, 2002; Levy, Beechler, Taylor, & Boyacigiller, 2007). Global mindset provides the basis for a leader to understand diversity and complexity at a broader level of abstraction, with more patterns and systems integrated into the worldview. Considered the critical antecedent to intercultural competence, global mindset is viewed as a constellation comprised of awareness and openness to the systems complexity of cultures and polities, and the capability to navigate across the diversity that this environment entails.

Built on cognitive feedback mechanisms, a global mindset is one that seeks experiences from which to build broader patterns of cultural relativity and general cultural understanding, which influence the leader's worldview and the approach a leader takes to applying culture-specific intercultural competences. Javidan and Bowne (2013) argue that the model of global mindset they propose, consisting of intellectual, psychological, and social capital, includes competencies such as business savvy; thus, global mindset is broader in scope than related constructs of cross-cultural intelligence and cross-cultural leadership (p. 150).

Developing a global mindset focuses on knowledge input, advanced cognitive skills, and sense-making interventions designed to inform experience and influence growth of global capabilities. Providing the cognitively-oriented strategic and cultural approach to dilemma management, global mindset supports "the ability to cope with strategic dilemmas in multinational decision-making processes with cognitive strength and flexibility, [built on a cultural data base] of general and specific knowledge of other cultures" (Bücker & Poutsma, 2010, p. 835). Lovvorn and Chen (2011) provided a link between the two developmental components as they suggested that cultural intelligence is moderator in the "transformation of the international experience into a global mindset" (p. 2 of special issue).

Bird and Mendenhall (2016) concluded that global mindset is, indeed, a core antecedent to cultural intelligence as well as intercultural competence. Without a global mindset, the way one approaches intercultural interactions and culturally different others would be severely limited with still ethnocentric lens.

The many forms that cultural intelligence, intercultural competence, and global mindset take in the global leadership literature offer valuable global competency development support. However, these concepts appear to be based predominantly on externally sourced cognitive data and framed as aspirational competency constructs that, if applied, would lead to enhanced individual efficacy and performance across cultures (Early, 2002; Early & Ang, 2003; Gupta & Govindarajan, 2002; Javidan & Bowne, 2013; Rhinesmith, 1993; Rosen, Digh, Singer, & Phillips, 2001).

Further, Kedia and Mukheriji (1999) asserted that global leaders also need "to have openness that allows a global mindset to form, evolve and develop" (p. 232), which suggests that an identity and "activity of being" (Kegan, 1982) are missing in the typical configuration of global leadership.

These approaches attempt to develop a leader from the *outside in* (Fig. 1), from knowing to doing, which is crucial for global leaders in their development of skills and awareness of personal values, perspectives, and approaches. Yet, in order to be truly effective in the international arena, global and international development leaders also need close, connected

Fig. 1. Outside-in: Becoming a Global Leader.

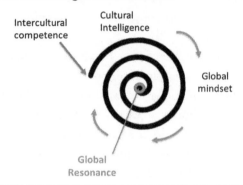

Fig. 2. Inside-out: BEING a Global Leader.

relationships, which can only be achieved *with* another, which ultimately transforms from the inside out. "Such experiences can reorient their values and significantly alter their worldviews" (Vaughn, 2002, p. 26), and provide a much needed expansion to becoming, then *being*, a global leader (Jokinen, 2005) (see Fig. 2).

GLOBAL RESONANCE: INSIDE-OUT GLOBAL LEADERSHIP

Global Resonance, both a concept and an inspirational process, is a dynamic state of receptivity and *intent to connect*, which generates attitudes and

Fig. 3. Global Resonance: Being a Global Leader, Inside-out.

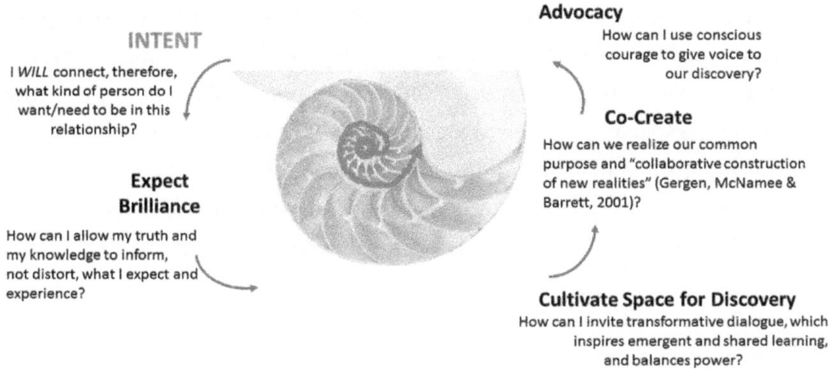

Advocacy
How can I use conscious
courage to give voice to
our discovery?

INTENT

I *WILL* connect, therefore,
what kind of person do I
want/need to be in this
relationship?

Co-Create
How can we realize our common
purpose and "collaborative construction
of new realities" (Gergen, McNamee &
Barrett, 2001)?

**Expect
Brilliance**

How can I allow my truth and
my knowledge to inform,
not distort, what I expect and
experience?

Cultivate Space for Discovery
How can I invite transformative dialogue, which
inspires emergent and shared learning,
and balances power?

behaviors that propel co-creation. Intercultural competence, cultural intelligence, and global mindset plus Global Resonance create a cyclical *knowing-doing-being* transformative developmental process. Once developed, Global Resonance becomes a global leadership identity and provides the source from which embodiment and practice of Global Resonance flow and from which global mindset, cultural intelligence, and intercultural competence are put into practice.

Generated from the inside-out, Global Resonance completes a global leader's *being-knowing-doing cycle* (**Fig. 3**) and proceeds through the following phases:

INTENT: CONSCIOUS RECEPTIVITY

Global Resonance begins from a place of conscious receptivity, not only accepting difference but expecting and inviting the possibility to be changed by the interaction with another. Not if, not hopefully, but WILL as both a state of being and thus identity, and a process of connection from which co-creation and advocacy grows. Another is "welcomed unconditionally, without prior knowledge of the other or without a name or passport. Unconditionality implies a total openness, of house, of being, of culture, to the other" (Peters, 2012, p. 43).

It is not a preplanned place but a state of being of openness to possibilities, referred to as "open will" (Scharmer, 2013). Rogers (1961) described this state as an empathic, other-centered praxis based on unconditional positive regard; others suggested that this state is a sense of readiness that sets the stage for connection to happen (Keller & Brown, 1968). Intent, the vital motivating perspective of Global Resonance is the consciously held goal to connect and to co-create possibilities. Surpassing the *hope* that connection will be made, *intent* includes the conscious decision around what kind of person a leader wants to be in the relationship with another.

EXPECT BRILLIANCE

This phase catalyzes an emergent process that is underpinned by honor and respect for the belief in the brilliance of the other, not as a hope, but as an expectation. Global Resonance assumes that a certain level of cross-cultural and intercultural competence, cultural intelligence, and global mindset exist. Cultural complexity is expected in any interaction, yet as cultural resonance develops, cultural differences are acknowledged, and then allowed to move off center stage, as two individuals connect and bring whole selves to the dynamic and evolving interaction. In fact, only by consciously acknowledging culturally influenced perspectives and expectations can an individual allow them to move aside to become resources to draw on, not filters that can distort.

Clearing space of cultural clutter, therefore, also allows for discovered patterns of sense-making and personal reactions. Assumptions are challenged, judgments suspended, and dialectical thinking practiced, bringing inflections to bear that "redefine relational connections" (Poulos, 2008). *Not knowing* is embraced and sparks that challenge preconceptions or prior judgments of good and bad, or right and wrong, are suspended, and increased awareness and compassion for another springs from within which facilitate the intent to connect.

CULTIVATE SPACE FOR DISCOVERY

Cultivating transformative space for discovery begins co-creation possibilities; unfolding and emergent meaning is allowed for and uninterrupted. This dialogic space is where the "I" is transformed to "We." In other words, the "we" begins to take on a collective and meaningful shape. Again, the behavioral skills of intercultural competence, cultural intelligence, and global mindset are not completely undeveloped; they are just now being engaged in differently.

Facilitating diversity of thinking is fundamental to co-creating Global Resonance and the basis of co-creating is exploration and discovery. Critical in the global context of complexity, the process of transformative dialogue, an asking orientation based on curiosity, openness and respect, and full expression of thought and feeling, minus cultural influences, contributes to Global Resonance. There is a consciousness in operationalizing one's INTENT. For example, if a leader is intent on connecting, then *how* she or he engages in dialogue is influenced by this intent. Advised by Gergen, McNamee, and Barrett (2001), there are no universal rules for transformative dialogue for dialogue itself will alter the character of transformative utility (p. 686).

CO-CREATE

In the space of co-creation, an issue of concern is seen as an object facing global leaders and stakeholders; the focus therefore shifts to an individual's contributions to the partnership and shared vision, and away from potentially adversarial blame or responsibility. Acknowledging their co-created partnership and balancing power differentials open a window to their diverse influences, enrich both the connection and the shared outcome, and promote commitment to action. "Collaborative construction of new realities emerges. Collectively knowing, [conspirators are] moving and doing together, co-creating the change, solution or direction from within their connected state of being" (Gergen et al., 2001). The outcome is greater than one could have created alone.

Advocacy: Courageous Consciousness

Consciousness of what is and has been discovered increases awareness of influences, differences, and possibilities that can longer be ignored; courage to give voice to them is the global leader's responsibility. In spiralic fashion, advocacy, therefore, completes the cycle and again touches INTENT, a place that is "childlike in simplicity … walking into each day and each moment with an open heart, active imagination and desire to connect, while holding the capacity for risk, passion for story, love of possibility" (Poulos, 2008).

In summary, Global Resonance brings the inherent and somewhat neglected attention to the dynamic relational aspects of global leadership. In fact, this is the essence of the dynamism of Global Resonance: One cannot resonate alone. Whether in physical science, human communication, or music, it takes two.

CONCLUDING INSPIRATION

Importantly, Global Resonance expands on western ways of knowing and inclusively reflects non-western models, for example, Ma thinking (Kodama, 2017), Taoism (Prince, 2005), and Jugalbandi, a classical Indian music art form based on diversity and defined literally in Sanskrit as "intertwined twins."

Years ago, I attended a Jugalbandi performance performed by the requisite two diverse instruments. The musicians, who are exceptionally skilled through years of committed practice at the feet of masters, breathe life into their instruments and make the two diverse instruments musically dance and converse testing and stretching each one's capacity in response to the other, further than either musician knew was possible.

I watched and listened, entranced, as the sarod and tabla conversed. Each musician and instrument focused on each other and tuned in completely to listen to what the other was emotionally expressing, not just playing. Back and forth, their limitations and boundaries were stretched as well as reshaped by invention and improvisation, as Jugalbandi is unique to each experience, just like a human exchange. The musicians' intense presence allowed for honoring attunement; in fact, during the performance, one musician paused in order to retune his instrument! Connection was prioritized over scripted performance. At one point, the Sarod player stopped and told the audience, "We are trying to reach resonance, but we aren't there yet. But you can see, we are having a great time doing it!"

That's it! A shared intention by two, founded on mutual trust, respect and support to find connection, and a collectively co-created resonance that would take them deeper and further than either was capable of achieving individually.

The ability to develop relational Global Resonance with another is both the most challenging and the most profoundly crucial capability that global leaders can develop. Instead of trying to rationally define *culture*, we are called to dynamically engage with culture, not only cognitively, but emotionally, physically, and spiritually. Global Resonance, an interdependent process built on trust and connection, cannot be achieved alone or cognitively only. "In order for a holistic transformation to take place, it requires the involvement of the whole person, that is addressing all mind, body and spirit," as well as in relation to others (Papastamatis & Panitsides, 2014).

In the end, "there are no necessary truths or essences to be discovered or analyzed. There is only conversation that rests on our preparedness to listen and learn from others, and in this conversation, based on mutual respect and recognition, manage to keep it going" (Rorty, 2008). Global Resonance encompasses the intent to enter the intercultural dialogue and the will to keep the conversation going.

GLOBAL RESONANCE EXPERIMENT

Consider these global leadership challenges; using Global Resonance, how would you approach them? How is this different from your present way? How can you regularly practice this shift in intent, perspective, and interaction with others, within the context of your global leadership?

(1) You are going into a country to set up women's health clinics. You need to develop relationships with government officials, including ministry of health officials, as well as local officials such as mayors, local councils, local village leaders, and doctors.

(2) You are working in the education sector. Your job is to increase access to education for girls and marginalized groups.

REFERENCES

Ananthram, S., & Nankervis, A. R. (2014). Outcomes and benefits of a managerial global mind-set: An exploratory study with senior executives in

North America and India. *Thunderbird International Business Review*, 56(2), 193–209. doi:10.1002/tie.21611

Bird, A. (2013). Mapping the content domain of global leadership competencies. In M. E. Mendenhall, J. S. Osland, A. Bird, G. R. Oddou, M. J. Stevens, M. L. Maznevski, & G. K. Stahl (Eds), *Global leadership: Research, practice and development* (2nd ed.). London: Routledge.

Bird, A., & Mendenhall, M. E. (2016). From cross-cultural management to global leadership: Evolution and adaptation. *Journal of World Business*, 51, 115–126.

Bücker, J., & Poutsma, E. (2010). Global management competencies: A theoretical foundation. *Journal of Managerial Psychology*, 25(8), 829–844. doi:10.1108/02683941011089116

Early, P. C. (2002). Redefining intelligence across cultural and organizations: Moving Forward Cultural Intelligence. *Research in Organizational Behavior*, 24, 271–299.

Early, P. C., & Ang, S. (2003). *Cultural intelligence: Individual interactions across cultures*. Stanford, CA: Stanford University Press.

Gergen, K. J., McNamee, S., & Barrett, F. J. (2001). Toward transformative dialogue. *International Journal of Public Administration*, 24(7,8), 679–707.

Gupta, A. K., & Govindarajan, V. (2002). Cultivating a global mindset. *Academy of Management Perspectives*, 16(1), 116–126.

Hall, E. T. (1981). *Beyond culture*. New York, NY: Doubleday.

Hammer, M. R., Bennett, M. J., & Wiseman, R. (2003). Measuring intercultural sensitivity: The intercultural development inventory. *International Journal of Intercultural Relations*, 27(4), 421–443.

Hammerich, K., & Lewis, R. D. (2013). *Fish can't see water: How national culture can make or break your corporate strategy*. West Sussex: John Wiley & Sons.

Hermans, H. J., & Kempen, H. J. (1998). Moving cultures: The perilous problems of cultural dichotomies in a globalizing society. *American Psychologist*, 53(10), 1111. doi:10.1037/0003-066X.53.10.1111

Hofstede, G. (1991). *Culture's consequences: Software of the mind*. London: McGrawHill.

House, R., Javidan, M., Hanges, P., & Dorfman, P. (2002). Understanding cultures and implicit leadership theories across the globe: An introduction to project GLOBE. *Journal of World Business*, 37(1), 3–10. doi:10.1016/S1090-9516(01)00069-4

Jarvis, P. (1999). *The practitioner-researcher: Developing theory from practice*. San Francisco, CA: Jossey-Bass.

Javidan, M., & Bowne, D. (2013). The "global mindset" of managers: What it is, why it matters, and how to develop it. *Organizational Dynamics*, 42, 145–155.

Johnson, J. P., Lenartowicz, T., & Apud, S. (2006). Cross-cultural competence in international business: Toward a definition and a model. *Journal of International Business Studies*, 37(4), 525–543.

Jokinen, T. (2005). Global leadership competencies: A review and discussion. *Journal of European Industrial Training*, 29(3), 199–216.

Kedia, B. L., & Mukheriji, A. (1999). Global managers: Developing a mindset for global competitiveness. *Journal of World Business*, 34(3), 230–251. doi:10.1016/S1090-9516(99)00017-6

Kegan, R. (1982). *The evolving self*. Cambridge, MA: Harvard University Press.

Keller, P. W., & Brown, C. T. (1968). An interpersonal ethic for communication. *Journal of Communication*, 18, 73–81.

Kluckhohn, F. R., & Strodtbeck, F. L. (1961). *Variations in value orientations*. Oxford: Row, Peterson.

Kodama, M. (2017). Knowledge convergence through "Ma Thinking". *Knowledge and Process Management*, 24(3), 170–187.

Levy, O., Beechler, S., Taylor, S., & Boyacigiller, N. A. (2007). What we talk about when we talk about 'global mindset': Managerial cognition in multinational corporations. *Journal of International Business Studies*, 38, 231–258.

Lovvorn, A. S., & Chen, J. S. (2011). Developing a global mindset: The relationship between an international assignment and cultural intelligence. *International Journal of Business and Social Science*, 2(9), [Special Issue].

Mendenhall, M. E. (2013). Leadership and the birth of global leadership. In M. E. Mendenhall, J. S. Osland, A. L. Bird, G. R. Oddou, M. L. Maznevski, M. J. Stevens, & G. K. Stahl (Eds.), *Global leadership: Research, practice, and development* (2nd ed., pp. 2–20). New York, NY: Routledge.

Meyer, E. (2014). *The culture map: Breaking through the invisible boundaries of global business*. New York: PublicAffairs.

Papastamatis, A., & Panitsides, E. A. (2014). Transformative learning: Advocating for a holistic approach. *Review of European Studies*, 6(4), 74–81. doi:10.5539/res.v6n4p74

Peters, M. A. (2012). Western models of intercultural philosophy. *Analysis and Metaphysics*, 11, 30–53.

Poulos, C. N. (2008). Accidental dialogue. *Communication Theory*, 18(1), 117–138.

Prince, L. (2005). Eating the menu rather than the dinner: Tao and leadership. *Leadership*, 1(1), 105–126.

Reiche, B. S., Bird, A., Mendenhall, M. E., & Osland, J. S. (2016). Contextualizing leadership: a typology of global leadership roles. *Journal of International Business Studies*, 48(5). doi:10.1057/s41267-016-0030-3

Rhinesmith, S. H. (1993). *A manager's guide to globalization: Six keys to success in a changing world*. San Francisco: McGraw-Hill.

Rogers, C. R. (1961). *On becoming a person*. Boston, MA: Houghton Mifflin.

Rogers, P., & Tan, J. S. (2008). *Fifty years of intercultural studies: A continuum of perspectives for research and teaching*. Working Paper Series, Working Paper No. 1104 University of Michigan. Ann Arbor, MI: Ross School of Business. Retrieved from http://ssrn.com/abstract=1132328

Rorty, R. (2008). Philosophy and the hybridization of culture. In T. Roger Ames & P. D. Hershock (Eds.), *Educations and their purposes: A conversation among cultures*. Honolulu, HI: University of Hawaii Press & East-West Philosophers Center.

Rosen, R., Digh, P., Singer, M., & Phillips, C. (2000). Global literacies. *Lessons on business leaderships and national cultures*. New York, NY: Simon and Schuster.

Rosenmann, A., Reese, G., & Cameron, J. E. (2016). Social identities in a globalized world challenges and opportunities for collective action. *Perspectives on Psychological Science, 11*(2), 202–221.

Scharmer, C. O. (2013). Addressing the blind spot of our time: An executive summary: Theory U: leading from the future as it emerges. San Francisco: Berrett-Koehler Publishers, Inc.

Thomas, D. C., Elron, E., Stahl, G., Ekelund, B. Z., Ravlin, E. C., Cerdin, J. L., & Maznevski, M. (2008). Cultural intelligence domain and assessment. *International Journal of Cross Cultural Management, 8*(2), 123–143.

Trompenaars, F. (1993). *Riding the waves of culture*. London: The Economist Books.

Vaughn, F. (2002). What is spiritual intelligence? *Journal of Humanistic Psychology, 42*(2), 16–33. doi:10.1177/0022167802422003

INDEX